Best

To Kathleen

I'm looking forward
to working together

Best,

WOMEN
IN
POWER

WOMEN IN POWER

THE SECRETS OF LEADERSHIP

Dorothy W. Cantor and Toni Bernay

With Jean Stoess

Houghton Mifflin Company
Boston • New York • London

For information about permission to reproduce selections from
this book, write to Permissions, Houghton Mifflin Company,
215 Park Avenue South, New York, New York 10003.

Library of Congress Cataloging-in-Publication Data

Cantor, Dorothy W.
Women in power : the secrets of leadership / Dorothy W. Cantor and
Toni Bernay ; with Jean Stoess.
p.   cm.
Includes index.
ISBN 0-395-53755-X
1. Women in politics — United States.   I. Bernay, Toni.
II. Stoess, Jean.   III. Title.
HQ1236.5.U6C36   1992   91-36633
303.3'4'082 — dc20   CIP

Printed in the United States of America

BP 10 9 8 7 6 5 4 3 2

To my beloved husband, Gerry, my children, Josh and Laura, and their spouses, Karen and David, who learned about the Leadership Equation along with me, and my darling grandchildren, Brad, Scott, Andrew, Alex, and Molly, to whom I hope it will be the norm.

DOROTHY W. CANTOR

To my always best supporter, my dearest husband, Saar, and to my best support team, my children, Mitch, Ellen, and Laura, who taught me how to lead as we all created dreams, followed and fulfilled them, and helped each other in the struggle to see life's possibilities rather than its obstacles.

TONI BERNAY

Contents

Acknowledgments

This book could not have come about without the loving support of the many people who gave to us so generously of their time, their suggestions, their editorial comments, and their introductions to fascinating, talented, and courageous women to interview.

Our heartfelt thanks to our colleagues Carol Gilligan and Lyn Mikel Brown, who shared their ground-breaking research on adolescent female development with us and who guided and helped us to shape our study in unique ways.

Thanks also to Diana Diamond, Steve Morin, Pat De Leon, Diana Zuckerman, and the staff of the American Psychological Association Practice Directorate, particularly Bryant Welch and Donna Daley, who made creative suggestions and immeasurably improved our book by helping us to add interviews of wonderful women to our study.

Thanks also to Joan Willens, who giggled with us and generously gave us her ideas on healthy narcissism, and to Mel Kinder, whose mentoring, kindness, and patience helped us to "know" our expertise and to write a more readable book.

And to our research assistant, Alisa Michaels, who dug up the impossible, a big, big thank you.

To the women in the women's PACs to which we belong who lent us their enduring support, we are eternally grateful:

To Laura Barbanel, Patricia Bricklin, Cynthia Deutsch, Carol Goodheart, Rebecca Hudsmith, Phyllis Katz, Ellen Kimmel,

Vickie Mays, Alisa Michaels, Lynne Rosewater, Nancy Felipe-Russo, Melba Vasquez, Lenore Walker, and Jerry Simmons of the Women in Psychology for Legislative Action, who helped us with their thoughtfulness and energy to bring a sense of activism to women leaders in psychology.

To Marsha Kwalwasser, cochair of the Women's Political Committee, for her ever-present friendship, loyalty, and help and to her cochair, Peg Yorkin, and the rest of our WPC "kitchen cabinet," who influenced much of our thinking about women and politics, our thanks for your political sophistication and savvy, our gratitude for your tutelage and inspiration and for being there for so long: Michelle Andelson, Barbara Barnes, Esther M. Berger, Sharrell Blakely, Louise Brinsley, Kathleen Brown, Sally Burkett, Diane Cooke, Jodie Evans, Susie Field, Marcia Herman, Dorothy Jonas, Betsy Kenny, Lyn Lear, Cindy Miscikowski, Marie Moretti, Vicki Reynolds, Muriel Sherman, Lisa Specht, Madeleine Stoner, Cathy Unger, Karen Weinstein, Mimi West, and Adele Yellin.

To Marge Tabankin, Corinne Levy, Kathy Garmezy, and their staff at the Hollywood Women's Political Committee and the Hollywood Policy Committee, who cheered us on all the way and inspired the drama in the book.

To Ellen Malcolm, president, Wendy Sherman, then executive director, and Jody Franklin, then political analyst, of EMILY's List, who keep us posted and pepped up and march with us at gubernatorial inaugurations.

To Mary Rapaport and Jane Hasler Henick, longtime activists and leaders in the National Women's Political Caucus, L.A. Westside, who always remember and include us in the fun and excitement of women in politics, L.A. style.

To Jane Danowitz of the National Women's Campaign Fund, who brainstormed with us early and introduced us to many political women.

And to the women of the California Women's Political Sum-

mit, who are WomanPower personified and who helped us to
define it.

To those special women without whom we felt the book
would not be complete but whom we could not include in our
formal study because their positions at the time of the interviews did not fulfill the research criteria — our gratitude for
your graciousness, your special contributions, and your pioneering spirit: Dianne Feinstein, former mayor of San Francisco, candidate for California governor in 1990 and U.S. Senate
in 1992; Geraldine Ferraro, former New York congresswoman,
vice presidential candidate, and 1992 New York senatorial candidate; Gloria Molina, former member of the Los Angeles city
council, elected in 1991 to Los Angeles County's powerful
board of supervisors; Maureen Ogden, New Jersey assembly-
woman; and Vicki Reynolds, mayor of Beverly Hills, who
helped us validate our research.

Special thanks to Jean Stoess, who did far more than was
called for in her contract to write with us and did it with grace
and good cheer; to our assistants Hannah Rosen, Linda Bates,
Alison Ronsheim, and Miriam Skaar, who waded endlessly
through our chickenscratch and manuscripts with patience,
fortitude, and smiles; to Andrew Lightwood, whose quiet presence and wonderful caretaking always feels like loving support,
especially on long writing weekends; and to Peter Medlock,
who seamlessly took over, knowing just how to support us in
his own wonderful, caring way.

And, of course, thanks to Harold T. Miller, our "guardian
angel" at Houghton Mifflin, for trusting this project to be exciting and worthwhile, and to Janet Silver for teaching us how to
make it work.

To the staffs of the women we interviewed for the book, who
opened the doors, did the scheduling and arranging that made
the interviewing possible, calmed our nerves in many waiting
rooms, and rooted us on, thank you once again.

And most important, to the twenty-five courageous and risk-taking women whose vision and dreams made this research happen, who participated in the study, who made time for us in their impossibly busy schedules, and whose cooperation, openness, and thoughtfulness made this book possible and as rich as it is — we were, are, and ever will be touched by your generosity of spirit as will all women who aspire to be leaders. (The following list gives the women's offices at the time of the interviews.)

Suzie Azar	Mayor, El Paso, Texas
Elaine Baxter	Secretary of State, Iowa
Barbara Boxer	U.S. House of Representatives, California
Betty Castor	Commissioner of Education, Florida
Kathleen Connell	Secretary of State, Rhode Island
Nancy Johnson	U.S. House of Representatives, Connecticut
Barbara Kennelly	U.S. House of Representatives, Connecticut
Catherine Baker Knoll	State Treasurer, Pennsylvania
Mary Landrieu	State Treasurer, Louisiana
Nita Lowey	U.S. House of Representatives, New York
Ruth Messinger	President, Borough of Manhattan, New York
Barbara Mikulski	U.S. Senator, Maryland
Constance Morella	U.S. House of Representatives, Maryland
Evelyn Murphy	Lieutenant Governor, Massachusetts
Nancy Pelosi	U.S. House of Representatives, California

Ann Richards	State Treasurer, Texas
Marge Roukema	U.S. House of Representatives, New Jersey
Patricia Saiki	U.S. House of Representatives, Hawaii
Claudine Schneider	U.S. House of Representatives, Rhode Island
Gail Schoettler	State Treasurer, Colorado
Pat Schroeder	U.S. House of Representatives, Colorado
Olympia Snowe	U.S. House of Representatives, Maine
Jolene Unsoeld	U.S. House of Representatives, Washington
Rebecca Vigil-Giron	Secretary of State, New Mexico
Jo Ann Zimmerman	Lieutenant Governor, Iowa

Foreword

Dianne Feinstein

Taking that first step in running for office is always the most difficult. How well I remember visiting many of San Francisco's "movers and shakers" in 1969 to ask how they felt about my running for the Board of Supervisors, the eleven-member legislative body that governs both the city and county of San Francisco. To a person, the reaction was "You shouldn't run. There's only one woman's seat on the board, and it's already filled." I didn't take their advice. Instead, I met their challenge, campaigned for a year — and won.

Since I received the most votes of any candidate, I was entitled to be elected president of the board by my new colleagues. But, again, the pundits said, "Feinstein has no experience. She should do the 'states*man*like' thing and let the second highest vote getter be president of the board." It just so happened that the person who came in second was a real estate broker who had *no* experience in elective office. But he was a man.

When I became the first woman mayor of San Francisco, I realized I was always being tested — by the press, by staff, by department heads. Did I know my stuff? Would I follow up? My state of the city messages were carefully critiqued, as were my press conferences. I was frequently criticized for some minor comment that got blown up into a full-scale controversy, unlike most males in similar positions, whose statements often went unchallenged.

It is clearly more difficult for women to succeed in politics than for men. Women have to prove themselves effective and credible time and time again. Experience has taught me that the keys to a woman's effectiveness in public office are to be "trustable": to give directions clearly and to follow up, to verify every statement for accuracy, to guard her integrity carefully, and to observe the public's trust one hundred percent. Most important, she must be a team player and build relationships with her colleagues that are based on integrity and respect. She must be able to get the job done. She must be a leader in the true sense of the word.

Despite the fact that good enough is not enough where women candidates and officeholders are concerned, I am glad to see more and more women entering the political arena. They often begin at the local level, perhaps on a school board, city council, board of supervisors, or a legislator's campaign staff or government agency. Working their way up the political ladder, they launch their political careers based on the "portfolio of expertise" they have acquired through community or work involvement. Then, after being reelected and putting in eight years or so in an entry-level position, they look up to the next challenge.

By then they have learned to negotiate, mediate, champion causes, and, yes, even compromise. They have become team players, not headline seekers. They do their homework, are prepared, speak concisely, lobby intensively, and work long hours.

Over the years, such a woman becomes a leader with an electoral base who looks to her for leadership. She is sought out and consulted. She is respected. Her legislation is enacted and direction carried out. She can win elections now. Her colleagues support her. She understands power, and can wield it constructively. She moves people to act. She demonstrates that she understands leadership and how to use it. The community looks to her to solve problems and to lead them.

She now knows that power is essentially the force or action necessary to get something accomplished for the greater good. She knows that its roots lie in wanting to make life better for others. She knows that the source of a leader's power is no different from that used by a mother or father to direct a family, by a supervisor to a manage the workplace, by an elected official to govern. She knows that, ultimately, power is a synthesis of the desire to make the world a better place and the experience of learning how to make it happen in political and other arenas.

While power is neutral in itself, it can be used for good or for evil. In politics, power used well translates into effectiveness, change, and making a difference. But just getting into office doesn't guarantee that an officeholder will have power. Power, I believe, must be earned with substance. What one *does* when in office and *how* one does it are critical to political success. In other words, how leaders use power often determines the quality and effectiveness of their leadership. I find I must continually learn the how-to of both power and leadership. It doesn't happen automatically. By harnessing her or his power in the service of good leadership, a leader can transform power into a force for positive change.

As you can see, in this country elected officials in every jurisdiction, large or small, have the potential to use power and leadership wisely and well. Some do; others do not. We earn the right to work for change through the vote of the people, but by our actions and relationships we develop the clout and reputation to bring about change. We are evaluated all along the way, and the criteria for women are often more stringent than those for men. As I have said, respect and credibility are hard for women to achieve, and this difficulty has its consequences throughout the political world. For example, legislation is often evaluated on the basis of its author. A good bill by someone who is not respected by her or his peers may die a lonely death in committee, while a poor bill by a respected author will gain a floor vote.

The secrets of power and leadership shared by the women in this book tell us that there is no one path to political success or to successful leadership. Rather, the road goes in many directions and is steep and rocky. But we can learn much from the political women chronicled here. By understanding them better, we can understand not only how they learned their secrets of leadership and how they use them now, but how all women can learn from them to develop their own ability to lead others, whether it be in politics, business, education, or whatever field they choose.

Dear reader, I hope you enjoy, as I did, *Women in Power: The Secrets of Leadership* and that in it you find the role models of leadership and insights that are right for you. Then, if you are willing to commit the twenty years or so I believe it takes to become a true leader — go for it!

WOMEN
IN
POWER

Prologue:
How This Book Came to Be

In 1988, as we were flying to San Francisco to meet with the executive committee of Women Executives in State Government (WESG), we began to reminisce about how the meeting had come to be.

It all began in the late 1980s, when we became charter members of Women in Psychology for Legislative Action (WPLA), a political action committee for women in psychology and other mental health professions. Everyone at WPLA's organizational meeting had long been active in the leadership and politics of the American Psychological Association (APA). We had all focused our efforts on helping women become more active and more politically powerful in the APA.

Using the experience and knowledge we had gained in APA politics as a springboard, we decided to get involved in "real" politics, particularly women's politics. Since then we have raised funds and otherwise supported the campaigns of many women candidates. We have been excited and satisfied by the growing numbers of women who are getting elected to high public office. And as our political experience grew, so did our curiosity about the women we were supporting.

We often wondered why these women so passionately desired to be in powerful policymaking positions that they were willing to run for public office. Why did they feel so strongly about advancing an agenda that they were willing to campaign for admission to the male bastion of politics? We also wondered what makes them strong enough to survive a grueling campaign and then stay in office long enough to make a difference. In essence, we wondered about the seeds and roots of women's power and leadership. Rather than just wondering, we decided to find out. We set out to find a way to interview enough political women to constitute a research population.

In February 1988, at the second annual luncheon that WPLA sponsored in conjunction with the Congressional Caucus for Women's Issues on Capitol Hill, we met Meg Armstrong, executive director of Women Executives in State Government. WESG is a national organization open only to women governors, lieutenant governors, secretaries of state, treasurers, and cabinet officers. It seemed like the perfect group from which to learn the secrets of women's power and leadership.

When we told Armstrong about our proposed research project and the questions we wanted to ask, she immediately became interested. She said that she and the other members of WESG had been batting the same questions around but needed our kind of expertise to get any answers. "You've got to meet 'my women,'" she said excitedly. "They're the perfect subjects for you to interview!" Armstrong made arrangements for us to meet with the WESG executive committee to see whether we could persuade these powerful, successful women to agree to be interviewed.

We first met Evelyn Murphy in 1988 in the coffee shop of the Stanford Court Hotel in San Francisco. At that time she was lieutenant governor of Massachusetts. She and the others at the breakfast table that morning were all members of WESG. The group consisted of Murphy; Gail Schoettler, treasurer of Colorado; and two other women. It quickly became obvious that Murphy, the chair, was the leader of these leaders.

Both of us were excited, as any psychologist would be when confronted with a ready-made research population. We could hardly stand the tension. Were they going to agree to be interviewed or not? We just couldn't tell. They seemed very businesslike about the whole thing, and we weren't sure how to read them.

Lieutenant Governor Murphy asked us what we wanted to know. We explained that we wanted to identify the qualities or strengths that enabled these women to get elected and to persevere in high positions. For example, we wondered why each of them chose such an unusual career path and what *internal strengths* enabled them to succeed in this predominantly male field. After all, most of the women in WESG belong to a generation in which career options were usually limited to teaching, secretarial work, and nursing. Even for the younger women, whose career horizon may have seemed wider, politics was obviously still not a popular choice. Yet these women have been elected and reelected, often by increasing margins. Many have moved up the ladder to highly visible and influential positions. How did they do it?

We weren't interested in how they dealt with the external political barriers that often impede the progress of women candidates, such as lack of party support, fundraising problems, or the uphill battle that candidates, especially women, face when trying to unseat an incumbent. Those questions belong in the realm of political science. As psychologists, we look at the world differently and pose different questions.

Psychologists are interested in human behavior, particularly how today's behavior developed out of earlier life experiences. Therefore, we view people with an eye toward what got them to where they are today. As we explained to the WESG executive committee, we wanted to ask such questions as the following.

• What was life like for them as children?
• How did their parents treat them?

- What messages did they get about success?
- How did they develop enough self-confidence to overcome the obstacles to women achieving political power?

In response to this last question, they all looked at us as if we were crazy. "What obstacles?" they asked.

One of us sputtered: "You know — all those things that are so hard for women to do in politics. Like how to be aggressive enough to break into the old boys' club. How to get those early leadership positions that can propel you to elective positions. Raising money. Building a strong network. Getting and wielding power in a male bastion." Surely, we both thought, these obstacles were just a matter of conventional wisdom and common sense.

The group began to fire responses at us. After Evelyn Murphy restored order, she asked us what on earth we were talking about. Then she summarized their responses, breaking the message to us gently: "We don't see it that way. We don't see the obstacles." We were stunned.

One by one the others chimed in: "I always knew I could do what I wanted." "I always knew I could be whatever I wanted to be." Gail Schoettler was the most vehement, and the others concurred with her responses. Murphy finally said to us, "If you're going to work with us, you'd better rethink your premise."

We walked away muttering. "Can you believe what just happened? They're denying that they've had to overcome obstacles. Imagine that!"

We decided that we definitely had to bring this group around to our point of view, so we spent the next several months negotiating with them. We did our best to convince them of the rightness of our psychological knowledge and positions. But every time we asked, "How about the obstacles?" they asked us, "What obstacles?" They held on to this position no matter what approach we used.

Many months later we met with Murphy in her office. By that time we had finally realized what she and the others had been saying: they didn't see the political problems confronting women as obstacles — they saw only the possibilities. Had there been a law preventing women from holding office, they would have seen that as an obstacle, a stone wall that had to be removed before they could proceed. But they interpreted anything else, such as the problems of fundraising or negative attitudes toward women candidates, merely as hurdles to be jumped.

Their experience was different from ours. So was astronaut Sally Ride's. When she went up in the space shuttle she was exhilarated; most of us would have been terrified. What you have inside you becomes the lens and organizing principle through which you see and experience life.[1] This perspective is reflected in other researchers' findings.

Why Most Little Girls
Don't Dream of Power

Men have long had male role models after whom to pattern their lives. From time immemorial, scholars have been able to analyze the seeds of male leadership by studying the lives of presidents and generals. It's not uncommon for little boys to grow up saying they want to be firemen or policemen or even president of the United States. But until now, little girls didn't have political role models to dream about or learn from.

The women we interviewed for this book are the first cadre

of top political women leaders to be analyzed as models of power and leadership. Women are making greater inroads into politics these days, but they have a long way to go to reach parity with men. The Center for the American Woman and Politics (CAWP) at Rutgers University estimates that at the current rate at which women are being elected, it will take 410 years before the proportion of women in Congress equals their percentage in the overall population.[2]

It is true that more women are being elected at local and most state levels. After the 1990 election, CAWP reported that women held 17 percent of statewide elective executive offices and about 18 percent of state legislative positions. Although 18 percent of state legislative positions is far below the percentage of women in the population, it is a major increase over the rate in 1973, when only 7 percent of state legislators were women. Using their finding that the number of women state legislators increases by one percentage point each election, CAWP predicts that by the year 2054, *half* of all state legislators will be women.[3]

Although more women get elected at lower levels, female candidates did not fare too well in high statewide and federal positions in 1990. Feminists were jubilant when three of the eight women gubernatorial candidates were elected: Joan Finney of Kansas, Ann Richards of Texas, and Barbara Roberts of Oregon. However, because of the retirement of two incumbent female governors and the defeat of a third, the number of women governors remained at three. In addition, the number of women in the House of Representatives remained at twenty-nine (including Eleanor Holmes Norton, the nonvoting delegate from the District of Columbia) and the number of female senators at two after the 1990 election.

Women are moving into various legislative and executive positions that historically have been male-dominated. In 1990, with Finney's election as governor, Kansas became the only state in history to simultaneously have a woman governor, a woman U.S. senator (Nancy Landon Kassebaum), and a congresswoman (Jan Meyers).[4] And women for the first time held three elective statewide positions in each of four states (Colorado, Iowa, Nevada, and Oregon).[5] A record four women were elected attorneys general and fourteen state treasurers. Women also held such elective executive positions as corporation commissioner, labor commissioner, and superintendent of public instruction.[6]

Because state legislative and executive offices are the traditional staging areas for campaigns for statewide and federal positions, more women can be expected to run for higher offices in the next few years. Obviously, many more must be elected to achieve the critical mass that will enable them to exercise the power that should be theirs. We hope it won't take 410 years — or 64 years at the state level.

This uphill political battle for women has been under way for the last two hundred years. Between 1776 and 1976, men outnumbered women 1,715 to 11 in the U.S. Senate. There were 9,591 men and only 87 women in the House of Representatives during the same period. And until Sandra Day O'Connor was appointed in 1981, no woman had served on the U.S. Supreme Court. Finally, 507 men and a mere five women served in the president's cabinet during those two hundred years.[7]

Clearly, politics and political behavior are seen as masculine endeavors. Political behavior, as we define it, includes autonomy, independent opinions, and aggressive action. By definition, in our society women who are aggressive and autonomous have been seen as deviant and have been considered unacceptable and undesirable as women.

Given these societal attitudes, it's hardly surprising that young women have so few political role models. Few women dare to challenge the stereotype. How can they dream if they don't have any cultural images to show them the way? No wonder it has been so hard for young women to so much as fleetingly dream about going into politics or assuming positions of leadership in businesses and other institutions. *It is the intent of this book to redefine political behavior as being appropriate to men and women alike.*

Political Women
as Models of Leadership

We began to wonder how the lack of role models affects the whole idea of women's leadership. We asked ourselves what kinds of role models would enable young girls to dream about attaining leadership positions. How would role models help them select the proper career path? What was it in the background and development of successful political women that enabled them to succeed when they had no role models? In other words, we wondered if they had some secrets of leadership and power that other women did not have.

The best way to answer these questions, we decided, was to conduct in-depth interviews with twenty-five successful political women. In addition to the interviews, we asked each woman to complete a three-page questionnaire (the Appendix contains the interview questions and the questionnaire).

We chose the women we studied because they are the most visible women in the world of politics. To put it bluntly, governmental politics allows the most blatant display of raw power. It provides the most dramatic and universal examples of power and of the capacity to lead and to change that we can point to. All of us have grown up with politics. Everybody experiences it, at least vicariously, even when not involved in the political system.

We studied successful women in elective politics, but the lessons we learned from them also apply to political environments in the broader sense: corporations, school systems, churches, or any other hierarchy whose political ins and outs must be successfully negotiated by a women if she is to advance her agenda.

As we were discussing the political workings of a particular corporation, a friend of ours said, "You know, sometimes we get so passionate and so involved and so political in this corporation that we forget we're not a nuclear power." Every field of endeavor has its own particular politics. Government is just one example of an institution that has a political life of its own.

We realized that if we could understand women in governmental politics, we could better understand women in leadership positions in other walks of life as well. The women we studied could therefore serve as role models to other women, who could then dream of being leaders themselves.

Selecting Political Women to Study

We decided that a bipartisan sample of twenty-five women from all parts of the country would give us a good idea if trends and patterns exist among women in politics. Our choice of subjects was already limited by the small number of women in government; nevertheless, we narrowed the field even further to eliminate as many extraneous variables as possible.

We adopted four basic criteria for our sample: (1) The women were elected rather than appointed. (2) They were in office when they were interviewed. (3) They held high federal, state, or local offices. (4) They were involved in U.S. politics.

1. *The women had been elected rather than appointed.* We chose this criterion because we assumed that women who have gone through the election process might have different attributes from their appointed colleagues. Again, we wanted to narrow the field so we would have people who were comparable.

Elective office is the only position that requires prospective employees to raise money, campaign, and be elected by their constituents as opposed to simply landing a political appointment. We wondered what allows elected women to hang in there over time, to go out and campaign and withstand the hassles of political life.

A broader approach might have been to study a group that was more representative of the public at large. After all, most people in other political systems are not elected. But we felt that the ability to create and manage an entire campaign organization is the most dramatic example of leadership.

2. *They were in office at the time of the interview.* We selected only women incumbents to avoid the possibility that women who had held office earlier might have been different from the current officeholders. (Unless we indicate otherwise, we refer throughout this book to the positions the women held at the time of the interviews.)

While we were working on this book people asked us if we had interviewed Geraldine Ferraro, Bella Abzug, or Dianne Feinstein. They were always surprised when we said that we hadn't. The reason we didn't interview these political trailblazers was that they were not in office at the time.

3. *The women we studied held high federal, state, or local offices.* Our sample included a U.S. senator, members of the U.S. House of Representatives, lieutenant governors, state cabinet and constitutional officers, and mayors of large cities or the equivalent. We felt that these offices were the most powerful elective positions.

One might argue that there is a difference between a senator and a mayor. We agree; yes, there are differences. But again, with such a small cadre of politically eminent women leaders to choose from, we did not feel we had the luxury of interviewing only congresswomen. And because there were only two women in the U.S. Senate when this book was written, we had to mix the classes of women we interviewed for confidentiality while at the same time diminishing the differences as much as we could.

4. *Only women in U.S. politics were interviewed.* We limited our sample to women in American politics to avoid complicating matters with differences among countries. This eliminated powerful world leaders such as Margaret Thatcher and Benazir Bhutto from consideration.

We originally intended to exclude women who had succeeded their husbands into office or whose fathers had been politically prominent. We reasoned that women from politically active families had an obvious psychological advantage just by growing up in the world of politics. We also felt that the name recognition accruing to political daughters would have given them a leg up on the political ladder over other women. Therefore, we did not interview such officeholders as Congresswoman Lindy Boggs of Louisiana, who was elected to the seat held by her husband, Hale, after his death, or U.S. Senator Nancy Kassebaum, daughter of vice presidential candidate Alf Landon. So much for our good intentions.

During the interviews we were surprised to learn that the fathers of 24 percent of the women had been in politics in some way (although none of the mothers had held office). Several fathers had served on school boards, and four had been mayors of small towns. Also represented were several mayors of large cities and the national chairman of a political party. We did include one interviewee who, although elected to fill her late husband's state senate seat years ago, has gone on to distinguish herself in her own right.

Interestingly, part of the reason we didn't know about the

political fathers in advance was that all six of the daughters were married, and five chose not to use the family name. This eliminated any political advantage they might enjoy from name recognition. In addition, several had attained office in a part of the country far removed from where their fathers had achieved political eminence. And in most cases, these women were serving in high state or federal offices while their fathers had been local elected officials.

We felt somewhat better about including these women when we learned that in most cases they were the only ones among their siblings to have entered high-level politics — even when they had brothers. This is significant because of the tendency for the sons in politically active families to carry on the family tradition in office. For example, in almost every generation of Kennedys, Rockefellers, and Roosevelts the male offspring have distinguished themselves in public service and political office.

Sometimes we found striking differences among the twenty-five women we studied. At the same time, however, we also found a number of similar personality characteristics weaving their way throughout all of the interviews. The patterns made by these unifying threads form the substance of this book.

Arranging Twenty-Five Interviews

We learned some things about women in politics that, although beyond the scope of this book, are interesting because they tell us something about the world in which political people — women and men — live.

We were particularly startled by the degree to which the political woman's life, like that of any high-ranking executive — man or woman — is not her own. This was brought home to us repeatedly as we tried to set up the interviews. We asked for an hour and a half (knowing we would settle for an hour) of each woman's time. And for their convenience, we offered to travel to Washington or their local office. We thought we were making it easy for them.

An hour or so of time, it turned out, is a lot to ask when most visitors seem to be scheduled for twenty minutes at the most. And as we learned several times, even a confirmed appointment could be rescheduled or canceled because of an unexpected congressional session or unanticipated meeting with the governor.

Our initial contacts, even when we had introductions, were made through a battery of appointment secretaries, chiefs of staff, or administrative assistants — the people who controlled the calendar. The lone exception was the midwestern woman who returned Dr. Cantor's initial call late one evening to discuss the project before she turned the scheduling over to her staff.

Any interview scheduled for the first thing on a Monday morning provided us with an interesting glimpse into a political woman's life. When she arrived at her office, her staff gave her the schedule for the day that they had prepared. After a briefing on who, what, why, when, and where, she launched into her programmed day. If the timing of the schedule was thrown off (as it was for one interviewee by an overlong dental appointment), everything else had to be collapsed into shorter time periods.

The women we interviewed rarely had to watch the clock, however. Their staffs did it for them. When time was up, a staffer knocked on the door and politely but firmly directed the boss to her next appointment.

Almost all of the women we interviewed were intrigued by the project and gave us as much of their time as they could. To take advantage of their generosity, we sometimes found ourselves conducting interviews under unusual conditions. For example, the only way Dr. Cantor could finish interviewing the congresswoman whose schedule had been disrupted by her dental appointment was to ride along on a mad dash to a "photo opportunity." The part of the interview done in the car was somewhat guarded, perhaps because of the presence of the driver.

In addition to the back seats of automobiles, interviews were conducted in congressional offices in Washington, local offices in the congresswomen's home states, state agencies, a storefront campaign headquarters, and a mayor's home. One interview took place in Dr. Bernay's living room with a congresswoman sitting on the couch and her daughter stretched out on the floor.

When a malfunctioning tape recorder ruined the interview with Ann Richards, she graciously agreed to do a second one. The first interview had been conducted at the Beverly Hilton during a whirlwind trip to California. The second took place in the office of a Texas law firm two days before the 1990 gubernatorial primary runoff election, where an exhausted Ann Richards was making last-minute phone calls. P.S.: She won the runoff and went on to become governor of Texas.

At times the task that we set before us was exceedingly frustrating. Because the process of setting up appointments proved to be so difficult, the interviewing stretched over a longer period than we had intended. A few women turned us down, citing scheduling difficulties, although that may not have actually been the case.

Much to the embarrassment of her staff, one congresswoman stood up the interviewer, who had flown to Washington for the occasion. We were annoyed but not particularly surprised because the same woman had previously broken several other appointments. So we interviewed a more available public official in her place. Generally, though, the women we talked with — and their staffs — were considerate, helpful, and very supportive of what we were doing.

Preserving Confidentiality

We told our subjects that either their comments would be anonymous or, if their names were used, they would have the right to approve the material. In either case, we assumed that their responses were somewhat restrained because, as public figures, everything published about them is scrutinized and held to an extremely high standard.

We interpreted their interviews with this in mind. We would not expect to reach a thorough understanding of *any* individual in a single interview — and perhaps even less so with a political woman, who must always be wary of how the public will view her.

It was hardly surprising to learn that women in politics, on the whole, do *not* think like we psychologists do. Even though the women we interviewed knew we were psychologists and had seen a brief summary of our ideas, they seemed quite unprepared for the kinds of questions we posed.

Most were taken aback when we asked for their earliest memory. Apparently they had never before made the connections between their early life experiences and their present status. A number of the women were intrigued and thanked us for opening a new line of inquiry to them.

We tried to ignore political issues, even those that were especially meaningful to us. Again, because we are not political scientists, the issue of political ideology was not critical to us. We asked no questions about politics, although several women did volunteer information. After all, political women are more accustomed to speaking about their political positions than about their psychological history and makeup. Each time an interview ended, we felt energized and heartened by what we were learning.

What These Women Can Teach Us

We will talk a great deal in this book about how the twenty-five women leaders we interviewed developed the leadership qualities that have enabled them to succeed in politics. We will analyze the elements of their upbringing and early development that nurtured those qualities and how they drew on them in political life. We will also look at how those attributes can help empower the lives of other women who want to be leaders in business, educational, professional, and other organizational spheres as well as political spheres.

We will translate these women's secrets of leadership into empowering messages that mothers can give their daughters to facilitate development of those leadership qualities. We will also look at how those attributes can empower our adult readers. Finally, we will suggest ways in which women who did not develop these strengths as children can compensate for or acquire them now to use throughout the rest of their lives.

We hope we can convey what we learned in a way that will help you and your daughters and granddaughters to claim your birthright: the effectiveness of your leadership capacities, power, and, as we have defined it, political behavior.

1

The Leadership Equation: Leadership = Competent Self + Creative Aggression + WomanPower

Competent Self, Creative Aggression, and WomanPower are the three critical elements guaranteed to add up to leadership. As we interviewed the twenty-five women in this study, we discovered these common threads that seemed to make up the leadership fabric in each woman. As we went from woman to woman, city to city, we were excited to see the Leadership Equation emerge, revealing the unique ingredients of women's leadership as well as the sources from which it springs. We will illustrate our findings with the stories of Barbara Gallagher and Marjorie Lockwood.

Barbara Gallagher
A Woman Who Made It

"My dad always told me I could do anything I wanted to do," said U.S. Congresswoman Barbara Gallagher. "But neither of us ever expected that it would turn out like this!"

Recently elected to her fourth term in the House of Representatives, she talked with us in her local office over a hurried lunch. "I *love* this job! I thoroughly enjoy being a mover and a shaker. I like being able to get things done for people. Frankly, I love having the power to make a difference," she told us enthusiastically.

Congresswoman Gallagher never dreamed when she was growing up of going into politics. That's not surprising. Since hardly any women held political leadership positions forty years ago, there simply were no political role models for young girls.

The second of six children (two brothers and three sisters), she was reared in a loving, stable midwestern family. Her mother and father made sure that she and each of her siblings felt deeply loved and very special.

During summer vacations, Mr. Gallagher sometimes took young Barbara on the road while he sold building materials. He introduced her to his customers and included her in conversations as if she were an adult. She felt comfortable in this male bastion and soon learned to banter with men as easily as with her classmates. During those trips, her father taught her some practical automotive skills, and by sixteen she could change a tire and repair minor engine problems better than either of her brothers.

Mrs. Gallagher devoted her life to making a good home for her family. She was a den mother when the boys were in cub scouts. Bluebird leader. Room mother. Field trip chaperon. Library volunteer. She cheerfully chauffeured her children to music lessons, ball games, and school events.

Whenever someone in the neighborhood needed help, Mrs. Gallagher was there for them, too. "You should always take care of the less fortunate," she used to say. Although she never held a paid job outside the home, her desire to make a difference in her community led her to civic activities. These were the secrets of leadership that Mrs. Gallagher passed on to her children. As a woman and a role model of competent femininity, she especially gave her daughters this legacy of leadership and power.

All six siblings developed a strong sense of self-worth, strength, and independence. The empowering message they heard constantly from their parents was "You can do anything you want if you try hard enough." It was repeated in so many ways: "You can do it! I know you can make the tennis team." "Let me help you with this hard problem so you can finish your science project on time." "I know it hurts now, but you'll win if you try out for cheerleading next year." "We know you're going to take first in extemporaneous."

Like the rest of the kids in elementary school, young Barbara Gallagher always listened to "Captain Midnight" and the other afternoon radio serials. Although women occasionally appeared in the serials, Gallagher became disgusted with them because they usually got into trouble and had to be rescued by a male star.

One of her other favorite pastimes was reading. She was especially proud of having read the entire Nancy Drew collection in the town library. When she read *Little Women* she loved Jo's strength and independence, but she was terribly disappointed when free-spirited Jo became a sedate housewife and mother.

Besides her own mother, the only strong female role model Gallagher had while growing up was Wonder Woman, whose exploits she followed in comic books. Although she knew that Wonder Woman's magical powers really didn't exist, she dreamed of acquiring her secrets of power and of being as powerful and smart as her heroine.

At ten, Barbara would spend hours sitting in the window seat of the bedroom she shared with two of her sisters, dreaming of the future. Wonder Woman lost her attraction after Gallagher saw *The Red Shoes* (which she sat through three times). She dreamed endlessly of Moira Shearer, the movie's star. And although her brothers made fun of her, she liked to dance around the house pretending to be a ballerina.

Gallagher attended public school through the eighth grade. She loved school and was somewhat of a tomboy. Her teachers often complimented Mr. and Mrs. Gallagher on having such a smart and congenial daughter. At a time when most girls tried to attract boys by appearing helpless and feminine, she avidly participated in tennis and the few other team sports available to girls. And having recognized her leadership abilities, her classmates often made her captain of the team.

When Gallagher was a freshman in high school, her parents enrolled her in a Catholic all-girls school. She was active in debate and drama and served as a class officer all four years.

The nuns who operated the school fascinated her. She saw them as strong, well-educated women who could run hospitals, schools, and other institutions. They were her first role models of strong women in leadership positions. "They were *it* as far as I was concerned," she said.

She didn't even mind wearing the blue plaid school uniform. Since everyone dressed alike, she didn't worry about not being able to afford the expensive cashmere sweaters and Pendleton skirts that were the rage in the public high schools. The expense of supporting and educating six kids stretched her father's paycheck to the limit, and her younger brothers and sisters wore far more hand-me-downs than they cared to admit. But the Gallagher boys and girls never thought of themselves as poor. They simply accepted their life as it was, and everyone was happy and healthy.

The constant messages from their mother helped all the siblings develop inner strength and weather difficult times. "Remember, Barbara, you're just as good as everyone else," her mother used to say. "Don't be afraid of someone just because they have more money than you do."

Then one day in her sophomore year she saw Rosalind Russell as newspaperwoman Hildy Parks in *His Girl Friday*. Russell seemed so strong. Such vision and drive! Gallagher was enthralled. Up on the shelf went the satin ballet slippers. Now she was going to be a movie star.

As Gallagher approached eighteen, reality set in. She always knew she would go to college. Her parents valued education and had promised to help each child with at least some college expenses. After surveying the conventional career options for young women at the time, Gallagher decided to become either a nurse or a teacher. Later that spring she selected a small coeducational liberal arts college about four hours' drive from home.

At the beginning of her sophomore year she became so fascinated by an introductory class that she switched her major to economics. During all four years she studied hard enough to earn her usual good grades, but she also found some time for intramural sports and student government. And somehow she made the time to be president of her sorority in her senior year.

After graduation, Gallagher spent two years traveling around the country as an analyst for a major corporation. Then she married one of the attorneys who consulted with her firm and moved back to her home state. She had three children during her first four years of marriage. She enjoyed motherhood but missed the stimulation of other adults. "Whatever became of *me?*" she sometimes wondered.

As an outlet for her energies she began to get involved in community affairs. She started as a volunteer at her children's school and later became a lobbyist for educational issues. Her husband, a successful attorney, encouraged her involvement in the community and was proud of her achievements.

Running for public office was not Gallagher's idea. To this day, she swears, "The only reason I got into politics was because I was at the right place at the right time." The right time she refers to was an opening on the school board. When the

incumbent decided not to seek reelection, several highly respected community leaders encouraged her to run. After much
soul-searching, she decided to enter the race.

"I figured I could do at least as well as the other trustees," she
thought, "and probably better than some of them. Besides, I'd
have more impact as one of the board's five votes than as a
lobbyist." She had the vision. Now she needed the power to
make it happen.

Since she wasn't able to raise much money for her campaign,
she recruited family and friends to help her. Her friend Susan
wrote the press releases and brochure copy. On the morning her
candidacy was announced, Susan introduced the new candidate
to the radio and TV news departments. When Susan and Barbara arrived at the newspaper, the editor greeted them with a
yawn and a look that said, "Oh, no, not another politician from
nowhere." "Don't worry, Barbara," consoled her friend. "You'll
do a great job. The press will come to you from now on."

As a donation to the campaign, her next-door neighbor, Jerry
Davis, did the photography for her campaign materials. But
when it came time to take the obligatory family photo, she had
to coax her kids to stand behind her and her husband. "Oh,
mother — how gross! Do we really have to do this?" whined
one of her teenage daughters. "Everybody at school's going to
laugh at us!" But the girl eventually relented and later bragged
to her friends about posing with her mother.

After Susan designed an eye-catching yellow and navy logo,
the campaign literature was ready to be printed. The only hand-
out Gallagher could afford was an inexpensive, quick-printed
brochure brightened up with the logo and the photographs.
Then, armed with brochures, the novice candidate began campaigning in earnest — knocking on every door in her district,
some of them twice.

No one was more surprised than Gallagher when she won by
a substantial margin. And once sworn into office, she quickly

earned the community's respect as an outstanding board member who always did her homework. Four years later, she was easily reelected and then was named chair of the board.

After two terms in local politics, Gallagher decided she was ready to move up to the state legislature. But this time, although she campaigned hard, she lost in a close race that wasn't final for two days.

"It really hurt because I worked so hard and ran a good campaign," she said. "But it wasn't the end of the world. My family was very supportive, and that meant a lot. It just wasn't meant to be this time."

After several weeks of inactivity, she bounced back and resumed her high-profile community involvement. Two years later she ran for the state legislature again and won 62 percent of the vote. Six years after that, she defeated the incumbent U.S. congressman for the seat she now holds.

Congresswoman Gallagher is pleased that as an incumbent, fundraising is no longer a problem for her. And even the leaders of the opposing party grudgingly admit that running against her is always an uphill battle. Her reputation as a tough and well-financed campaigner discourages all but the most foolhardy opponents.

Her congressional district is too large to permit her to knock on every door, as she did at the beginning of her political career. But she tirelessly makes the rounds of the "rubber chicken circuit" — even during nonelection years — talking to people and listening to what they have to say. She has been careful to stay in touch with the people who elected her. It pays off. Her margin of victory has increased by at least 3 percent in each of her past four elections.

At campaign time now an ad agency prepares slick mailings; and she can afford to saturate the district with TV, radio, and newspaper advertisements. But to this day she still uses the original logo in all of her campaign materials. Her kids no longer balk at the family photo, and *their* kids think Grandma's really something special.

Gallagher feels more comfortable in Congress now than she did as a freshman, having learned how the system works and how to make it work for her. She can be counted on to support family and women's issues and is becoming known as an expert in economics and business affairs.

Often, however, legislation she supports goes nowhere because she still can't round up the votes. She remembers trying to get support for the Family and Medical Leave Act. One congressman derisively said the bill was "just what you'd expect from a woman." Another scornfully dismissed it as "bleeding heart" legislation that would cost American industry millions of dollars. Although she was able to line up all of the other congresswomen and a few congressmen, she couldn't muster enough votes to pass the bill.

"Getting more women elected would make my job so much easier. They're far more likely than most men to support the issues that interest me," she said. She fears that most family-oriented legislation probably won't go anywhere until a critical mass of women is elected.

Congresswoman Gallagher's biggest source of stress is a schedule that is out of her control. Her schedule is relentlessly demanding both in Washington and during frequent trips back to her district. She conscientiously sets aside time for her husband, grown children, and their families but sometimes feels sad because she can't get away long enough to enjoy her friends.

Despite the stresses of the job, she's contented because she feels she's making a difference. When the timing is right, she would like to move up to the U.S. Senate. After that, who knows?

The Leadership Equation

If you're wondering why you've never heard of Barbara Gallagher, relax. She isn't a real woman. Barbara Gallagher is a composite elected official who embodies many of the qualities we frequently encountered in our interviews and who lives the Leadership Equation. We can use Barbara Gallagher's story to describe the elements of leadership that make up the Leadership Equation.

A Competent Self

Barbara Gallagher's most important characteristic is that she knows who she is at all times. She does not feel defined by situations, people, or events. She doesn't feel she has to change the way she acts to please the people around her. This is what we mean by having a *Competent Self*. Gallagher's strong sense of self enables her to promote the principles she believes in even though she knows that some people will disapprove, some quite vehemently.

A Competent Self protects her from feeling threatened when she takes risks. Losing her first campaign for the state legislature hurt, of course. Nobody likes to lose. But she didn't feel as if her identity had been taken away — all she did was lose an election. She hadn't been destroyed as a person.

People with an inadequate or not good enough sense of self are reluctant to take even smaller and less public risks than Barbara Gallagher did. They feel threatened by changing jobs, getting married, or even traveling alone. This is because the blow to their identity would be too great to bear if they were to be unsuccessful at *anything*, regardless of what it is. They would feel as though they had lost themselves. They would be overwhelmed by self-doubt, constantly wondering, Maybe I should have done something different. What if I had done this? Or that?

A Competent Self enables a woman to see the possibilities instead of the obstacles. Even when a possibility doesn't materialize and instead turns into an obstacle, the political woman will be able to draw on her Competent Self for the strength to weather the bad times and then continue to pursue her vision.

Creative Aggression

When we speak of *Creative Aggression*, we include such notions as taking initiative, leading others, and speaking out. We consider all of these attributes to be positive. One important aspect of Barbara Gallagher's sense of self-worth was her capacity to feel comfortable with her aggression and competitiveness.

Unfortunately, women's aggression has had a bad rap for a long time. Portrayals of aggressive women as fearsome and destructive can be found in literature as old as Greek mythology. Think of Scylla and Charybdis, women who took the forms of a rock and a whirlpool and destroyed unwitting sailors, or of Medusa, with snakes protruding from her head, whose look turned people into stone.

Even today, men and women themselves are afraid of female aggression. We need only look at examples in the current culture, such as the female protagonist played by Glenn Close in *Fatal Attraction*, whose intense love and aggression make her a psychotic killer, and Sigourney Weaver in *Working Girl*, the female boss whose aggression and anger make her a destructive bitch. Women's aggression in contemporary society is still considered unacceptable, unfeminine, and dangerous.

However, all that is changing. Women's aggression is being redefined as being in the service of life and growth and not of destruction. We call this Creative Aggression and borrow Karen Horney's description of "adequate aggression":

> Capacities for work . . . taking initiative; making efforts; carrying through to completion; attaining success; insisting upon one's rights; defending oneself when attacked; forming and expressing autonomous views; recognizing one's goals and being able to plan one's life according to them.[1]

Despite the positive elements embodied in this definition of aggression, women's aggression continues to be feared in many social contexts, including politics. Political analyst Celinda Lake, in her study "Campaigning in a Different Voice," claims that political managers have observed that "ambition is not a good thing for a woman to have. If voters sense ambition, they won't like it. It is the exact opposite for male candidates."[2]

Lake offers this comment from a campaign worker after the candidate lost an election:

> Mary was more male than female. I mean she was aggressive, she was a fighter, she was all of these things . . . our opponent was a nice guy, the family man. . . . And I think that probably people didn't like such an aggressive woman.[3]

Mary encountered the traditional double standard by which aggression is measured in the world of politics. The same catch-22 applies to women in business, the professions, and other institutions.

Since female aggression still carries such a stigma, it is not surprising that young girls suppress rather than express it. They do so because they believe it is wrong to be noticed and to let others know their desires. They fear that their opinions are unacceptable to others. Because they assume that the people they are closest to also feel the same way, girls automatically conclude that showing aggression will cost them a critical loving connection to their family and friends. Thus, they feel guilty and ashamed about what they think and feel. So to comfort themselves and to reach a psychologically safe place, they compliantly shove what they know, think, and desire into the closet of the unknown and unthought. Isolation from their own experience becomes a routine way of life. This should not happen.

Society has tried to temper the word *aggression* by substituting *assertiveness*, as if aggression were overloaded with destructive connotations. Whatever you choose to call it, we believe that aggression can be but is not necessarily destructive. It can be constructive and creative. It is a feeling like all other feelings. Creative Aggression can enhance personal growth if used creatively and wisely. When Barbara Gallagher fought for the Family and Medical Leave Act in Congress, lobbying and buttonholing her colleagues to get their votes, she was using and enjoying her Creative Aggression for the benefit of her career and society. What each of us does with our aggression is a matter of choice.

WomanPower

As Creative Aggression is aggression in the service of life and growth, *WomanPower* is power used to make society a better place. It is not power for its own sake or for manipulating others. The political women we studied enjoy using their power to advance a specific agenda, and of course they enjoy the pleasures of the spotlight.

Barbara Gallagher made her first foray into politics not because the life of an elected official seemed glamorous but rather because she wanted to make a difference in educational issues that came to her attention while her children were in school. She started out as a school volunteer and later became a lobbyist for educational issues. The driving force behind her political activity was the desire to help others and help society. She enjoyed the recognition and the spotlight and loved it when she was asked to run for the school board. She was flattered and thought, "Now I really have an opportunity to change the school system."

The concept of WomanPower is so critical to understanding women's political behavior that we will discuss it thoroughly in the following chapter.

Marjorie Lockwood
A Political Woman Who Didn't Succeed

In contrast, Marjorie Lockwood is a hypothetical woman who can't make it in politics because she doesn't have enough of the ingredients of the Leadership Equation that enabled Congresswoman Gallagher to succeed. Marjorie Lockwood and Barbara Gallagher are similar in many ways. They're almost the same age. They're well educated, bright, and personable. They live in the same medium-sized city. Both are married and have children. And neither one launched her career until her children were old enough to help care for themselves.

The major difference between these two women is the status of their sense of self and their use of Creative Aggression. Barbara Gallagher's Competent Self contributed to her successful climb up the political ladder. But as you will see, Marjorie Lockwood's shaky, inadequate sense of self is one of the personal characteristics that cost her a promising political career. Barbara Gallagher's aggressive energy was available to her for campaigning, for making her mark on the school board, and for becoming a spokeswoman for family and women's issues in Congress. She is a leader of women and men. In contrast, Marjorie Lockwood was so frightened by her aggressive energy that she began to withdraw into herself.

Marjorie Lockwood's father, a construction worker, was constantly involved in get-rich-quick schemes. Her mother was a shy, frightened woman who wanted her only child to be happy and secure. The feminine legacy of "secrets" that she passed on did not empower Marjorie to feel comfortable with her Creative Aggression and success. Both parents were delighted in their own ways but also overwhelmed by their daughter's intelligence, drive, and personality. They had conflicting expectations of her. "My father wanted me to be a rich and famous actress. My mother wanted me to be safe and secure," she said. "I didn't know what to do. I felt torn apart. I couldn't satisfy both of them."

Not knowing which parent to satisfy, Lockwood grew up confused and unhappy. Although she always got high grades and her teachers considered her to have leadership potential, school was not a happy time for her. "As a teenager I was lonely and scared," she said poignantly. "I didn't know whom to try to satisfy or what I wanted to do with my life. I didn't feel like I belonged in school. I didn't feel like I belonged anywhere."

As she sadly learned, the risks of being "popular" at school weren't worth the threats she felt of losing her parents' love. In high school she participated in a number of student activities but never wanted to be a leader. She always volunteered for positions that kept her out of the limelight; she was always the committee member, never the chair.

The only reason she tried out for the cheerleading team when she was a junior was that her friends kept bugging her to do it. She was absolutely amazed when she was selected. After a year on the team she ran for captain, again at her friends' insistence, and won that, too. Suddenly she began to feel that nobody liked her anymore because she was too stuck up, too self-important. At least she thought her girlfriends felt that way.

When her mother said, "Marjorie, you sure are getting a lot of calls from boys these days," she thought her mother meant that if she stood out too much, something must be wrong. And her father gave her the impression that he disapproved of the crowd with whom she was hanging out.

She received mixed messages from her parents. Here she was, a success at cheerleading, and in effect her parents were saying: "We don't think that's a great idea." Her father worried that since she was now hanging around with the "jocks" instead of the good students she could no longer attract the "right" boys.

As a cheerleader she had earned status but had lost the loving connections to the most valuable people in her life. Somehow she finished out the year, graduated, and went off to college. But in college she took a different route, having discovered that success didn't breed the kind of connections she wanted.

In her late teens and early twenties Lockwood dreamed of becoming a fashion editor for Paris *Vogue*. "I wanted a glamorous and exciting life, traveling the world covering openings and shows, maybe even winning a Pulitzer Prize," she said.

In her freshman year in college she started to live her dream. She happily discovered a flair for reporting and newswriting in a journalism course. The following year she became absorbed in photojournalism. "I just loved working in the darkroom. I could size and crop my photographs and then add captions that told a whole story," she remembered. Photojournalism certainly would be glamorous and exciting, just the kind of thing her father would have expected her to do.

But she couldn't get her mother's constant messages about safety and security out of her head. Freelancing in photojournalism wouldn't guarantee either safety or security unless she was one of the lucky few who made it big. That kind of life would be one big risk.

She unwittingly searched for a way to please both parents in this no-win situation. After agonizing over her plight for several months she finally took the easy way out — and reluctantly changed her major to elementary education. Her reasoning was that although teachers are relatively underpaid, they usually get good benefits and the work would be steady once she got established in a school system. After graduation she taught second grade for three years and then married her college sweetheart.

Shortly before the wedding her husband-to-be laid down the law: "I want you to devote your full attention to being my wife and making a good home for me and the kids." She silently nodded in agreement. She had abandoned her vision of a glamorous globe-trotting career for the life of a full-time housewife and mother of two. In doing so, she clearly satisfied her mother's and her husband's dreams, but not her father's or her own. Predictably, because these roles were only part, not all, of her dreams, during early adulthood she felt unhappy and unfulfilled.

When both of Lockwood's children were in school she began to develop some interests outside the home, just as Barbara Gallagher had done. It wasn't long before her name began to be recognized in community activities. She was particularly interested in environmental matters and became known as a well-informed, level-headed advocate of environmental education. She enjoyed the role.

Her husband wasn't crazy about her being away from home during the day, but he didn't complain as long as she was always home when the kids were there. "Now I know how Cinderella felt," she said. "I was afraid if I didn't get in the house before the kids came home from school, my car would turn into a pumpkin and I would be dressed in rags."

As her children got older, Lockwood volunteered even more time to community affairs. In no time the media began to seek her out because they knew she would always give them a good interview. She earned such a high profile in the community that strangers began to recognize and talk to her at the supermarket.

When the death of an incumbent created a vacancy on the city council, the mayor asked Lockwood to apply for the unexpired term. She accepted on the spot and felt a tremendous high for several months after her appointment. She was deeply touched by the deluge of phone calls, cards, and letters when the appointment was announced. Now she (and usually her husband) got invited to the best social functions in town. Everybody always returned her phone calls. She met the city's most influential men and women. She had arrived!

Lockwood devoted her energies to bringing herself up to speed on council matters. Soon she was immersed in esoteric subjects that ranged from airport operations to personnel matters to zoning laws. The front seat of her car was littered with agendas and reports. "Why don't you leave the car unlocked, Mommy?" her son asked one day. "Maybe somebody will steal all this stuff so you won't have so much work to do." She wasn't sure whether he was kidding.

After several months in office, her enjoyable high was replaced by worry and self-doubt. She soon learned that most of the issues she dealt with weren't as black and white as she had thought. There were two sides, if not more, to almost every situation. Consequently, she could no more please everybody now than she could please both parents as a child. When the council made a decision on a controversial issue, half of the audience would be pleased — and the other half would stomp out the door in anger.

Lockwood now doubted whether she was really good enough to sit on the council, whether she was making the right decisions. She had begun to feel guilty about the power she held. And she was beginning to feel embarrassed when people made a fuss over her, especially when they ignored her husband.

When the general election rolled around, she had to run for election to her own four-year term. The polls showed that she had good name recognition and a high approval rating. But she continued to grow even more uncomfortable being in the limelight. Despite her accomplishments, good looks, talents, basic sense of goodness, sharp mind, and charming personality, she felt worthless. "I know I've got a lot going for me, but I just can't feel it," she moaned.

Her opponent conducted an aggressive, well-financed campaign that he clearly intended to win. The more he attacked Lockwood, the more she wanted to hide. Her feelings of wanting to be loved by everyone controlled her life. When attacked, she felt unworthy, unwanted, boring, and selfish.

When her opponent called her too passive, she didn't fight back. And when he went door to door in the community, she couldn't make herself campaign even on her own street. Politically knowledgeable people were not surprised when she was defeated.

She was devastated. "It's the public's loss," she grumbled. "After all I did for this community — and look what they did to me!" She withdrew from the public eye and rarely left home. Her political career had come to an end, and she was sorry that anybody had ever talked her into going into politics in the first place.

Finding Their Political Selves

Why did it take so long for Barbara Gallagher and Marjorie Lockwood, as well as most of the women in our sample, to find their political selves? By *political* we mean having aspirations and seeking leadership positions in both corporate and elective political life.[4] For the most part, women's political aspirations seem blunted and delayed. Why is this so? The answers lie in what happened to them, what didn't happen, and what needs to happen while they are growing up. The purpose of this book is to provide those answers.

2

WomanPower in the 1990s

"Power and women."

"Women in power."

"Powerful women."

Why do these phrases seem incongruous? It's because not enough people are likely to connect women and power in the same thought. The phrases don't seem incongruous when you substitute the word *men:*

"Power and men."

"Men in power."

"Powerful men."

Why does equating men with power seem perfectly normal, while *women* and *power* come across as mutually exclusive terms? Why is it typical to talk about women or to talk about power, but not to combine them?

It's because the classical stereotype of women and femininity just doesn't include the idea of power, and although things are changing gradually, the stereotype is still hard to overcome. The old-fashioned spectrum of femininity typically encompasses attributes such as affectionate, sympathetic, sensitive to the needs of others, understanding, compassionate, warm, tender, fond of children, gentle, yielding, cheerful, shy, responsive to flattery, loyal, soft-spoken, gullible, or even childlike. There is no room in the traditional female stereotype for powerful. Femininity doesn't imply tough, strong, or decisive.

It is not surprising, then, that women traditionally have not thought of themselves as powerful in the male definition of the term and that society doesn't attribute power to them. This is because feminine qualities such as those listed in the previous paragraph are the exact opposite of those traditionally used to define power. We want to change this.

What *Is* Power?

The Random House *Dictionary of the English Language* lists eleven definitions of power, including "ability to do or act; capability of doing or accomplishing something; . . . great or marked ability to do or act; strength; might; force . . . the possession of control or command over others; authority; ascendancy: *power over men's minds;* . . . political ascendancy or control in the government of a country, state, etc.: *They attained power by overthrowing the legal government;* . . . one who or that which possesses or exercises authority or influence."[1]

In their book *Power Failure,* Barbara Booles and Lydia Swan call power a force:

> It is the ability to do or act. It is the ability to mobilize resources — money, people — to influence results. It is the capacity to affect part of the world in which we live. As such, power is neither good nor evil. It is neutral in value. Both Jesus and Hitler had power and used it to effect different types of change, to rally people toward different ends. Corporate and organizational power is similar in nature. In a corporate hierarchy the ability to get things done translates to having the responsibility and authority to command people and spend money. Corporate power is measured in tangible, sometimes palpable terms — how many people does it give an executive to manage, how indispensable are these people, what are their combined salaries, etc.?[2]

What qualities does power bring to mind? Strength. Force. Authority over others. Getting other people to do what you want them to do. These have never been considered feminine traits. The emphasis here is on strength, authority, decisiveness, getting things done, running other people's lives — all considered masculine traits. As our society defines power, one can't be powerful without being tough.

Not only doesn't society attribute power to women, but women themselves have not been comfortable with using power as long as it is defined in the classic terms. They don't think of themselves as powerful. And when women try to put on the mantle of male-style power — force and strength, devoid of the feminine caring aspect — they frequently feel extremely uncomfortable. They sense that power is "not me."

That's why the feminist drive in the 1970s and 1980s to gain and wield male-style power at the expense of feminine qualities just didn't feel right. But times have changed. As more women move into leadership positions in government, business, and other institutions, they have begun to feel less need to emulate male dress and manner. Gone are the severe blue suit, white blouse, and floppy necktie of the "dress for success" crowd of the 1970s. Femininity is in — softer-looking dresses and suits, bright colors, and attractive jewelry. The attitude of achievement-driven yuppies of the 1980s has given way to a work ethic that values quality of life as well as material possessions.

Now, instead of exhorting women to put aside their femininity and learn how to manage like a man — to paraphrase *My Fair Lady*'s Henry Higgins — books, magazine articles, and plays praise the feminine strengths that women contribute to politics and business. Society is finally beginning to appreciate the fact that women complement rather than compete with the strength of male managers.

In its 1990 special edition devoted to women, *Time* recognized, as we have, that "the emerging female style of management" is becoming more prevalent because women are achieving more positions of power. In addition, *Time* predicted that women's "flexible, mediating approach" will play a vital role in managing America's heterogeneous work force, with its increasingly varied cultural ground rules.[3] It seems that women shouldn't have to permanently hang up their aprons to share in the power that men have always enjoyed. In fact, men may find themselves adopting female qualities to adapt their managerial styles to the changing needs of the workplace.

The stirrings of the same theme can be detected in the world of politics. For example, some female candidates have tailored their campaigns to appeal to men as well as to women by emphasizing both male and female strengths. When former San Francisco mayor Dianne Feinstein ran for California governor in 1990, she used this tag line in her campaign: "Dianne Feinstein: Tough *and* caring." Note the emphasis on *and*. For her first campaign for Congress in 1978, Geraldine Ferraro's slogan was "Finally, a tough Democrat."

When a political story appeared in a Massachusetts newspaper under the headline GOV HOPEFULS JAB AT EACH OTHER during the 1990 campaign, Lieutenant Governor Evelyn Murphy, then a candidate for governor, thought it sent a positive message about women and power. She told us:

> You only need one of those to be thought, "Oh, yeah, she's tough enough, she slugs back." Then you can go back to a far more cooperative and thoughtful style of leading. This kind of news coverage works to your advantage to some extent because you don't spend time on the defensive trying to show how tough you are and being too aggressive and too harsh.

Female candidates, who must be very careful not to come across as either wimps or shrews, could find far better uses for the campaign energy and resources they are forced to expend to deal with the problem of public perception. This necessity to counter society's stereotypes won't change until female candidates *and* the voters are comfortable with associating the idea of women and power in the same thought.

Women are never going to want to be powerful if we perpetuate the macho male ideal of power. But power redefined to include the ability to make a difference in society for the greater good would no longer conflict with feminine nurturing and caring. Why not combine the best of both masculine and feminine identities into a broadened definition of power that men as well as women can reach for? As we've just seen, this kind of power is already making headway in business and politics, although no one has yet given it a name. Society at large can only benefit from male and female leaders who exercise it. We call it *WomanPower*.

In the remainder of this chapter we will analyze why women back away from conventional ideas of power. We'll also talk about some ways to reconcile male and female qualities into a definition of power — WomanPower — that can be acceptable to everyone.

Power — the Ability to Make People's Lives Better

We asked all of the women we studied what power means to them. Although we interviewed each woman separately, nine responded identically: Power is "the ability to get things done." Several other responses, although not identical, said basically the same thing.

In addition to getting things done, most of the women we

talked with said they used their power to make other people's lives better. That is the way they experience power.

When we probed further, four of the women elaborated on their ideas about power:

- "Power in itself means nothing. . . . I think power is the opportunity to really have an impact on your community."
- "My goal is to be a powerful advocate on the part of my constituents."
- "Power is basically that sense of strength and understanding about how to pull together resources to get your agendas done."
- "To me power means being able to do something for others. I use the power of my office to help other people . . . the potential of helping somebody else out, that's how I view my office. I feel that what I'm doing is worthwhile and rewarding and has direct benefits for other people."

There is nothing in what they have said that suggests that women should not have power. These women are comfortable with it and do not feel that it makes them any less feminine, although our society has historically not seen things that way.

Women's Traditional Ways of "Getting Things Done"

Our culture has maintained the myth that women should not have power because it's deviant and unacceptable if they want to be loved. To get what they want, women have had to learn how to exercise power in ways that were not obviously masculine. Once learned, these ways of controlling others were passed down from mother to daughter through the generations. They can be summarized as follows: (1) the power of manipulation, (2) personal power, and (3) the power of helplessness.

The Power of Manipulation

Someone who manipulates others acts as if the person being influenced doesn't know what's happening. The woman who manipulates people does not herself feel strong. The exact opposite of manipulation is straightforwardness: Both the person exerting the power and the one being influenced know exactly what is happening.

In her 1990 best seller *You Just Don't Understand,* Deborah Tannen demonstrates the difference between men's and women's styles of communication with the following anecdote: A married couple were on their way home one night when the woman decided she'd like to stop for a drink. But when she asked her husband if *he'd* like to stop, he said no and continued driving. By the time they got home, she was obviously upset. Surprised by his wife's behavior, the husband wondered why she didn't come right out and ask him to stop instead of playing games.

Tannen explains that the woman was angry not because her husband hadn't stopped but because she felt he hadn't shown any concern for her wishes. In contrast, she felt she had been considerate of his wishes by asking *if* he wanted to stop. Tannen concludes that although these styles of conversation are different, they are equally valid.[4]

Effective as straightforwardness is, women exert it at the risk of being labeled "tough," "bitchy," or "overbearing." According to Congresswoman Jolene Unsoeld of Washington, this happens because "the public does not know what the 'proper' image of a woman with power is. Somebody in Washington who wrote an article a couple years ago on people in power inevitably described the women as 'bitchy,' having tantrums and losing control. The men were described as 'tough,' not tolerating dissent, and this kind of thing. So the activities being described were identical, but the perceptions were so different." In other words, when women are direct, which would make them feel powerful, they are castigated by both men and other women. What a bind!

Unsoeld lamented that both men and women automatically assume men are effective simply because they are men. "It is assumed by both men and unfortunately women, too, that women are not — and they have to prove it."

Personal Power

Personal power is a capacity that causes people to do things for you because they know and like you. For example, when your neighbor surprises your family with a dinner casserole because you have the flu, she is responding to your personal power. The drawback of personal power is that it is dependent on others for a personal relationship.

By contrast, if you control resources such as money, knowledge, and physical strength, people do things for you not because of anything personal but because of what you control. In our society, men have traditionally controlled the resources. Mr. Tycoon, who routinely gets the best table and special service from the maître d' at an exclusive restaurant, benefits from the power of wealth. Obviously the maître d' knows him, but it is immaterial whether he does or does not like his customer. Mr. Tycoon always gets exceptional treatment because of his power and influence. Furthermore, he expects and enjoys it.

Unlike men, women have been more comfortable using personal power. It feels better to them than to men because it depends on interpersonal connections. The power of controlling resources by itself hasn't satisfied women because it doesn't convey love and good feelings in addition to the tangible reward.[5]

Even when women do control essential resources, they are discouraged from exerting their power directly. How many times have you seen a waiter automatically give the lunch check to the only man at the table — and then return the credit card to the man even though the signature on the charge slip is Helen's or Miriam's? From past experience, the waiter simply assumed that the man was in control.

Evelyn Murphy clearly understands the value of controlling resources: "Power is basically that sense of strength and understanding about how you pull together *resources* to get your agenda done." In other words, women shouldn't abandon that power in their zeal to accumulate the pleasurable feelings of personal power. The best way for women to accomplish their objectives is to combine both kinds of power and then sit back and savor the delayed satisfaction of seeing their agendas move.

The Power of Helplessness

Helplessness can be a very effective way to get others to do things for you. Women have learned over the years that helplessness is an effective and socially accepted way to control their worlds. Those who lack concrete resources and also think they lack competency, the ability to do a certain task, often rely on helplessness to get their way.

Let's consider the woman who never learned to drive. When she needs transportation, someone will have to be interrupted to drive her wherever she wants to go. She uses helplessness to exert power over her husband, her children who are old enough to drive, and probably relatives, friends, and neighbors. It should be clear that helplessness does not lead to strong leadership.

We All Have an Intuitive Sense of Power

A sense of power is inherent in all of us, male and female. It comes from a feeling of effectiveness and mastery. Children experience this sense of power as they stand erect and walk for the first time. You can see the obvious joy on the face of a child when she lets go of the sofa and takes her first unsupported steps into your arms. Althea Horner calls it *intrinsic power*, or the power of the self.[6] Intrinsic power develops in boys and girls alike. If you don't believe that you have power over yourself, your fate, your decisions and choices, you are unlikely to feel as if you have power to make things happen.

"I Am. I Can. I Will."

When we talk about power over yourself, we mean a sense of mastery and the ability to make things happen. Althea Horner sums up the sense of power beautifully as a feeling of "I am. I can. I will."[7] She explains that "I am" implies "I have an identity," "I can" suggests mastery, and "I will" describes the intention to take a certain action.

You can see that sense of power in toddlers who are beginning to do things alone, without the assistance or presence of a parent. But Horner would point out that the sense of power develops even earlier in the baby's development, when she is so dependent on and synchronized with her mother that she shares her power. The baby is hungry. She cries. She can't get her own food and would feel powerless if her cries didn't summon the mother. When the bonding between mother and child is satisfactory, the child develops early feelings of security and self-esteem, which are very much tied to the ability to control the mother and her power. The child's intrinsic power will gradually take over as she does more and more on her own and practices using her skills and abilities.

At the same time her intrinsic power is developing, the child will come up against a greater power: that of the parent. It is the reaction of mother and other family members to the child's autonomy that most strongly will affect her development from this age onward. According to Horner, the way that power struggle plays out will very much influence how the child will use power later in life, or refuse to use it. It will influence whether in later life she seeks or clings to power, hates or envies it, or rebels against it.

Some parents applaud and beam at their children's independence and interfere only when it is really necessary. Children from such families will develop a healthy sense of power. Other parents criticize and chastise independent behavior. Their children, to stay in their parents' good graces, will retreat and allow their parents to direct them. Still other parents fail to exercise sufficient parental power, leaving too much responsibility in the hands of children who are not yet ready for it. These children become premature adults. They do not have the tools to run their own lives. They feel frightened that their power will destroy the parents on whom they depend. The building of this delicate balance of power recurs over and over again as children develop physically and intellectually.

At about the same time, children begin to encounter what Horner calls "formal power," which is held by teachers, police officers, coaches, employers, and other authority figures. Experiences of formal power reinforce children's perceptions of their

parents as all-powerful giants. If the parents and authority figures loom too large the child will feel powerless. If they're not
large enough the child will feel overwhelmed with the weight
of her own power.

Adolescence provides another opportunity to solidify a sense
of power. Teenagers have to reconcile their sense of self with a
changing pubescent body. They have to move further away
from their parents and assume more responsibility. Once again,
the parents' response to this behavior is critical to development.

"I Don't Know What I Once Knew"

Another strong influence in adolescence is society's expectations of appropriate behavior for girls and boys. This is the
point at which Carol Gilligan in *Making Connections* describes
how girls retreat from their early sense of power to achieve
social approval.

Gilligan uses the example of Tanya, an eighth grader who
was unable to confront an unpopular girl who had begun to
follow her around. Tanya explained, "I don't like this girl at all
. . . I absolutely hate her, but I don't know how to act because I
have to be nice."[8]

Had Tanya encountered this problem several years earlier,
she might have said, "I don't like this girl, and I don't want to
play with her." Gilligan would call this reaction an eleven-year-
old's "moment of resistance." She believes that an eleven-year-
old has a particularly sharp, clear vision; almost perfect confidence in what she knows and sees; and a strong belief in her
integrity and in her highly complex responsibilities toward the
world. Eleven-year-olds are not for sale. One of the other girls
Gilligan studied illustrates this point by her Creatively Aggressive response to a sentence completion test: "What gets me

into trouble is . . . chewing gum and not tucking my shirt in —
but it's usually worth it!" she adds rebelliously.[9]

At the time Gilligan interviewed her, Tanya's budding sense
of Creative Aggression had been stifled for the sake of acceptance and approval. She had experienced the crisis in adolescence in response to society's demand that girls "keep quiet
and notice the absence of women and say nothing." Her rebel-
lious resistance had been replaced by self-doubt based on societal or cultural expectations. Her self-messages had been translated into "I don't know. I don't know. I don't know what I once
knew."

Reclaiming Power

Although little girls and little boys experience the same developmental delight in mastery, societal expectations keep adult
women, as a group, from having the same sense of power that
adult men have. Yet the women we studied differ from the
female stereotype of being docile, passive, and subservient. For
them, something different happened. Either their power never
went underground during their teenage years, or they were able
to reclaim it and use it constructively as they matured. (In
Chapter 7 we discuss how these women were able to retain or
reclaim their power late in life.)

Several women we talked with didn't hold back about explaining how they feel about being able to get things done. "I
like power," one said. "I get a big rev out of it!" said another. "I
like being powerful. Hopefully I do not have too much problem
dealing with it, even though it is frightening. But I feel like
somebody's going to have it, so it might just as well be me."

A few of the political women we interviewed described remaining out of touch with their power even after they had achieved high political office. For example, Jo Ann Zimmerman, lieutenant governor of Iowa, told us:

> I didn't think about having power myself. There are just things to do, and you get them done. I never thought that I had power until I realized that other people were telling me that I did. I realized I was getting all those signals, that I had power, and that I had better step in and use it or somebody else would use it. Power's not set; it's amorphous. It's not just there because you think it's there. It's there because people give it to you and you think it's there. And if somebody doesn't use it there's a vacuum that somebody else will step into. There's always something to be done, and if you can see power and find the right time to use it, it's yours. So you reach out and you take it.

Evelyn Murphy had a solid enough sense of power to see herself as the one who could step into the vacuum. But she wasn't conscious of having that power. She didn't *think* about it. She had buried it somewhere along the line, but not so deeply that it couldn't be used.

Similarly, Congresswoman Claudine Schneider of Rhode Island observed:

> Somebody once said to me, "You're influential and powerful." And that just knocked me over. I never considered it. But I went home that night and I thought, "Yes, I am definitely influential. I can pick up the phone and reach almost anyone, strategize how to make things happen, and then just do it." Now *powerful*, I couldn't relate to that word because I identify it more with a *position* of power.

Schneider, too, had progressed to elective office without registering in her mind that she was powerful. But as we talked further she added, "I feel very powerful as a person, not so much as a politician." Perhaps she was saying that her sense of personal power was solid because it had been there since childhood, whereas her sense of political power was still new, developing, and less secure.

Overcoming the Stereotype
of Powerlessness

Males dominate our culture and regard females as powerless beings. Perhaps this phenomenon is men's reaction to the power struggle against their mothers, rooted in the natural division of labor that emerged during the earliest days of history: men were the hunters and women the nurturers. Over time, males evolved as the doers and females as the ones who expressed feelings. (We will talk more of maternal power later.)

It is not surprising that once men achieved power and dominance in society they would not be in a hurry to give them up. Between societal development and the struggle against maternal power, men had every reason to keep women from acquiring power. As Congresswoman Nancy Pelosi observed:

> Power is not anything that anybody has given away in the history of the world. I tell women all the time that if you want it, you have to go for it and you have to be very serious about getting it and holding it. It's not anything antiwoman or anything else. It's just that men don't want to give up their power to another man or to a woman.

This is not to say that men today go around plotting with each other how to keep women in their place. As Jeane Kirkpatrick pointed out in *Political Woman*, her trailblazing book published in 1974, even after legal barriers to women's participation in politics came down, cultural norms continued to identify politics as "man's work."[10] There are few links between a "woman's world" and politics. Thus, the careers that lead to politics — law, business, and unions — have been male-dominated, and the political positions themselves are filled by men.

Unconscious processes and societal constrictions perpetuate the notion that power is masculine. Here's a subtle example: When a man wants to discuss a power tactic, in politics or business or any other field, he will use football or war metaphors, activities that are not traditionally part of women's experience. This symbolically, and sometimes practically, leaves women out of the experience. How many times is the leader described as the "quarterback," in an allusion to a game that few women have ever played? Do men really sell their ideas by "making an end run" around someone who is standing in their way? No, not literally. But they use sports metaphors to explain their successes in the big game of life. Consciously or unconsciously, they exclude women from the playing field of power.

The Need for Attachment to Others

It might seem from what we've said thus far that it's all men's fault that women don't have power. But the truth is that women themselves can perpetuate the notion that power is unfeminine. They may even reject power. As Suzie Azar said about being invited to join an all-male board after her election as mayor of El Paso: "I got so involved in this male world for the first few months, it felt like I had stepped into this new arena, that one day going into the women's room I almost felt like I should be going into the men's room now." Translation: "If I have power, I'm no longer a woman." Fortunately, she was able to integrate her power and her female identity and reports that she now brings women along with her and caucuses in the ladies' room.

Many women *do* reject power as part of themselves and their self-images. Congresswoman Nancy Johnson of Connecticut told us candidly that "power is something I was always very, very afraid of. It was a word I didn't like." She certainly is not alone in that fear.

Why do women commonly fear power? To answer that question we have to first state an assumption: Relationships are critically important to women. This is because a woman's sense of self is tied to her need for connection or attachment to others.

How does this happen? It has to do with the fact that little girls are the same as their mothers and little boys are different. As infants, boys and girls alike are closer to their mothers than to their fathers. After a few years, however, the little boys begin to identify with and make a closer connection with Daddy. And they stay there. The little girls also leave their mothers and make a connection with Daddy, but they come back to Mommy by way of identifying with her.

The little boy's "task" is to move away from Mommy and become independent. He looks at his mother and thinks, "That's not me. I have to be something else. I have to find a different way to be because Mommy and I are different." He glances at his father and decides, "Oh, I'm like him." But that means he first has to tear himself away psychologically from this cozy lady.

The little girl doesn't have to move away from her mother to develop her gender identity. She may move away later for other reasons, but from the beginning her connection with Mother is unbroken. As a result, girls are more defined by the continuity of relationships and closeness.

With that assumption in place, we can appreciate Jean Baker

Miller's thoughtful explanation about why women fear power: Their fear is based on a belief that if they are powerful they will destroy their relationships. Miller explains that women fear power because of what she calls "a troublesome equation" that they experience.[11] They fear they would be acting selfishly if they were to use power. This is because exercising power conflicts with the lifelong messages they have received about devoting their energies to enhance the power of others. Thus, women equate selfishness with destructiveness. They come to fear that such selfishness and destructiveness may result in abandonment by those around them. It is easy to see why women feel threatened by isolation and a loss of their feminine need to serve and connect with others if they were to gather and exert power.

Clarice Kestenbaum entitled an article in a psychoanalytic journal "The Professional Woman's Dilemma: Love and/or Power." The very title expresses the conflict and fear with which women contend: If I exert power, will I still be lovable? Kestenbaum noted that in Roman mythology, women with their own power had no men in their lives. The powerful goddess Minerva was never married and never had love affairs, while beautiful Venus attracted men but had no power.[12] The differences between them were clearly delineated. Minerva's powerful attributes were never integrated with Venus's loving, nurturing qualities into the same person.

Often that's still the case today. As Kathleen Connell, Rhode Island's secretary of state, said, "Many of us, at least our generation, are man pleasers." She explained that when she disagreed with a man in her role as a registered nurse she learned to broach the subject of the disagreement with a question or subservient suggestion. She would ask, "Do you think this is a good idea?" or suggest, "This might be a good way to proceed," rather than stating, "This is how I think we should go. Are you going to join me in this?" What's the message here? To please men and keep them liking you, always defer to them. Hardly a message of power.

Since relationships are so critical to women, it's no wonder that they fear power. As a result, they sabotage their power by continuing to operate in smaller, more comfortable worlds, of which the most obvious is the family.

Mothers' Power

Although power and nurturance have been viewed as contradictory, in truth Mother is an extremely powerful figure in the household. Raising children is a powerful position. Mothers' power has both obvious and hidden dimensions.

Mother wields *obvious* power in her role as director of the family — shopping, planning meals and vacations, directing bedtime and homework time, and the like. Remember the old joke about the man who said he had all the power in the family because although his wife decided what they did every day, he could decide whether to admit Red China to the United Nations? In other words, within the household men defer to the female. However, as long as men were the sole breadwinners and therefore controlled the resources, the ultimate veto power belonged to them.

How often have you heard mothers disciplining their children, "Wait until your father gets home!" It's not hard for the kids to figure out who holds the final power in the house. Some women use that threat because they do not believe they are as powerful as their husbands, while others are afraid to take on disciplinary power for fear of alienating their children and losing the connection to them.

The hidden dimensions of mothers' power enable Mother to

foster her children's growth. She is able to do this through her role as caretaker. In doing so, she empowers others and vicariously finds the measure of her success in their success. Although women are aware of the influence they have on their children's lives, they do not usually recognize that influence as "power." Yet our culture perpetuates the myth that if you go into psychotherapy, you'll come out hating your mother.

Although the myth is untrue, the notion behind it needs to be considered: No matter what has happened to you in your life, your mother is responsible. The reality of the power of motherhood lies somewhere between the denial that there is *any* power in motherhood and the myth that the mother is omnipotent and controls everything in her children's lives.

Because she is the primary caretaker, the mother's needs do influence her children's development. Some mothers, those whose lives are satisfying, move away from the children and experience their own sense of competency and power. Other mothers, with less satisfying lives, either try to keep their children close and stifle their independent development or push them away before they are ready. This turns the children out into a frightening world without sufficient resources to function properly. As you can see, it is important for mothers to recognize the power they have, positive or negative, in their children's lives. It is also important that they recognize that they are not the child's only influence.

What keeps mothers' power from being the sole factor in children's development? Other influences on children include fathers, siblings, grandparents, extended family, friends, teachers, and other authority figures that children encounter throughout their lives. In addition, there is a natural developmental thrust that slowly moves children forward in preparation for separation from mother.

Mothers are powerful figures. Society tolerates mothers' power, and women feel comfortable with it. But neither society nor mothers define what they have as *truly* powerful because its sphere of influence seems so small. As Jean Baker Miller has pointed out, the real world doesn't define power as enhancing other people's power, and that's what mothers' power is all about.[13]

Politicians and Power

When we asked Congresswoman Nancy Johnson what power means to her, she told us, "The more I thought about it, the more I realized how much power I had as a parent and how much I exercised it." She added that she felt the same way when she worked in volunteer activities. Then she made this critical observation: "I came to see that taking responsibility is taking power." Once she made the connection to her power in other areas of life, she was able to move out into the world with it. Johnson, who had told us earlier that at one time power was a word she didn't like, later said, "I *am* a politician. I am a damned good one, and I'm proud of it. And, yes, I exercise power. That's my job."

We asked Johnson if wielding power was all right with her. Her answer was unequivocal:

My goal is to be a powerful advocate on behalf of my constituents. I enjoy that sense of "Yes, I have power." And I exercise it responsibly, but forcefully. One of the things that always amuses me is that when we really get into issues, my constituents or my colleagues will say, "I wouldn't want to be on the wrong side of your fence." All of that power that I saw in my father I now see in myself. And to exercise it responsibly and to not let it drive me is a challenge.

WomanPower in the World
of Politics

Must women abandon their style and behave like men to feel powerful and be perceived as leaders? Congresswoman Pat Saiki of Hawaii thinks men are more sensitive about this question than women are:

> I think men tend to be a lot more nervous about the male-female relationship in a professional or powerful body than the women do. I don't think women are as affected by the power that's around them. They're not often as awed by it. I don't think women aspire to powerful positions as eagerly as men do. Maybe it's because we don't aspire to the use of power for our own purposes.

Saiki's view of women and power redefines power through feminine eyes. It is a caring kind of power. It's not self-serving; instead, it's directed toward advancing an agenda. It's what we mean by WomanPower.

Traditionally, the male model of behavior is used as the standard. Someone who wants to compliment a woman is likely to say that she's "as good as a man." And all too often, to emulate men in the corporate world women give up their feelings of connection, warmth, friendship, and empathy.[14] The assumption is that male power is the *only* legitimate kind of power and that women are afraid or unable to seize it.

We like Jean Baker Miller's response to that idea:

> Frankly, I think women are absolutely right to fear the use of power as it has been generally conceptualized and used. The very fact that this is more often said to be a defensive or neurotic fear is, I believe, a more telling commentary on the state of our culture than it was on women.[15]

As we have said, WomanPower integrates typically female qualities with some male characteristics, and it values both kinds of attributes equally. For those who still see aggression and nurturance as incompatible qualities, we reply that it is possible to be assertive and achievement-oriented while at the same time owning maternal strengths and power. The key is in recognizing that there is strength rather than weakness in tenderness and caring.

Congresswoman Olympia Snowe told us, "I'm very much of a realist, and I don't like to hurt anybody, even in politics." Does that mean she can't and won't engage in debate or put forward her point of view? Not at all. She went on to say, "I'm pretty much straightforward in a conflict. I'm not interested in the game playing and maneuvering that I think is more commonly associated with men than women."

Jo Ann Zimmerman, lieutenant governor of Iowa, had been trained as a nurse to confront men in a nonthreatening manner. She described how she once took advantage of the vacuum that was created when the balance of power in the legislature shifted: "I said, 'OK, guys, here I am. I'll help you solve some of these squabbles.' I think it was the nurse thing coming back. They started coming in and saying, 'Got this problem.' And I could reach out and do things with them." When she talks about "the nurse thing," she means her nurturing side that responds to someone else's needs. But now she uses that part of her personality to implement her agenda.

WomanPower also encompasses the notion of empowering others, a page taken from the mothers' power book. Contrast that with the common notion that, to be powerful, one must stomp on people on the way up. Ruth Messinger, president of the borough of Manhattan, expressed annoyance at that kind of power, contrasting it with her view of power as the ability to get things done. "More often," she said, "it's used as the ability to make other people do things or to control other people in ways that I don't think are appropriate. That's how I run into it. It makes me angry."

Congresswoman Snowe expressed clearly what so many of the women told us: "Power means to me being able to do something for others. I use the power of my office to help other people. I view this office as the potential of helping somebody else out."

We want to emphasize that WomanPower includes a reason for being, a purpose, an agenda to be advanced. This is diametrically opposite to the tendency of men to enter politics for power and influence with no particular agenda in mind.[16] Indeed, Sidney Verba of Harvard University suggests that women's most distinctive contribution to politics is that they are more interested in doing things for the public good than in simply expanding their own sphere of power.[17]

Many of the women we interviewed have witnessed the undirected acquisition of an appearance of power. As Congresswoman Snowe said, "Some people just like to acquire power, but they do nothing with it and they fail to exercise their leadership." And Nita Lowey, Congresswoman from New York, put it this way: "The thing about this job that's so gratifying is that it gives you the power to really set an agenda and to get things done. *Power in itself means nothing.*" That last sentence says it clearly. It isn't the appearance of power suggested in an impressive title that has real meaning. Real strength lies in the capacity to lead others to achieve a meaningful agenda, whether in politics or in the business world.

Power and the Ability
to Lead

U.S. Senator Barbara Mikulski gave a good definition of leadership:

> I think leadership is creating a state of mind in others. President Kennedy's legislative accomplishments were skimpy, but he created a state of mind in this country that endures long after his death. Churchill created a state of mind in Great Britain and enabled the British to endure the blitz and marshal the resources to help turn the tide of World War II. Martin Luther King, Jr., created a state of mind. Florence Nightingale created a state of mind in people about what nursing should be, that it shouldn't be those who were derelicts and ladies of the night, that it was a profession.

The acquisition of power, whether by males or females, does not guarantee that leadership, the ability to influence others, will emerge automatically. Power in itself is not enough. The successful leader must believe strongly enough in his or her ideas to want to put them forth to others, and others must look to this person as an authority figure. Congresswoman Barbara Boxer said it best:

> If you want to be a leader, it doesn't mean that you have to have an opinion on everything. But if you do have an opinion and it is clear and you feel strongly about it, then you should say it.

Congresswoman Nancy Johnson carried this thought one step further: "In a sense if you have ideas and always put them to use, then you're automatically a leader."

When we asked Congresswoman Olympia Snowe to distinguish between power and leadership, she said:

I see leadership as the willingness to move to the forefront on an issue. You may have the power, but you may not be a leader. I've seen that here in Congress. I think there are some truly natural leaders and there are those who are not. I've been disappointed over the years by people who've failed to exercise their leadership. They just haven't grabbed the issue and moved to the forefront with it. Either they were unwilling to lead or wouldn't take a position that might not be extremely popular even though it would have been the right thing to do. Some people just like to acquire power, but they do nothing with it and fail to exercise their leadership.

Congresswoman Marge Roukema of New Jersey agreed that an elected official should be willing to take unpopular positions:

Sometimes you must reflect the views of your constituents. But there are other times when you have to be an educator. Even when your people don't understand, you have to educate them to the issue. Governance is leadership and moving issues forward even when they're unpopular. That's leadership.

Becoming a Leader in a Male Environment

Leadership opportunities exist not only in politics but in everyday life and in the business world. Paula Johnson, who studied men's and women's effectiveness in daily life situations, found that men could employ both the typically male and female forms of power, which we discussed earlier, whereas women were restricted to the less effective, female forms.[18]

What a dilemma this poses for women. When a man leads other men, they relate to each other as equals. The situation is much different when women lead men because women have been taught from girlhood not to be assertive around men. Many men have a hard time relating to a female supervisor. That's one reason why a woman manager, even if she feels that her ideas are worth presenting, may have a harder time getting and keeping men's attention than a male supervisor would.

A number of recent studies have confirmed differences in men's and women's managerial styles. For example, the autonomy and power related to management are more important to men than to women.[19] Women managers inspire their subordinates to excel by creating an atmosphere in which people feel good about the place in which they work and what they do.[20] Doesn't that sound like a traditional mother's role in creating a happy home? New management techniques include acknowledging other people's feelings. That doesn't sound new at all. It is a shift to acceptance of the value of a more feminine perspective.

The problem for women is that they are often assessed by men with a preference for the male-style approach, or they have to reconcile contradictory expectations to succeed, contradictions not imposed on men. Here are four examples:

- *Take risks, but be consistently outstanding.* The obvious dilemma — if success were guaranteed, it wouldn't be a risk.
- *Be tough, but don't be macho.* We certainly have heard that theme before from our political women.
- *Be ambitious, but don't expect equal treatment* — in pay, perks, and rate of advancement.
- *Take responsibility, but follow others' advice.*[21]

Another leadership problem for women is that males, beginning as early as second grade, talk more than females. Also, men's opinions are more likely to influence others. If taking action is perceived as leadership and men take more opportunities to talk and act, then women are less likely to be seen as leaders. In addition, leadership is in the eyes of the led, that is, in their willingness to accept the leader's authority. Men are more respectful of the authority of other men, whom they see as being inside the system.[22]

Finally, males grow up in a competitive environment. They are accustomed to being team players. They are used to losing as well as winning. Sports, for men, is a training ground that prepares them to get along in large structured groups, even with people they don't particularly like. In contrast, women are traditionally socialized in small play groups that emphasize cooperation rather than competition.

What all this means is that to be taken seriously as leaders, women have to work harder than their male colleagues do, whatever environment they are in. And in the corporate world, as in politics, the ultimate "boys' club" is at the top. In politics, the incumbency of men makes it difficult for women to get elected (as it does male newcomers).

The women we interviewed told us repeatedly how hard they have to work now to be perceived as leaders. But they also recalled *always* leading their friends and classmates as they grew up, so that leadership felt natural. Mary Landrieu, treasurer of Louisiana, feels that she sharpened her leadership skills between seventh grade and senior year in high school: "You never feel more powerful than when you're a senior in high school. I mean, I thought I could change the world single-handedly when I was seventeen years old." Doesn't that sound familiar?

Congresswoman Nita Lowey too has felt comfortable with leadership since childhood:

> I guess somehow I was always in a position of leadership. When you're president of a class, I don't know that it takes *great* courage. I don't look at any of this as great courage because I feel comfortable in that role. My natural instinct is to be a facilitator or a compromiser because I do see most issues as gray rather than black and white.

So leadership was something that came naturally. In high school, for example, I became president of the senior class because none of my friends would run against me. My opponent wasn't as well known and didn't have as many friends in the "leadership ranks" as I did.

Although being a leader means, as Congresswoman Connie Morella said, "you work damn hard," there is still personal gratification for women who are in positions of power. New York Congresswoman Nita Lowey noted:

You're constantly expanding your knowledge, and that's tremendously gratifying, too. In the course of the day in Washington you can be meeting with a Robert McNamara or the prime minister of Pakistan or prime minister of Israel and going to a workshop to discuss drugs or going to a Select Committee on Narcotics and hearing from every expert in the world — or at least the United States — on these issues. It's tremendously expansive, and that's very exciting.

Often there's a real kick to the experience. Mayor Suzie Azar described how excited she felt when first elected:

I got invited to be on the downtown board, the board of executives. It's all of the bank presidents, all of the big muckety-mucks. And it's all men. I liked that. I liked all of a sudden being raised up to their level. I became a peer with the guys downtown. I have a lot of very strong opinions about a lot of subjects, but all of a sudden everybody was listening to my opinions. The newspaper was asking for my opinion with every issue. I had had the same opinions earlier as a councilwoman for four years, but I never got to put them in print. And now all of a sudden my opinions were valuable and all of a sudden what I thought was very worthwhile. *That's power.*

There can be pleasure in feeling powerful and anger at those who use power for their own benefit. As you read on and learn about the messages that the women we studied received as they were growing up, ask yourself whether your experiences were the same as or different from theirs. In the final two chapters we will suggest ways you can enhance your sense of power and develop it in your daughters.

We close with the words of Louisiana Treasurer Mary Landrieu, who said it all:

> I like being powerful. I hope it doesn't go to my head. If somebody's going to have it, it might just as soon be me. There's always power, and it's just a matter of in whose hands it falls. I don't think women have enough of those power levers in their hands. It is a little scary, but I'd like to use the power that comes from this office to help other people and to really make our state and the world better. I think it's the only reason one should want power. It shouldn't be for one's self-enrichment or to make your ego feel better. I really believe that power should be used to serve other people. If it can't be, then it should be taken away.

3

The Legitimacy
of WomanPower and Politics

In 1988, before the Republicans and the Democrats had selected their presidential candidates, *Life* magazine ran a photo story featuring the major presidential hopefuls of both parties. The article was titled "So What Do You Want to Be When You Grow Up? PRESIDENT!" *Life* asked what the candidates had wanted to be at age twelve and the earliest age at which they wanted to be president. The following were their responses.

Candidate	Wanted to Be at Age 12	Earliest Age Wanted to Be President
Bruce Babbitt	Ski instructor	16
George Bush	Major league baseball player	18
Robert Dole	Doctor or baseball player	50
Michael Dukakis	Doctor	53
Pete DuPont	"Something different than at age 11"	47
Richard Gephardt	Cardinals center fielder	44
Albert Gore, Jr.	Professional football player	39
Jesse Jackson	Professional baseball or football player	42
Jack Kemp	Pro football quarterback	51
Paul Simon	Journalist	8

Not a woman in the bunch, or so it seems. *Life* did interview a woman, Jeane Kirkpatrick, former U.S. ambassador to the United Nations and a respected political scientist, who was being touted as a possible presidential candidate; but her responses and photo didn't appear in the article. Obviously she didn't fit the conventional pattern of a presidential hopeful. When asked at what age she decided she wanted to be president, Kirkpatrick retorted: "Girls don't dream of becoming President."[1] *Life* called her response "refreshingly candid."

Candid, yes. But not refreshing, at least from the female viewpoint. Kirkpatrick's comment, coming as it does from a successful, highly regarded political woman, is just another indicator that, as a rule, girls don't grow up dreaming of a career in politics — or in leadership in general. (Chapter 5 will examine the crucial role that dreams play in the lives of children and young adults, both women and men.)

In Chapter 2 we discussed some of the psychological reasons that the general public, and women themselves, do not feel comfortable with the idea of women in positions of power. In this chapter we will examine some of the social and political factors — some might call them obstacles — that have impeded women's political progress over the years.

Moving Beyond the Women's Agenda

Implicit in any discussion about women's share of power and their political behavior, says Jeane Kirkpatrick in *Political Woman*,[2] is the assumption that sexual differences are relevant to politics. If this assumption is not made, Kirkpatrick says, then there would be no point in talking about the political behavior of women as a group.

Why should we be interested in the political behavior of women as a group? For one thing, we chose politics as our model because it is the field in which the use and abuse of power and leadership are most evident. Aside from the fact that women are represented in office so disproportionately to their numbers in the population, are there reasons other than equity why more women should hold public office? What's so special about female officeholders? Can they really make a difference?

Congresswoman Claudine Schneider of Rhode Island stated in an article that women don't claim to have all the answers, but their unique perspective on life enables them to bring a valuable new dimension to politics. She attributes this to the fact that females' growing-up experiences are so different from those of males. Thus, the female perspective, based on nurturing and caring, can be manifested by a range of social and intellectual concerns (shades of what we talked about in Chapter 2). Women, she says, are more sensitive to issues ranging from child and family care to how to deal with "the day-to-day frustrations of rising costs." But she believes that until the number of women in office is about even with men, these contributions from the female experience will continue to be largely lost.[3]

Former Governor Madeleine Kunin of Vermont agrees that women in politics do make a difference:

> I'm not of the school that thinks by putting 50 women in a legislative body you automatically bring in peace, goodwill, and perfection. But I do think we reflect our own values and value systems, our own lifetime experience as we take part in the political process. Women in our legislature generally promote a progressive agenda and they've moved some of the women's issues onto the general agenda.[4]

Programs put forth by political women, such as federal funding for abortions and family and medical leave, are examples of issues that women have advocated so strongly that they eventually were moved to this country's "general agenda." Thus far women haven't achieved the critical mass in American politics that would enable them to change the course or style of the political process, but we expect this will occur when women in office becomes the rule rather than the exception. As former vice presidential candidate Geraldine Ferraro aptly remarked in 1991, "When women stop making history women can start making policy."[5]

The Center for American Women in Politics has reported that a majority of women officeholders take liberal stands on women's issues. For example, women officeholders are more likely than their male colleagues to support ratification of the Equal Rights Amendment and to oppose a constitutional amendment to ban abortion.[6]

The Gender Gulf

Although women's organized efforts dating back to the mid-1800s did culminate in ratification of the Nineteenth Amendment — and the right to vote in 1920 for the first time — no strong women's voting bloc developed until very recently. Certainly ratification of the Nineteenth Amendment symbolized women's access to political power. But women's suffrage, Jeane Kirkpatrick writes, did not significantly affect the social makeup of government. This contrasted sharply with the actions of other newly enfranchised groups such as blacks and immigrants when they received the right to vote. For example, "As Irish and Italian men gained the right to vote they elected more Irish and Italian men to party and public office. But when Irish women gained the right to vote, they also elected more Irish men to office."[7]

Much has been written in the last few years about the prospective impact of a gender gap on politics. But only recently has the gender gap proved to be as viable as was anticipated by candidates and party workers in the past decade.

In an article entitled "The Gender Gulf," pollster Louis Harris writes that in late 1990 women as a bloc swayed American public opinion on the national level for the first time. The issue was whether the United States should use military force in the Persian Gulf after the Iraqi invasion of Kuwait. When Harris compared polls taken in 1964 and 1965, before the outbreak of the Vietnam War, against some taken a month prior to the war in the Persian Gulf, he noted the dramatic growth in the impact of women's opinion.

Harris found that men and women had basically the same views in regard to strategies, such as trade embargoes, that did not involve the loss of human life. However, men were equally divided when it came to strategies such as attacking Iraqi forces, while 73 percent of women opposed an attack. It was the opposition to the use of military force by three-quarters of American women that swayed the entire poll against the war. Nevertheless, this groundswell of public opinion against the war did not affect policy, as members of Congress demonstrated in January 1991 when they supported President Bush's stand in the Persian Gulf. What if a larger percentage of women had been in power or there had been a woman president? Would things have been different? Might the same goal have been accomplished without the loss of life?

Harris believes one of the repercussions of the gender gap effect may be changes in the traditional roles of the Republican and Democratic parties in regard to war. And repercussions from the "gender gulf," concludes Harris, are only going to increase in the future.[8]

Bridging the Gender Gulf

To better understand why it has been difficult for women to acquire and wield political power — let alone dream of becoming president — we must examine some of the social, political, and environmental barriers that political women have encountered over the years. We'll give these roadblocks a psychological spin as we discuss ways that politically minded women can help themselves and their daughters turn these barriers into opportunities.

"Amateur" Status

From early childhood Americans learn about the following three aspects of politics:

1. The role of the citizen: voting and so on
2. The relationship of the citizen to the state: loyalty, patriotism, and so on
3. Performance of specialized political roles

Boys learn all three. But girls generally learn only the first two — they know that to be a good citizen they must vote and support their government. But they aren't taught how to perform specialized political roles.[9] Because women aren't prepared for these roles, most never dream of themselves in such positions. As Booles and Swan observe in *Power Failure*, "most men don't doubt that they are entitled to become president; most women do."[10]

An organized system of keeping people out of power makes no sense, especially to those on the outside. One effective way to bring home to those on the inside what it's like to be excluded is with a sort of role reversal. The following humorous poke at men's suffrage was written by Alice Duer Miller, a novelist and poet who lived from 1874 to 1942. She wrote this in 1915, five years before the Nineteenth Amendment gave women the right to vote.

Why We Don't Want Men to Vote

1. Because man's place is in the army.
2. Because no really manly man wants to settle any question otherwise than by fighting about it.
3. Because if men should adopt peaceable methods women will no longer look up to them.
4. Because men will lose their charm if they step out of their natural sphere and interest themselves in other matters than feats of arms, uniforms and drums.
5. Because men are too emotional to vote. Their conduct at baseball games and political conventions shows this, while their innate tendency to appeal to force renders them unfit for government.[11]

We're not charging that there is a nationwide male conspiracy to keep women out of power. However, we agree with Jeane Kirkpatrick's observation that men tend to bar women from influential positions to protect the status quo:

> Society has never barred women from breadwinning roles, but only from economic roles that are profitable and respectable. . . . Men do not bar women from taking part in politics, but only hamper their efforts to participate in power.[12]

Traditionally, a common — and acceptable by male standards — political job for women is doing volunteer clerical duties at party headquarters or in an individual campaign. Spending many hours stuffing envelopes for the party isn't likely to advance a devoted female party worker too far in the system.

As Millicent Fenwick, former New Jersey congresswoman, complained: "Women are on the outside when the door to the smoke-filled room is closed." She believes that one reason for this exclusion is that

> women are new in politics; we come to it with some zeal and idealism. . . . The result is that the political operators have a sense that we will not understand the political realities — and they are often right. Maybe it's not a female characteristic as much as an amateur characteristic. Maybe some day we'll lose our amateur standing.[13]

Naturally, those in command aren't about to share their power with "amateurs." As Shirley Chisholm observed during her presidential campaign in the 1970s, "No one is giving it away."[14] Women have to learn to aggressively seek out and grasp power for themselves.

We don't mean to imply that women shouldn't get involved in their party's menial chores. Candidates can learn much from their experience with nuts-and-bolts aspects of political campaigns. In fact, several of the women we talked with mentioned that their early experience with the party gave them the confidence and knowledge to embark on their own campaigns years later.

What we do mean is that a woman who dreams of entering politics shouldn't be content doing only clerical work. Instead, she should climb upward through the party hierarchy to more responsible, managerial positions that will not only enhance her knowledge but also increase her visibility within the party and the community.

Congresswoman Nancy Pelosi of San Francisco is one of the few who have made the quantum leap from party worker to the U.S. House of Representatives without first serving in a lesser elective position. She was elected to Congress in a hard-fought special election to fill the seat vacated by the death of Congresswoman Sala Burton. Pelosi, whose father had been a congressman from Maryland and later mayor of Baltimore, earned a high profile of her own through her many years of devotion to the Democratic party. Among other positions, she had been a major fundraiser and a contender for the party's national chair. Hardly the envelope-stuffing category.

The world of politics, especially at the highest level, continues to be dominated and controlled by men. Although more and more women are winning elections, particularly at the state, county, and city levels, politics is one of the last male bastions. The failure of female candidates in 1990 to show a net increase in the U.S. Senate, House, and governorships demonstrates once again that women have made little progress toward shattering the "glass ceiling" that separates women politicians from the highest offices in the land. Yet women have as much at stake as men do in determining "who gets what, when and how."[15]

One would think that with so few women in politics those who are there would become household names. Unfortunately, that is not the case, as we suspect you'll discover as you take the following quiz. Do you know what the following groups of political women have in common?

A. Jane Byrne, Sharon Pratt Dixon, Dianne Feinstein, and Maureen O'Connor
B. Barbara Mikulski and Margaret Chase Smith
C. Shirley Chisholm, Patsy Takemoto Mink, and Ileana Ros-Lehtinen
D. Hattie Wyatt Caraway, Martha Griffiths, Mary Norton, and Leonor Sullivan
E. Jeannette Rankin, Hattie Wyatt Caraway, Susanna Salter, and Ella Grasso

The answers: A, mayors of major cities; B, women who have served in both the U.S. Senate and House of Representatives; C, first black (Chisholm), Asian-Pacific-American (Mink), and

Cuban-American women (Ros-Lehtinen) to be elected to the House of Representatives; D, women who have chaired congressional committees; E, first women to be elected to high positions: U.S. House of Representatives (Rankin), U.S. Senate (Caraway, appointed to succeed her husband and subsequently elected to two full terms), mayor (Salter), and governor (Grasso).[16]

We hope to be able to add the names of the first female president and vice president to this list in the not too distant future. Until then, we encourage aspiring female politicians to use those listed here and their peers as role models of politically savvy women.

Sexism

Occasionally voters wonder if a male candidate is tough enough to hold office, but women office seekers are always expected to prove their competency, strength, and experience. They have to walk a fine line between reassuring the voters about their toughness and not appearing too aggressive or — horrors — shrill. This is particularly true of Democratic women candidates because the stereotypes of being liberal, supporting family and children's issues, and being female reinforce one another.[17]

Probably the most notorious example of a toughness test administered to a female candidate occurred in 1984 during the vice presidential debate between Geraldine Ferraro and George Bush. The final question in the debate, directed to Ferraro, asked how she proposed to convince the public and potential enemies that she would be able to protect the security of the United States should it become necessary. Ferraro assured the questioner that as president she would do whatever was required to protect the country militarily, but first she would do everything possible to avoid getting to the point where war was the only alternative. In response, Bush stressed his record as a pilot during World War II, emphasizing his strength and toughness as qualifications for the presidency. The irony is that George Bush lost the 1980 presidential nomination to Ronald Reagan because Bush had been perceived as a "wimp."

In *Ferraro: My Story*, an account of her role in the unsuccessful 1984 Democratic campaign, Ferraro commented poignantly on the implications of this line of reasoning for women:

> What a pointless resumé for leadership, excluding over half the population from the top rungs of government. If you hadn't fought at the halls of Montezuma, ran the argument, you couldn't understand the need for peace on the shores of Tripoli.

This line of reasoning, she continued, was "as valid as saying you would have to be black in order to despise racism, that you'd have to be female in order to be terribly offended by sexism. And that's just not so."[18]

The toughness test also conceals a double standard. Women are judged more harshly than men for showing emotion in public. Colorado's Congresswoman Pat Schroeder says she wishes she hadn't cried the day she withdrew from the presidential race, but the tears just came. Some women who supported her felt betrayed by her tears: "I wish she hadn't cried. How could she do that to us?" But when President Reagan read letters from children on television he almost always had tears in his eyes, and Michael Dukakis was applauded for his emotional tribute to his family at the Democratic convention.

Factors such as personal appearance tend to color voters' perceptions about female far more than male candidates. Hair styles, height, weight, dress, and general grooming of the female candidate provide daily fodder for the news media. Congresswoman Olympia Snowe stoically has learned to live with it:

You can't always ascertain how people will react to you personally. One of the first things you have to get a handle on is the way people react to the way you wear your hair, the way you walk, the way you talk, the way you dress, the way you think. You really have to accept those things in a way that doesn't affect you. You take it for what it is, constructive suggestions for the most part. You have to be confident enough in other ways to think that people will approve of you.

When Claudine Schneider was challenging Claiborne Pell for the U.S. Senate in Rhode Island in 1990, *Business Week* quoted a cab driver who said he hadn't made up his mind whether he could support a woman. Then he said: "Claudine's O.K. But tell her to do something about that hair."[19]

In contrast, the media pay scant attention to a male candidate's appearance. It's highly unlikely that a newspaper, for example, would print a story such as the following, dwelling on the wardrobe and grooming of a male office seeker:

Alex Grant, candidate for governor, appeared at three political functions here today. For a prayer breakfast he chose a color-coordinated suit, shirt, and tie that accented the gray in his stylishly blow-dried hair. At an appearance before members of the construction industry later in the morning he changed into a green turtleneck with a tweedy jacket and neutral slacks. Unfortunately, this ensemble couldn't quite disguise a slight paunch, the result of too many meals on the rubber chicken campaign circuit. For the final event of the day, a fundraising luncheon with the banking community, Grant chose a charcoal gray pin-stripe suit, white shirt, and trendy power necktie that neatly set off his healthy tan. After strategically combing several strands of hair over his bald spot, Grant managed to charm the bankers with his comic flair for slightly off-color stories, first apologizing to the women for his bad language and then delivering the punch lines with gusto. And although his rough, chapped hands obviously needed a manicure, Grant nevertheless plowed into the audience at all three appearances to press the flesh with the voters.

Language Barriers

Female candidates encounter two language barriers: the words they speak and the words spoken or written about them. As Deborah Tannen observed in *You Just Don't Understand*, gender distinctions built into our language result in the use of different terms to describe men and women.

Tannen contends that although speakers and writers may not intentionally use sexist terminology, they very often inadvertently resort to terms with very different connotations in their search for punchy, catchy words. Calling an aggressive woman "feisty" but an aggressive man "forceful" immediately categorizes the woman as a small, nonthreatening creature and the man as strong and in charge. In 1984 Geraldine Ferraro was feisty; George Bush was forceful. A woman faints; a man passes out.[20]

Women are also constrained by body language in their quest for power and leadership. Visualize the traditional family photo in a male candidate's campaign brochure. He looks straight at the camera, while his wife and children gaze adoringly up at him.

Tannen cites a widely distributed campaign photo of Geraldine Ferraro in which she is looking at her husband while he looks at the camera. Although the photo says she is a good woman, it is inappropriate because she, not her husband, was the candidate. However, had Ferraro looked at the camera and her husband gazed downward at her, the photo wouldn't be nearly as effective. Its unintended message would have been "Here is a dominating woman with a wimp for a husband."[21] Talk about catch-22.

Similarly, the Democrats considered Ferraro's height of five feet four inches to be a disadvantage against Bush, who is over six feet tall. Ferraro's advisers were particularly concerned that he might look down at her during the 1984 debate or, worse yet, she would look up at him. To minimize that possibility, the Democrats built (over Republican objections) a ramp behind the podium so Ferraro would appear to be closer to Bush's height without obviously having to step up on a riser when she reached the podium.[22]

Gender Roles

Women aren't always accepted in nontraditional sex roles. Many members of the public still don't feel comfortable when women — and men — choose positions that society considers unusual for their sex. For example, we look askance at women in construction jobs and still raise our eyebrows at male nurses. We are distrustful of couples in which the women hold highly prestigious positions of power and leadership and the men choose to be "house-husbands."

We in the United States simply have no experience with women in the highest leadership positions, as Antonia Frazier pointed out in *The Warrior Queens:*

> Almost every culture throughout history has had its warrior queen or queens, either in fact or in fiction or in some combination of them both. The United States of America is so far one of the significant exceptions in spite of "the singular address and happy boldness" which Alexis de Tocqueville discovered in its unmarried young ladies as long ago as 1835. When a possible future warrior queen was presented in the 1984 vice presidential candidate Geraldine Ferraro, the reaction was . . . extremely uneasy.[23]

Sometimes public confusion over political gender roles is reflected in small, amusing details. For example, a female candidate or officeholder with an obviously female first name isn't exempt from the automatic assumption that all politicians are male. Although female politicians are more likely now to receive invitations addressed to "you and your spouse" than "you and your wife," this was not the case even ten years ago. Over the years many political women have received invitations to such stag events as a bawdy roast of a prominent male politico or a soiree in a males-only club. Few women whose first names can be either female or male, such as Frances Jones or Jean Smith, are enchanted when they receive mail addressed to Mr. Francis Jones or Mr. Gene Smith. We can think of a number of inspired ways in which a woman might want to respond to such correspondence.

Sarah Weddington, a former Texas state legislator, tells of the handsome plaque she received from the state bar association in honor of being named one of the state's ten outstanding legislators. Engraved in gold on the walnut plaque were the words: "With grateful appreciation to the honorable Sarah Weddington for his dedication and service to the state of Texas."[24] (Weddington, by the way, must feel particularly pleased that Ann Richards was elected governor of Texas. Richards honed many of her campaign skills while working on Weddington's campaign staff, and the two have remained close friends ever since.)

All too often the public, particularly men, feel threatened by women in nontraditional public roles. People may say to the husband of an assertive woman, "Your wife must be a handful," or may ask, "Can't you keep your wife under control?" But how often is the wife of a powerful man asked how she feels about his being a politician — or a doctor, a lawyer, a plumber, or any other traditional male role?

In the United States, indirect power — the notion that behind every successful man there's a strong woman — is a far more acceptable kind of power for women to wield. The American public feels comfortable if the woman is seen as an influence on the man as long as it's he, not she, who is out there in front, actually achieving political objectives. It could be said that Congresswoman Olympia Snowe of Maine enjoys the best of both possible worlds. She's a powerful woman in her own right and also the First Lady of Maine since her 1989 marriage to Governor John McKernan, Jr.

Ascribing sexual influence to a woman is another way that our society denigrates women's power. Look at all the power Delilah had, yet her power was totally sexual. The story of Delilah is just one example that invites generalizations, such as "It's really not power, it's just sex," which put down aggressive women.

Although many voters of both sexes don't feel comfortable with the woman who is aggressive, ambitious, and outspoken, these are the very qualities that political candidates, whether male or female, need to win an election. That's another reason why we feel that today's successful political women are so valuable as role models. Their lives and experiences will help break down sexist stereotypes and let the general public know that it's okay for women to enter politics.

Unseating Incumbents

Susan Carroll, senior research associate at the Center for the American Woman and Politics (CAWP) at Rutgers University, believes that two factors are mainly responsible for women's slow political progress: (1) the low rate of turnover in office and (2) the high reelection rate of incumbents.[25]

It is doubly important for women to quickly establish a beachhead in high office because opportunities to exercise leadership and power flow from seniority and longevity. In the legislative branch of government, good committee assignments and, ultimately, the committee chair are awarded on the basis of longevity. And in the executive branch, the ability to effect change depends on the successful planning and implementing of programs over a long period. One state legislator (who was not part of our study) blamed the stagnation of an eastern city on the fact that no mayor had served more than one term in over thirty years. The politics of that office had overshadowed its purpose.

Carroll says that the tendency for most officeholders to seek reelection is a major hindrance to challengers, men and women. This works together with the political advantages accrued by an incumbent to perpetuate the status quo. Incumbents going into a reelection campaign enjoy the advantages of greater name recognition, an established record on which to campaign (usually but not always a plus), and better access to fundraising. Donors are far more likely to give money to a known quantity, a successful vote getter with a track record, than to take a chance on a challenger.

The power of the incumbency is felt most strongly in the U.S. House of Representatives, where more than 90 percent of the candidates who run for reelection are successful. While this kind of staying power is good news for women incumbents, it nevertheless works against women who aspire to seats in Congress.[26]

If the pressure to maintain the male status quo is truly so strong, then why over the years have political parties sometimes fielded women candidates for high statewide or federal office? We aren't referring to successful female candidates or to the wives of former officeholders who ran to fill their husbands' unexpired terms. We're talking about those women who burst onto the political scene, enjoyed brief fame as a candidate, lost the election, and then returned to relative obscurity.

The answer is that the incumbents against whom these women ran were so powerful that no male would dare take them on. Running a woman as a "sacrificial lamb" in such cases not only prevented the incumbent from getting a free ride but also made it appear as if the party were supporting an aggressive woman who had "paid her dues." The only advantages we can see for a woman running as a sacrificial lamb these days are to build name recognition and campaign experience.

Sometimes, however, a sacrificial lamb ploy can backfire. In the 1990 general election in New Jersey, Republican newcomer Christine Todd Whitman almost defeated prominent Democratic incumbent Senator Bill Bradley. Bradley was widely regarded as a shoo-in. Yet Whitman, whose name was anything but a household word in New Jersey, lost the election by only 58,936 votes out of the almost 2 million ballots cast. Whitman tallied 918,874 votes to Bradley's 977,810. It is particularly interesting that the three minor-party senatorial candidates garnered a total of 41,770 votes.[27] Although their totals weren't enough to have put Whitman over the top, it is possible that had the Republicans put forth a better-known candidate they might have unseated a powerful incumbent.

We want to distinguish between a sacrificial lamb and the female candidate with "fire in the belly" who has decided she can be a viable candidate. But no matter how strongly a challenger campaigns, the chances of unseating an incumbent are rarely good. Therefore, unless women are willing to risk running against an incumbent, they must wait for an open or unchallenged seat to become available.[28]

The open congressional seats in 1992 due to reapportionment have provided an unusual opportunity for aspiring congresswomen in California, Florida, and other fast-growing Sunbelt states. That, coupled with voters' strong anti-incumbent and term-limitation attitudes in the early 1990s, may contribute to increasing the proportion of women in office.

In the Prologue we mentioned that women should not expect to be represented in Congress in proportion to their numbers in the general population for more than four hundred years, given their present rate of election. This is how the estimate was derived: "If 98% of U.S. Congressional incumbents get reelected and 95% of the U.S. Congress is male then women can expect to achieve parity in Federal legislative office in 410 years."[29] Obviously, incumbency as well as sexism present challenges for women seeking public office.

Fundraising

Fundraising has traditionally been more difficult for women. Most women learn from childhood that good girls don't ask for things, especially money, or call attention to themselves. Yet that's exactly what women candidates have to do to fund a respectable campaign. Many female candidates consider fundraising to be the most distasteful and difficult aspect of their political career.

Colorado's Pat Schroeder told us that she wishes there were better ways to raise funds than by accepting donations from special-interest groups, who may expect special consideration down the line. But she acknowledges that fundraising is a fact of life for all candidates, particularly at the statewide or national level: "So if you don't go to the fat cats, it takes a whole lot of fifteen-dollar checks to make up what you lose by not approaching special-interest groups. That to me has been the real dilemma, but I don't know how else you do it."

Ann Richards of Texas agreed that big bucks are essential when the stakes are as high as they were in her 1990 gubernatorial campaign: "Most people romantically think that putting together a strong grassroots organization doesn't cost any money, but that's not true. It costs a great deal of money." Richards credited her campaign staff's strong get-out-the-vote effort for the margin by which she won the election.

When we asked Kathleen Connell, Rhode Island's secretary of state, what aspect of politics she found most difficult, she immediately named fundraising: "I really hate running around asking for money. I'm getting better at it, but I still hate it."

Betty Castor, commissioner of education in Florida, said that since she dislikes asking for money, she now uses a different approach to fundraising: "I can't go to prospective donors and say, 'Write me a thousand-dollar check while I'm here in the room.' So I do everything leading up to that, and then somebody else comes in and closes the deal."

Claudine Schneider, congresswoman from Rhode Island, told us what happened when she lost her first election in 1978 and then ran for the same position two years later: "I won by fifty-six percent of the vote and raised about $365,000. I mention the money only because it's very important, and at that time it was twice as hard for women to raise money as it was (and oftentimes now is) for men, too." Schneider seems to be suggesting that fundraising is getting easier for women, or at least easier for her.

Interestingly, Connecticut Congresswoman Barbara Kennelly doesn't believe that fundraising is as difficult as most women seem to think:

> I haven't had much of a problem with fundraising, and I've known too many women candidates over the last ten years for whom money was not the problem. Then once we get in, we have no trouble whatsoever. You can't raise money if you're not a good candidate. And you can't raise money if you don't look like you have a fair chance of winning. Unfortunately, too many women run against incumbents, and when they lose, it somehow gets translated into "women can't raise money." It's becoming a cliché.

Women have been slow to support female candidates financially, to "write the big checks" that men often contribute. However, as increasing numbers of women are becoming established in the professions, business, and education, they will be better situated to donate large amounts to female candidates.

Credibility

Women constantly have to provide the credibility. Susan Carroll of CAWP has found that women candidates are just as qualified to hold office as are men; but women's political experience is likely to be different from men's. For example, before running for office women are more likely to have held appointive positions on boards and commissions, while it is probable that men have previously served in another elective office. In addition, female elected officials are more likely than their male counterparts to have worked for other candidates, either on a campaign or office staff, before running for office themselves.[30]

Carroll also found that although candidates of both sexes have comparable business and professional experiences, men are most likely to be lawyers while the women have chosen one of the helping professions.[31] This holds true for our sample as well, which includes one lawyer and a predominance of teachers, nurses, and social workers.

The ever-present demand for a woman office seeker to prove her competence brings us back to the dilemma confronting every female candidate: how to convince the voters she is strong, capable, and qualified enough to hold political office while at the same time avoiding being perceived as "bitchy" or "shrill."

Voters, especially men, find it unsettling, even threatening, to discover that a female politician also has some of the masculine traits they admire. All too often there is a contradiction between the attributes voters expect in a candidate and what they want in a woman. Ambition is a plus in a man but a drawback in a woman. Men should be tough, but strength in a woman is threatening. Male candidates should be aggressive, women compliant and deferential. In addition, a female candidate must be doubly vigilant about the image she is trying to project if she gets caught up in a negative campaign such as those go-for-the-jugular races in the early 1990s.

Support from Women

There has been much speculation about the impact of the gender gap, that is, about whether women en masse will support female candidates or issues of general interest to women. The Harris poll we cited earlier indicates such a trend, but it is still highly questionable whether the women's vote will determine the outcome of certain races. We have seen that women did not turn out in blocs after they won the right to vote, and even now the financial and other support they give female candidates is far less than what can be expected from the male political infrastructure. Fortunately, however, some women's organizations have begun to provide tangible help to women who are working their way up the political and leadership ladder.

Susan Carroll of CAWP reports that women's organizations and networks play increasingly important roles in recruiting and supporting female candidates. In addition, political action committees (PACs) that either support women candidates or comprise women grew rapidly in the 1980s and are expected to play an even more prominent role in the election process in the 1990s. Finally, Carroll recognizes the growing numbers of women helping other women achieve positions of leadership.[32]

Congresswoman Jolene Unsoeld from Washington State would agree that women have been slow to create a support system for female candidates:

> We are developing an "old boys' network," but it is not as well structured yet. Organizations such as the Women's Campaign Fund and EMILY's List [a Democratic women's donor network that supports women candidates] are certainly helping to

strengthen it, but professional women still do not view themselves as having power and authority within government and politics. They are so wrapped up in their own professions that they don't see the role they can play in opening up the system much more for women. So they tend not to make a political contribution in the size that would be commensurate with a similar amount a male might donate.

Now that we've reeled off accounts of fundraising difficulties for women, credibility problems, sexism, halfhearted support from other women, and other political horror stories, you may not find it surprising that women aren't exactly rushing out to file for office. These barriers should cause a woman to stop and think, to evaluate her viability as a candidate, and to pick her battles. However, she should also keep in mind that other women have already made it in politics. We know it can be done.

Women can succeed in politics, as the twenty-five women we interviewed for this book have demonstrated. Jeane Kirkpatrick has categorized such women as either *"office seekers"* or *"ready recruits"* when they first sought political office.

Kirkpatrick would say that the office seeker takes the initiative and makes up her mind to run without first talking to anyone else. In other words, she recruits herself. A ready recruit waits to be asked. It really doesn't matter who does the asking — co-workers, friends, family, party officials, or anyone else. But until someone gives a ready recruit the necessary encouragement, she probably hasn't dreamed that she would make a great public official.

Kirkpatrick doesn't think that ready recruits are necessarily more passive or ineffective than office seekers. Rather, ready recruits may be more tied to women's traditional socialization of not being too aggressive, not asking for things, not calling attention to themselves, and so on.[33] (We will talk in greater detail about political entry points in Chapter 7.)

Several of the youngest women we talked with, including Mary Landrieu, treasurer of Louisiana, and Rebecca Vigil-Giron, New Mexico's secretary of state, were office seekers. They made the decision to run on their own, before the music even started. So did Maryland's Senator Barbara Mikulski, undoubtedly motivated by what she calls her "zoom-zoom personality."

Vigil-Giron told us that she began her political career in high school as a delegate to Girls' State and then continued building political experience in college and later as a Young Democrat. Then, in 1985,

> I knew there was an election coming up, and that more than anything made me decide I wanted to run for this position I knew nothing about. But I knew I could do it — and I could do a better job, too. I was alone when I decided to run for office, all by myself. When I shared it with my friends, they must have thought I was crazy because I didn't have a political name. I didn't have money or a family with money. Running for office with no money, no political base, was a big risk, but it was one that I had to take at the time.

At the other end of the spectrum is Kathleen Connell, Rhode Island secretary of state, a ready recruit. She ran for office, she said, at her husband's request:

> I've been at it long enough to tell the truth — my husband was vice chairman of the town Democratic party. When the Democrats didn't elect anyone to fill the ticket, he decided I would be a ticket filler. "Sign these papers, will you?" he said one night.
> "What papers?" I asked.
> "You're gonna run for school committee," he informed me. "But don't worry. You won't win anyway."
> So I signed those papers, and I won.

And Connell found she liked politics so much that she made it her career.

The Bottom Line for Women Candidates

Susan Carroll, after analyzing many of the same challenges to women candidates we touched on in this chapter, concluded in her 1985 book *Women as Candidates in American Politics:*

> A woman's chances may be improved if she has elective office-holding experience, nontraditional sex-role attitudes, and an adequate supply of money, time, and campaign workers. Nevertheless, a woman candidate stands the best chance if she also is an incumbent or is running for an open seat.[34]

We hope that this book will help inspire a whole new crop of office seekers, or at least some ready recruits who will jump in before long. And we look forward to the day when this famous quote from Clare Boothe Luce will no longer ring true: "Because I am a woman I must make unusual efforts to succeed. If I fail, no one will say, 'She doesn't have what it takes.' They will say, 'Women don't have what it takes.'"

PROFILE

Pat Schroeder
The Family "Comfort Zone"

The women in our study received the secrets of their power and leadership from their families, who enabled and empowered them to become the leaders they are today. Colorado Congresswoman and presidential candidate Pat Schroeder's family life is an example of the kind of "comfort zone" that encourages the development of women leaders.

Congresswoman Pat Schroeder grew up in what she described as a very close family, which provided a warm environment to nurture the development of her Competent Self.

Schroeder credited three childhood experiences for helping her to not feel intimidated when she went to Harvard Law School and, later, entered politics: (1) her family provided an exceptionally strong "comfort zone" for her and her brother, (2) her mother was a somewhat nontraditional role model, and (3) her parents told her she could do anything she wanted and didn't send her mixed messages about her role as a woman.

During World War II the family moved frequently to be with Schroeder's father, a flight instructor for the Army Air Corps. "We moved around a lot because we had to be wherever they had a training facility," Schroeder said, "but we never went overseas." She compared the family to "tumbleweeds" as they followed her father to bases around the country. The frequent moves made the family the children's only anchor.

There was no "mainstream," she said. "In my childhood, there were ten mainstreams and ten churches" instead of a single community. "There never was that wonderful comfort zone of 'I've been known here forever and it's my hometown.'"

Instead, Schroeder and her brother depended on the family to provide them with a "comfort zone."

Pat learned how to make friends quickly when her family moved to a new post. She used to line up her toys along the sidewalk, and in no time the neighborhood children would come over to check out her inventory and play with her.

The family soon learned to do without possessions that didn't travel well as they moved around the country. One year when they didn't bring Christmas ornaments along, she and her family cut out the circles from the front of Lucky Strike cigarette packages to hang on their tree.

"Both of my parents were very much into kids," she said, "mainly because at that time they couldn't be into anything else. It's not like they were distracted by country club dances or things like that, and we usually had to move on before they were able to nurture close friendships. So they may have put a lot more energy into us than they would have in more normal times."

Schroeder values her experience of the ways an extended family can pull together in difficult times. When her brother was born her uncle got a leave and came to visit, and her grandmother also made the trip. Once, since her family couldn't travel by car because gasoline was rationed, they took the train to Chicago for her aunt's wedding. Being part of a close-knit family reinforced her feeling of being loved and special.

Schroeder recalled how impressed her mother was when, as a first grader, Pat won a storytelling contest for the city of Dallas and thus became eligible for the state contest. Since she hadn't mentioned the contest to anyone at home, none of her family came to see her win the citywide contest. But after a PTA member phoned with word of that victory, her mother attended the state contest. Standing on the stage, Schroeder recalled, "I looked down there and she was crying. I thought I had screwed up. Then I realized it was because she was so nervous, tense, and shy — she would never have gotten up on the stage to do something like that. She was blown away that *I* did."

Schroeder's mother thus encouraged her daughter to reach out, take a risk, and follow a dream of greatness, even though she herself could not have done what her child was doing. The approach her parents took to risk taking was one of "cautious encouragement," exemplified by her recollection of her parents' attitude toward her driving: "This is a car. We trust you, but, by God, if anything goes wrong —!"

As a first-grade teacher, Schroeder's mother provided her daughter with the role model of a working mother. Schroeder believes that her mother might have been a more traditional mom had it not been wartime, when in many occupations women replaced the men who had gone to war. So her mother worked full-time and wouldn't get a housekeeper because it just wasn't done at that time. Since Pat was in daycare while her mother worked, she doesn't believe that as an adult she felt any conflict about putting her own children into daycare. She recognizes that many of today's young mothers are torn between staying home and putting their children into daycare and that they expend a great deal of energy trying to resolve that dilemma. "Maybe my mom went through that," she said, "but being the second generation to do it wasn't quite so bad when my turn came."

Schroeder described how she has watched her mother become more aggressive:

> In one of our campaigns she was knocking on doors and someone said, "I wouldn't vote for Pat Schroeder, and I think she ought to stay home with her kids." My mother said, "Well, I was a working mother and I had two kids." And the lady said, "Oh, yeah? Well, what happened to 'em?" And my mother replied, "Well, one's a lawyer and the other one is Pat Schroeder."

Her father's role model had been his kid sister, who was

> the best archer in Nebraska. She could outshoot anybody. She could just do anything. So he assumed all women were like that. If I wanted to fly airplanes, fine; and if I wanted to do this, fine; and if I wanted to do that, fine. I was never "Daddy's little girl,

I'll put you in organdy and this is how it's supposed to be." And I think that was partly because of his experience with his sister.

According to Schroeder, her father encouraged both of his children to do things for themselves, giving them permission to "do whatever you want."

By second grade, when she was seven years old, Schroeder's father was giving her a whole month's allowance at a time. His advice to her was, "Now if you blow it the first day, it's a long time until the end of the month to be making peanut butter sandwiches. But you've got it, and it will be a good experience to see if you can manage it."

Schroeder heard the message of her father's trust in her, and it was repeated by the ways her parents always gave her and her brother some leeway. Their tacit encouragement translated into "Well, what would you like to do next?" In Schroeder's case that approach worked well, for she learned to fly an airplane at age fifteen and went off to Harvard Law School at a time when very few women were choosing law for a career.

Her family's political involvement over the years has helped her to feel comfortable in the world of politics. She told us that when her grandfather and his five brothers left Ireland to come to America, they were so excited they got on the wrong boat and ended up in Buenos Aires. They then worked their way to Philadelphia, and her grandfather homesteaded in Nebraska, where he eventually became a state legislator. As she put it: "The family has that prairie populism thing. They're a politically active, outgoing family."

Schroeder recalled going through a tumultuous time when she got out of law school, went to work, and then suddenly started having babies. For a while she tried her hand at being a full-time mother and vividly remembered thinking one day, as she was feeding babies and watching Barbara Walters on TV, "Oh, my God. What have I done to my life? Will I ever be anything other than a peas pusher?"

Her career direction changed from pushing peas one day in

1972 when she first decided to run for Congress. Although running as a Democrat in Denver was viewed as "a noble suicide mission," Schroeder saw the race as a tremendous challenge and an opportunity to present issues that needed discussion: "the Vietnam War, housing, the environment, children, the elderly," many of the same issues she has championed over the years.

Schroeder was a ready recruit when a group of Democratic liberals in Denver asked her to run. But the Democratic National Committee, which wasn't convinced that this newcomer could win, refused to support her campaign that year. So she and her friends ran an unconventional grassroots campaign and won with 52 percent of the vote. At the time, her son Scott was six and daughter Jamie was two. Schroeder said she has included them in her political life when they wanted to be included but has never required "command performances."

The bottom line for Schroeder was a sense that her parents were behind her. Their message was, "We're the roots. When you get your wings we share your wings, but we're not going to compile a score of who flew the highest or the longest." And, she added, "I was empowered by their being with me. And I always preferred having wings to having things."

Schroeder's husband and children have become this generation's counterpart of her family support team. When she was elected to Congress in 1972, her husband gave up his law practice in Denver and moved with her and the kids to Washington. He has practiced law in Washington since then, carefully avoiding any governmental legal matters that might be construed as a conflict of interest with his wife's position.

Congresswoman Pat Schroeder has been a very nontraditional wife and mother, yet her children have thrived and her family is always there for her. This is summed up in the dedication of her book *Champion of the Great American Family*: "To Jim, for giving up home-cooked meals, darned socks, and a dust-free home."[1]

4

"Your Best Support Team Is Your Family"

The title of this chapter came from our interview with Catherine Baker Knoll, treasurer of Pennsylvania, as she described how her family backed her when she was campaigning. It was a significant piece in the jigsaw puzzle we've been putting together in our search for the psychological traits of women in leadership positions. This is what the finished puzzle tells us about the women in our study: Whatever it was that they received from their families when they were growing up enabled them to become the leaders they are today.

As you read Chapters 4 through 7 please keep in mind that we're not saying that *every* woman we interviewed has *every* helpful characteristic we've identified. All we can talk about in this kind of research is the predominant themes we've found that contributed to the making of the Competent Self. Consequently, we decided that before a particular element was included, such as feeling loved and special, it had to be shared by a majority — but not necessarily all — of the women we interviewed.

If you don't share one of these traits, don't despair. The women in our sample who didn't share a particular element got where they are without it. Apparently their strengths in other areas compensated for the lack of a particular component as they were growing up. It's the whole puzzle we're looking at here: it was what these women received from their families of origin that prepared them so well for a lifetime of leadership.

The Importance of Internal Applause

As psychologists, we believe that who we are today depends to a great extent on our early development. The way we were raised and how we grew up are the main determinants of who we have become as adults and how we feel about ourselves.

We don't believe that chance or luck or fate play much of a role in shaping our makeup: it's our early life experiences that mold us. That is why we set out to learn about the young lives of political women and their relationships with their parents, grandparents, siblings, and extended families.

We wanted to learn what early messages these women received from their families that established and nurtured their Competent Self — that positive, indelible self-concept that won't be erased by challenge, confrontation, or failure. We wondered what family influences led these women to believe so much in themselves that they were not afraid to become leaders. We also wanted to discover what secrets of leadership enabled them to feel comfortable with their femininity even when they were engaging in "unfeminine" behaviors such as acting aggressively and assuming power.

We believe that the strong Competent Self in all the women we interviewed originated in early childhood. They all experienced a feeling of being loved and special, going back to their very earliest memories. To the young girl, this feeling resembles a kind of constant approval from those around her. She knows that everyone thinks what she does is wonderful. She believes the empowering message "*I* am lovable. People love me, even when I make mistakes."

She hears the message over and over again until she makes it part of her inner voice. It functions as a continuous round of internal applause, which after a while replaces her need for external applause in the form of constant positive feedback. With constant internal applause comes a sense of security that gives the young girl the inner strength to take risks and try new adventures.

Many of the women we interviewed volunteered that they felt loved and special before we even came to that question in the interview. And when we asked by whom they felt loved as a child, the answer would either be a confident, ebullient "Everybody!" or a list that included parents, grandparents, and other doting relatives.

Rhode Island Secretary of State Kathleen Connell spoke of a grandmother who "always rewarded me for milestones. I don't mean something that was terribly expensive, but it was something special." Her mother also was "very lavish with praise when I was little," and Connell was "the classic apple of my father's eye. He took great pride in anything that I did."

As Louisiana State Treasurer Mary Landrieu told us:

> I always felt pretty special because not *only* am I the oldest in my family, but I'm the oldest of nineteen grandchildren on one side and the oldest girl of thirty-four grandchildren on the other side. Since all of my grandparents were living until just a few years ago, I never had a problem with not feeling special because of the way they and my aunts and uncles treated me. I could tell it was important that I was the first child. Not that they didn't love my brothers and sisters or treat them as equally as possible, but you just kind of get the feeling that you're special when you're the oldest in a big family.

New Jersey Congresswoman Marge Roukema couldn't remember a time when she didn't feel special to her parents. She vividly remembered one incident that made it very clear that she was loved. When she was about four, she announced she was going to run away because her family didn't appreciate her:

> When I packed my bags, my mother came in and spanked me soundly. She told me that I should never even think about running away and to unpack my bags because I wasn't going anywhere. And I can remember saying to myself, "They really do love me. They don't want me to leave."

Growing up feeling loved and special is a boon for all children; it is the bedrock on which their personalities are built. We know that not all children are so fortunate, but for political women a loving childhood seems to be a common factor.

We are not implying that everything was or is perfect in the lives of these women, or anyone else. None of the women we interviewed had perfect parents — who does? None of them had perfect families. None have had perfect lives. However, their experiences in their families were good enough to contribute to the development of a strong, healthy Competent Self.

The idea that loving parents provide an environment in which healthy children can flourish is hardly surprising — sometimes research confirms what common sense has told us all along. John Gossett and his colleagues at the Timberlawn Psychiatric Research Foundation in Dallas determined that the best way for young parents to raise psychologically healthy children is to make their spouse their partner and best friend.[1] Therefore, we were not surprised to hear so often from the women we interviewed that their mothers and fathers consulted each other on household, childrearing, and professional matters.

What does such an atmosphere do for the children? It insulates them from feelings of hopelessness and from perceiving barriers to their own progress. A warm, stable family provides consistency so the children know what to expect of their world. It exposes them to less conflict. It frees them from the responsibility of negotiating between their parents. It allows them to focus on their own interests and development rather than having to look after their parents. Finally, it gives them a good model for their own interpersonal relationships.

It is extremely important that women see their mothers as equal partners to their fathers, not as second-class citizens who can't control their own lives. As children, the women we interviewed constantly received positive messages about women, which contributed to the positive image they developed of themselves as females.

When such a nurturing atmosphere exists, the socioeconomic status of the family has less impact on the children's development than it otherwise might have. This is illustrated by the fact that the families of the women we interviewed spanned the economic spectrum. Professionally their fathers ran the gamut: CPA, state policeman, farmer, owner of a small business, career military man, politician, tennis instructor, rancher, and lawyer. Most of the mothers were full-time wives and mothers, at least while their children were living at home, and many devoted considerable time to school, church, community, and other public service activities. Those mothers who worked outside the home tended to be teachers or retailers (several worked alongside their husbands in the family business).

Clearly, growing up in an affluent family was *not* a prerequisite for developing a Competent Self and moving out into the world. Some of our subjects talked of working in the family business to help make ends meet. Several worked their way through college, and after graduation a few in turn helped their younger siblings through school. Economic adversity for these women was an obstacle they were able to overcome, strengthening their evolving Competent Self in the process. This is consistent with the finding that only 20 percent of prominent political or organizational women come from wealthy families, whereas 62 percent of the women who are known because of their husbands' status come from wealthy families.[2]

Indeed, we wonder whether growing up in a privileged family might interfere with a girl's ability to hear and act on messages such as "You can *do* (or *earn*) what you want." However, even if affluence were to be disadvantageous to young women in this case, the problem wouldn't have to be insoluble. We would expect that a healthy combination of enough other messages could compensate for the inability to hear this message.

We found that 92 percent of our subjects grew up in the kind of warm family setting we're talking about, although Congresswoman Olympia Snowe's family environment was disrupted earlier than would be optimally desirable (her remarkable story is told in a profile later in this book). Almost all of the women in our sample grew up in intact families in which the relationship between their parents was caring, supportive, and communicative.

Family Values

In addition to a warm, nurturing family life, we identified certain family values that seem to contribute heavily to a career in politics. All of the women we interviewed came from families that placed a high premium on education, community service, and participation in politics.

All of our subjects are college-educated. Several have advanced degrees. A number were the first or only members of their families to go to college. And those with brothers indicated that their parents did not discriminate between the boys and the girls in regard to education.

For some, such as Senator Barbara Mikulski, a college education put a great strain on the family finances. When Mikulski was a high school senior in the process of deciding where to go to college, a fire destroyed the family grocery store. When she offered to go to night school instead of college so she could work in the rebuilt store, her father wouldn't hear of it. "If you don't go to college now you never will. Your mother and I will find a way to send you," he told her. Then they worked out a plan for her to attend college as a commuter student and work weekends at the store so they wouldn't have to hire additional help.

Congresswoman Pat Saiki's family also made sacrifices so the three daughters could go to college. To put aside money for the girls' education, the family economized by not owning a car or a piano, and Saiki's mother made all their clothes. The parents, particularly her father, also reminded the girls of the sacrifices they were making. This, Saiki told us, gave her a tremendous sense of responsibility, a need to excel, and great respect for her parents.

For Saiki, born in Hilo on Hawaii, going off to college in Honolulu was as big an event as going to college across the country would be for a mainlander. Before leaving for Oahu she made a pact with her father that she would not marry for at least two years after college, during which time she would earn money for her younger sister's college education. Then she and her sister would help the youngest sister.

Saiki kept her bargain, and in addition while in college she worked weekends, holidays, and vacations as a stewardess for Aloha Airlines. Since she was paid double time whenever a volcano erupted and as soon as the sun went down, she worked evening flights to double her income. Before long she was earning her own way and sending whatever she could spare to her sister, who was also in college by that time. And on top of that, Saiki bought her father his first car. We know that this story almost sounds like something out of Horatio Alger, but it's true. Saiki's extraordinary energy and dedication have helped make her a successful politician.

Community service was another strong family value ingrained in the women we interviewed. They grew up watching their mothers' involvement in PTA, church, and other volunteer organizations, doing good things for children and charities. Through this example they learned that both their family and the community at large respect such public service.

Manhattan Borough President Ruth Messinger believes the "give something back" message registered strongly with her because she felt so loved by everybody as a child. When she was growing up she learned that "you're supposed to be doing something for people who are less well off. You're supposed to be giving something back." This is another way of saying that her parents gave her so much in her early years that as an adult she could afford give to others.

By the time she was fourteen Messinger was spending her summers doing maintenance work for a settlement house camp. Anything but a glamorous "make-work" position, the job was consistent with her family's social service orientation, which she considers the key factor in getting her where she is today.

Senator Barbara Mikulski also grew up in a family that valued community service. Among the many examples of her family's generosity and concern for others is her recollection that in bad weather her parents would give her oranges from their store to deliver to diabetic senior citizens who couldn't get to the market themselves. Mikulski said, "You just got out there and you helped your neighbor."

Family participation in politics taught our subjects early in their lives that political involvement is valued. As we noted earlier, the fathers of 24 percent of the women we studied had been involved in politics in some fashion. Those six women saw the value of political involvement firsthand. In addition, many others in our sample whose parents weren't politically active except to vote told us that their families would discuss politics and world events at the dinner table or that their families felt it was important to cast a ballot in every election. From this as well as their mothers' involvement in community affairs our women learned the importance of participating in the democratic process. Congresswoman Marge Roukema's mother went one step further when she saw to it that her daughter joined the League of Women Voters immediately upon graduating from college. Women from politically active or involved families also learned that the world of politics isn't restricted just to men.

The Mother's Role

Popular thinking would have us believe that strong political women are the way they are because they identified with their fathers. This notion has been supported by earlier research, which tended to look solely for the father's influence on political women. And *The Managerial Woman,* the 1977 best-seller based on Margaret Hennig and Anne Jardim's study of highly successful managerial women, seemed to confirm the idea that to be powerful in any sphere, girls needed fathers who treated them like sons.[3]

We believe that the shortage of daughters of politically powerful mothers to study, until recently, led to the fallacious conclusion that the father always serves as the successful daughter's role model. And, conversely, the lack of politically successful female role models until recently has made it harder for women to dream directly and openly about assuming leadership roles. It is also possible that we have ignored the role the mother plays in approving and supporting her daughter's developing sense of competence as well as her political and leadership aspirations. It is possible that these factors make up the empowering female legacy and secrets of leadership that mothers can pass on to their daughters.

But other things we know should lead us to recognize the mother's role. For example, we know that children use the parent of the same sex as a role model. We also know that the earliest relationship any child has is with his or her mother; and since mothers feel a sameness with female children, a mother-daughter relationship is exceptionally close from the outset. As we explained in Chapter 2, it is through this relationship that girls learn to "listen" to feelings, to "hear" the sensual maternal secrets that help them to maintain an empathic connection with another person, and by having that connection to hear the empowering messages and to develop self-esteem.[4]

If the mother is herself a strong and competent individual, then the daughter can continue to identify with her and develop her own Competent Self. However, if the mother is perceived as weak and ineffective, then some girl children will turn to the father and give up the maternal values. The women that Hennig and Jardim studied had the latter kinds of mothers, rather quiet women who usually gave in to the final wishes of their husbands.[5] This experience, combined with the societal expectation of the proper role of women during the 1920s and 1930s, when the women in Hennig and Jardim's study grew up, led them to turn to their fathers as role models. But in doing so, they gave up the nurturant part of themselves. It is not surprising, therefore, that if the managerial women married at all, they did so later in life (after age thirty-five) and chose not to have children.

The women whom we studied and their mothers are products of different mothering styles and different eras. Although many of the women we interviewed grew up before the sexual revolution, they first ran for office in the 1970s, after the sexual revolution was under way. Consequently, they could look to contemporary political role models such as Bella Abzug, Shirley Chisholm, Barbara Jordan, and other pioneering political women of the 1960s and early 1970s.

The "glass ceiling" separating women from top male leadership positions was still intact, but in the 1970s political women were beginning to make inroads into elective office that might eventually put them within shattering distance. Furthermore, by that time society had begun to place more value on women's work, although most people still did not value it as highly as men's work.

Message from Mom:
"It's OK to Get Involved"

A few of the women we talked with think their mothers' dreams were thwarted by the time in which they lived because those closest to them did not support achievement by women outside the home. Nevertheless, our sample of women generally viewed their mothers, and sometimes even their grandmothers, as competent, influential people although most were described as "homemakers" and "housewives." In other words, our sample of political women did not see having a career as the only way to demonstrate one's capabilities. This is consistent with Kelly and Boutilier's statement in 1978 that "the key to a woman's participation in politics is her mother's competence within the family structure *as well as* in the public world as an equal with males.[6]

Catherine Baker Knoll, treasurer of Pennsylvania, vividly recalled an incident that occurred when her father was mayor of the town where they lived. Upon learning that the tax assessor had suddenly died, her father asked her mother what he should do.

"I can't understand you," Knoll's mother replied. "There shouldn't be a question in your mind. You're automatically going to appoint his wife to replace him."

"I can't appoint a woman!"

"Yes, you will," said her mother. And he did.

Knoll got two vital enabling messages from that exchange: (1) that her mother's view was respected by her father and (2) that a woman could hold a political job. As Knoll told us, "That's where I realized she *is* a power, besides being the power in the home."

Message from Mom:
"It's OK to Be Strong-Willed"

Congresswoman Claudine Schneider called her mother "a real survivor," a term several other women also used to describe their mothers. Schneider related a story about her mother, who came to this country as a Belgian war bride after World War II:

> She came over on the boat by herself, not speaking English very well, and she went to classes, learned English, and worked beside my father six out of seven days a week. By today's standards she was what we call a "superwoman" because she worked all day and then would come home, cook the dinner, do the laundry, iron the clothes, and then check our homework. She was a very hardworking woman.

Another term we often encountered for such mothers is "strong-willed." The depth of their strong will sometimes didn't become apparent until their husbands died, at which time some women had to take charge of the family business. The daughters felt it was as if their mothers had been waiting to blossom until the shadow of the more dominant man had been removed.

Betty Castor, Florida's commissioner of education, thinks that her mother would have gone much further in life had she had the right opportunities. She had been a traditional mother, who was "always there. She was watching out." But she also was her husband's "true partner" in the family business. When her husband died at fifty, she was left with a business to run and her youngest son still at home. "But she just picked up the pieces and ran the business and made more money than my father ever made at it," Castor told us proudly.

Castor believes her mother resented the fact that no one encouraged her to go to college, since she could have accomplished more had she gotten a college education. Castor also feels that while her mother supported her father's position as a small-town mayor she was disappointed that men were able to achieve in the political realm whereas women could not:

> She probably would have made a very good candidate because whenever she undertook a project she accomplished it well. Whether it was organizing a luncheon or doing something for my father or even in the business, she was a taskmaster. She just got it done, and yet she was never in a position where she got great credit for that.

What Betty Castor got from her mother was not only a role model, but the empowering message that she could be more successful than her mother had been.

Message from Mom: "It's OK to Be Both Nurturant and Aggressive"

The women whose mothers had been the "woman behind the man" respect their mothers' important role. Congresswoman Barbara Kennelly remembers that "Daddy said she was part of

his success because she walked behind him smiling and soothing the waters." And Louisiana Treasurer Mary Landrieu thinks
her mother

> is probably one of the best people I've ever known. She is quite
> remarkable in the sense of being a selfless individual and very
> generous and kind and very loving and very smart and commit-
> ted to raise a family and being a very good support partner for
> my father, who was very active in politics and in a very demand-
> ing business. They have a wonderful marriage and they are very
> happy together. I think she's a very strong role model for women,
> albeit in a more traditional avenue.

Those women whose mothers were still alive at the time of
the interview related how they still experience their mothers'
involvement and fortitude. For example, Congresswoman
Nancy Pelosi still spends the first half hour of phone conversations with her mother talking about "the Bush administration
and what they haven't done for people."

As we mentioned in the profile preceding this chapter, Congresswoman Pat Schroeder is very proud of the Creative Aggression her mother has developed, which she described when she
told us about her mother's experience campaigning door to door
for her daughter.

Finally, when Congresswoman Connie Morella was planning
a party for her mother's ninetieth birthday, she told us she
hoped her mother would show up for her party because "she's
an independent character" as well as Morella's role model. At
ninety, her mother was working part-time folding tablecloths
in a laundry. She wasn't doing it for the money, Morella's
mother had explained. Rather, "if I reach the point where I
don't have to get up and get dressed and get out early in the
morning, I'm just going to fall apart," she said.

In summary, the secrets of leadership and empowering messages the women we interviewed got from their mothers were
condensed into the gift of identification with both the nurturant and the aggressive, independent facets of their competent

personalities. This is what allowed them to integrate both aspects into the Competent Self.

The Father's Role

Although the women in our sample focused more attention on their mothers and could identify with their mothers' independent, aggressive components, we do not mean to imply that these women's fathers played no part in their daughters' development. Researchers are becoming more and more aware of the role that fathers play in their children's lives from the very first day. The father's role in child development has historically been devalued by society, but we are pleased to note that the father's contributions now are beginning to be more recognized and appreciated.

Message from Dad:
"It's OK to Do Whatever the Boys Do"

The mere presence of a father in a family is not enough. He must actively relate to his children. And to be effective with daughters, he must relate to them in nontraditional ways.[7] This means that fathers have to promote independence and task mastery as well as the friendliness and interpersonal skills they have traditionally encouraged in daughters. Truly nontraditional fathers would value the same degree of independence and achievement in both their male and female children.

The fathers of the political women we studied seem to be nontraditional by this definition. Some fathers had mothers or sisters, outstanding women in one way or another, who had been role models for them. For instance, Congresswoman Nancy Johnson's paternal grandmother had been one of the first graduates of John Marshall Law School and "a real mover and shaker in the settlement house movement in Chicago." Consequently, Johnson's father saw women as intellectually equal to men. But because he felt his mother's activities had kept her from mothering him as much as he wanted, he felt strongly that motherhood should take precedence over any other activities for the women in his family.

Almost all of the fathers were the traditional breadwinners for the family and generally were successful at their trade or profession. As they moved out into the world, they modeled competency for their daughters.

The daughters of political figures were generally not encouraged by their fathers to choose political careers. Congresswoman Barbara Kennelly believes that her father, who had been national chair of the Democratic party, would be proud of her; however, he never encouraged political aspirations in her or her brother and when she married he actively discouraged political aspirations in her husband. There was never, according to Kennelly, "any of the Kennedy-type nurturing" in her family.

One of Treasurer Mary Landrieu's goals was to marry a politician. She said she didn't dream as a teenager of running for political office. (We will speak more about the role of girls' dreams in Chapter 5.) Landrieu, who earlier in this section described her mother's selfless commitment to her husband, used her mother as a role model for serving and supporting others and both parents as models of competitiveness and independence. Her father had been mayor of a large city and secretary of housing and urban development in the Carter administration.

Congresswoman Nancy Johnson's father, a state legislator, brought his children up to believe they could do anything, yet his deep-seated assumption was that the three girls would marry, have children, and be homemakers. Johnson recalled that her father did not discriminate between what he expected of her brother and of Johnson and her two sisters. "So my sisters and I learned to do much heavier work than most girls ever were required to do," Johnson remembered.

The following story leaves no doubt in our minds about how truly nondiscriminatory he was. One of the most vivid memories of her adolescence, Johnson said, was her first formal dance. Here she was, a tenth grader in her first long dress, walking with her date and his friend out to the car when her father, who had been trying unsuccessfully to push his car out of the snow, asked:

> "Would you all mind giving me just a little push? I can't seem to get out." And the boys said, "Of course." Then he looked up at me and said, "Well, come on, Nancy." So I plowed over the snowbanks in my long dress and pushed the car, and we all got it out of the snow.

Congresswoman Nancy Pelosi, whose father was in Congress when she was born and later became mayor of Baltimore, developed a negative outlook toward politics as a career because she saw firsthand how hard her father worked. The adored little girl with six older brothers, Pelosi was raised in a loving environment. Her father protected her to the point of not permitting her to go too far away to college. And yet when she got engaged, he commented jokingly, "You mean, all that education and now she's going to scrub floors like everybody else?"

Message from Dad:
"It's OK to Be Both Nurturant and Aggressive"

These nontraditional fathers were not afraid to display a nurturant side of their personalities, their daughters recalled warmly. When Rhode Island Secretary of State Kathleen Connell was in nursing school, which she found to be a difficult and tedious experience, her dad would come up weekly to take her and some classmates out to dinner.

Colorado Treasurer Gail Schoettler recalled that her father, who came across as unemotional and dominating, was also extremely fair and generous. She remembered that when employees retired from working on his ranch, he took care of them financially, visited them in the hospital, and did whatever he could to make them comfortable.

Although Congresswoman Connie Morella's father disapproved of her flying across the country at age eighteen, the morning she was leaving he came in and kissed her and put money under her pillow for the trip. Thus he gave her the message that he still loved her, even when she behaved independently.

In their fathers these women found a model for moving out into the world. Their fathers' messages reinforced the young girls' value of nurturant behavior and encouraged them to do whatever they wanted. The fathers served as a quiet vision offering the possibility of politics when the time came for the daughters to make a career choice. All of these messages became a part of the daughters' Competent Self.

Most of the fathers who have lived long enough to see their daughters in action have been able to overcome any ambivalence they may have had about assertive, independent women. Congresswoman Marge Roukema told us how proud her father was of her political achievements: "He campaigned with me. He licked more envelopes and made more phone calls than anybody. He was my biggest volunteer."

Manhattan Borough President Ruth Messinger is proud of the way her father supports her:

> I believe my father talks about me to somebody every day of the year. He has this notion that if he can just meet and convert enough people, then he doesn't have to worry about my going up

before the voters. When he's riding the bus to work I'm sure he checks out the person sitting next to him and then tries to make a connection. He might say, "Oh, that looks like an interesting book. What's it about? Oh, that's funny — I thought it was a book about politics" and take it from there. People tell me that all the time.

Such support for the adult daughters tells us something about what life must have been like for them as children. Their fathers' support certainly must have played a vital role in their metamorphosis into political women.

Mixed Messages

Lest you believe that all of the women we interviewed came from idyllic families, let us add a note of reality. Some of the women had less than wonderful experiences with their parents. Among the parents were a punitive mother, a mother who never showed affection, a father who drank too much, and a few mothers and fathers who were generally unsympathetic to their daughters' advancement.

Because some parents couldn't resolve the conflict between their own nurturant and aggressive components, they sometimes sent mixed messages to their daughters. Confusion arose from such contradictory messages as "We know you can do anything you want" *but* "We expect you to be attractive and act like a lady at all times." Congresswoman Nancy Johnson heard that she could be anything she wanted to be *but* she was also expected to fulfill the traditional female role of wife, mother, and homemaker. (We will talk more about mixed messages in Chapter 5.)

Fortunately for the women we studied, their mothers and

fathers also sent enough other strong, unambiguous messages to outweigh the mixed messages. This made it possible for the women's political and leadership selves to emerge at some point in their lives.

Congresswoman Nancy Johnson, for example, also heard that not only could she do "heavier work" (implying manual tasks, such as pushing a car out of a snowbank), but she could also do the "heavier work" of a congresswoman instead of that of a secretary or teacher, typical careers in the era in which she grew up. And despite the mixed messages her father sent, he took obvious pride in her accomplishments. When she was elected, she recalled, he chuckled with pride: "Well, they'll never know what hit them."

Lieutenant Governor Evelyn Murphy told us how she rebelled against her father, a career army officer, even though she knew she was special in his eyes and thought he had treated her more leniently than he had her older sister. Murphy, who felt her father was too controlling, believes the turning point in her life occurred when she challenged his authority:

> I was going to take my things to school and he said, "No, you can't have a car to go down tonight. I plan to drive down and take you all over the place." I said please, but he told me no. So I just said, "But I'm taking it. You promised it to me."

Murphy realized she had to escape from the suffocating family atmosphere if she was going to blossom on her own:

> So when I left for college at age seventeen I intentionally left forever. There was more to what I wanted in life than I could seek from my parents at that time. I didn't know what it was, but I knew I had to get away.

When Murphy finished her degree, she returned to Boston, back to her roots, where she and her mother had lived with her grandmother during World War II. That strong grandmother, who had been the "pivot and focus" of the family, and her stoic mother were her models of strength.

Many of the women we interviewed spoke of grandparents, aunts, and uncles whose love, strength, and independence compensated for the messages their parents were unable to provide. In such cases, members of their extended family helped these women develop a Competent Self despite the lack of support and encouragement from home.

The Sibling Factor

Thus far we've talked about the important roles that the older generation of family members plays in development of the Competent Self. We intentionally saved one of the most significant family influences — the sibling factor — for last.

When we were writing this book many of our friends and associates thought they knew exactly how our research on the sibling factor would turn out. Frankly, so did we. The psychological literature on this subject led us to expect that the women in our sample probably were either only children or the firstborn in a family of girls.

For example, Hennig and Jardim's study of twenty-five female managers in *The Managerial Woman* was one indicator that achieving women are either only children or first in a family of girls. Hennig and Jardim concluded that these women had been chosen by their fathers to fill the role of the son the fathers never had. Consequently, each woman had a close relationship with her father, who exposed her to masculine experiences that later helped her compete and survive in the almost exclusively male world of management.[8]

Sometimes when we told people about our subjects, they'd say knowingly, "Oh, they're only children who get it all from their fathers." In fact, only children have been described by Kevin Leman in *Growing Up Firstborn* as "superfirstborns" who have the characteristics of first children magnified two or three times.[9]

Other people we told about our research commented, "They won't have any brothers, that's for sure." One of the studies that supports this prediction is Kelly and Boutilier's analysis of the biographies of political women. Kelly and Boutilier hypothesized that many of the women they studied would have older brothers who helped them learn male sex roles, much as the fathers had done for the managerial women. But this did not turn out to be the case. In fact, none of the women in their sample had an older brother.[10]

We drew further support for our expectations of only children or firstborn in a family of girls from our knowledge that oldest children have consistently been found to be more highly motivated to achieve than their siblings are. The differences in achievement motivation between only children and later-born children or those from large families are particularly striking. This is not surprising: parents with only one child on whom to place their hopes simply put more pressure on that child to succeed than do parents of larger families.

Finally, research has shown that female only children have a strong work ethic and are highly competitive, just what we would expect of successful political women.

As it turned out, everyone — including us — was wrong. Much to our surprise, there was just one only child among our twenty-five subjects. And only 16 percent of the twenty-five women were the oldest in a family of girls. Family sizes ranged from two to nine children, and brothers and sisters were widely distributed throughout the sample. The complete breakdown is as follows.

Category	Number	%
Only child	1	4
Firstborn	12	48
Middle	8	32
Last	4	16
Totals	25	100

We began to wonder whether male politicians fit the original sibling hypothesis of being only children or firstborns. To determine that, we phoned a sample of twenty-two congressmen as part of the only research conducted about political men for this book. We found seven oldest children, six middle, and nine last-borns. Their families ranged in size from two to six children, and brothers and sisters were about evenly represented.

Clearly, neither birth order nor sex of siblings was of great significance for the women (or the men) we studied. Neither was the size of the family important. This isn't at all what we expected.

Although there were only four firstborns in families of girls, some of the women we interviewed feel that their success would have been thwarted had there been male siblings. For example, Ruth Messinger told us,

> I'm absolutely convinced that if my sister had been a boy, my whole world would have been turned upside down. I have always thought that my father would have had a much tougher time being as respectful of intelligence and invested in future options in an evenhanded way if he'd had children of his sex.

We concluded that it was the *presence* rather than absence of siblings that was significant. Why? Growing up with siblings helped our women develop critical aspects of their Competent Self, such as aggression, competition, negotiation, coalition

building, and the other interpersonal skills that are so essential
to leadership success.

Siblings and Creative Aggression

A family with siblings provides a safe arena in which children
can develop Creative Aggressive behavior. Even today it may
be the only arena available to girls, whereas boys are more
likely to have opportunities to nurture and direct aggression
through competitive sports.

Mary Landrieu, Louisiana's treasurer, commented on the
mixed messages society sends about female aggression:

> I think my parents did a better job than most in helping me to be
> competitive and aggressive when I needed to be. But little girls
> still get messages that don't really serve them, such as "Sit down
> and be pretty and just don't say too much." And that comes
> across regardless of how much your parents want to overcom-
> pensate for the messages the world gives you.

Anyone who has siblings or has raised siblings (or has just
been around siblings) knows how much they fight. Such a
family environment provides a place to learn the limits of
aggressive behavior. Although parents may sometimes think
otherwise, sibs do learn when to stop, short of killing each
other. As Kathleen Connell put it, "My brothers and I used to
fight until the older one got so he could beat me up, and then
the fighting stopped. We stopped fighting when I started losing.
So I must have been the one causing fights, I suppose."

When the opportunity presents itself, it usually doesn't matter whether an older or younger sibling instigates the fight. As
Ruth Messinger remembered:

> I'm sorry to say how terrible I was to my younger sister when I
> was about five. She remembers it, too. I used to tease her when

nobody was looking. I made her so angry that she would bite me, and then I used to report her for biting.

Even when parents try to limit fighting, sibs will find another way to develop their Creative Aggression. According to Barbara Kennelly, "My parents never, never indulged us in fighting with each other. It was not acceptable. Oh, I'm sure we fought — my sister and I, eighteen months' difference — sure we fought. But I mean, spats." And Jo Ann Zimmerman said, "My brother and I had some fights, hitting each other. Of course, my parents weren't around then." She added that because her parents did permit her and her brother to yell at each other, the two of them learned to conduct physical combat in private.

Sibling fighting doesn't always have to mean physical contact, although it frequently occurs. Clearly, as Bank and Kahn observe in *The Sibling Bond*, there are positive aspects of fighting in childhood. Fighting helps siblings learn to manage and resolve conflict. It marks them as "a distinct subsystem, different from parents whom they have been taught to love and honor."[11] It allows them to understand rather than fear their own and someone else's aggression. Good parents know when to intervene and when to let their children resolve their fights themselves.

Why is it important for political women and men to possess Creative Aggression? (The answer is *not only* so they can sling mud at opponents!) Aggression energizes. It allows us to move out into the world with new ideas and try to make things happen. It stimulates us to make dreams come true by setting goals, making plans, and carrying out the actions that help us reach our goals and fulfill our dreams. In this sense, aggression is the opposite of passivity — and it is clear that passivity is not compatible with politics and leadership.

Day-to-day competition among siblings sharpens a lifetime skill. Siblings are natural competitors for parental attention and love. Whatever the birth order, competition is ever-present. The oldest child competes to maintain the advantage of being number one. Younger children struggle to catch up with their older sibs. Middle children try to get the attention that the oldest and the youngest naturally seem to get. Siblings compete to see who's tallest, brightest, prettiest, and so on.

Exposure to and experience with competition may be *the* critical factor that makes having grown up with siblings useful to women who run for public office, because outside the family, women have many fewer opportunities to compete than men do. Women are not socialized to be competitive. They are not encouraged to participate in sports to nearly the extent that boys are, even today.

Competition is so much a part of life that people tend to overlook its potential value. They don't see how sibling rivalry contributes to a person's ability to be competitive as an adult. Almost all of our subjects said they had never before made the connection between growing up with siblings and the development of their own competitiveness. During the interviews, they didn't "hear" how they compared themselves with their sibs or realize how important these comparisons were to themselves. For example, Education Commissioner Betty Castor at first denied being competitive with her siblings, but when we asked about her relationship with her twin brother she admitted:

> I thought I was smarter than my brother, and I suppose that I also competed with my sister. So I think there was competition in the family. I really haven't thought about it — competition being fostered in the family. But I was competitive with my older sister because she always appeared to get all the attention in the family, being the first child. And she did pretty well in school. When she graduated from eighth grade it was a very big deal, and when she graduated from high school that was a very big deal. I competed with her knowing that she started off as a

very good student and wound up a very good student. So I was trying to be at least as good a student, if not better. And I knew I was going to compete favorably with one of my brothers because he just did not seem to like school.

Competitive siblings will try almost anything to gain an edge over one another. But as Kathleen Connell demonstrated when she stopped fighting with her siblings when she began to lose, siblings also learn when *not* to compete. In other words, siblings learn to pick their battles and to take calculated risks. This is an extremely important skill for political women and men, not only during campaigns but also when they are advocating issues and working with others while in office. It is equally important for leaders in industry and other organizations. The willingness to take risks is so important that we discuss it much more fully in Chapter 6.

Living with siblings also presents an opportunity to learn how to negotiate among contemporaries and with the older generation. Congresswoman Nancy Johnson noted that she was the one who tried to get her father and sister, often at odds, to see both sides of an issue. The negotiator became a politician.

Successful negotiations involve trade-offs. Political women know that one way to get what they want from their colleagues is to have something to offer in return. Kathleen Connell, Rhode Island secretary of state, pointed out that a drawback of her position was that she had no chips to trade:

> To get things done in this office I've got to negotiate with the governor, the administration, and on and on and on. They don't need anything from me, so they play hardball. In this position I don't have a lot of trades. And that's the name of the game.

Political women need to build coalitions to be effective once they are elected, and multisibling families provide an early environment for developing that skill. Siblings also learn (if they're smart) a particularly useful coalition tactic: supportiveness. Congresswoman Barbara Kennelly, who said the childhood fights between her and her sister were merely spats, added, "We were always on the same side — against our parents, maybe." That kind of supportiveness can last into adulthood, as Congresswoman Claudine Schneider illustrated in this comment about her brother:

> We were, and we still are, very protective of one another. If my mother gives him grief, I will call her up and say, "Look, you're not going to hear from me again until you apologize to him." I am real tough on this front. If anybody messes with my baby brother, they're in deep trouble. And he's very protective of me.

Several of the women commented about how supportive adult siblings can be to the political woman. Catherine Baker Knoll said:

> All my brothers and sisters have always been active in my campaigns. This is crucial because you automatically have your own nucleus of family and then your friends. For instance, my oldest brother wrote to the presidents of his service club all across Pennsylvania telling them that he was my brother and he really would appreciate it if they'd read his letter at their meetings. They're not allowed to discuss politics, you know; but since he's been so involved in the club, they would do that. So I'm sure I got a lot of votes that way. And it all adds up, doesn't it?

So in spite of the aggression they may play out, most siblings develop fierce loyalty to each other. They're saying to the world, "We can do it to each other — but don't let any outsider try to do it to any of us." The ability to create and nurture loyalty is a valuable skill for leadership success.

It is not unusual for politicians, after tearing each other apart during a primary campaign, to put aside their hostility and work together to defeat the other party's candidate. Congresswoman Marge Roukema once even called for party unity with her primary platform, saying, "It's about time Republicans stopped fighting Republicans and started beating Democrats."

Party loyalty can be a big plus in political life. A number of the women we interviewed began their political careers as volunteers in the party structure, and some progressed to highly responsible positions. Their loyalty and work were rewarded with strong party support when they themselves ran for office. Many of these women, in turn, have helped other candidates move up the party ladder. But as we said in Chapter 3, we would urge women who are trying to enter politics by starting as party workers to seek leadership positions and avoid being trapped at the envelope-stuffing level.

Aside from loyalty, siblings provide an additional source of love, which somehow survives all their fighting and competition. The relationship with a sibling has a special permanence, especially in today's society when there is no assurance for children that their parents will stay together and always be there for them.

Some of the women we interviewed told us voluntarily how strongly they felt loved by their siblings: "We all loved each other." "When I was five, I felt loved by both parents and all my brothers and sisters." "My older sister's sense of caring for me meant a great deal, too." "My six older brothers always treated me magnificently." "I also felt loved by my brother, so there was a good family 'love network' there." "You always feel loved growing up in a big family. There's always somebody there to put their arms around you, to console you if you've fallen or had an accident or something."

That family love network includes parents, grandparents, aunts, uncles, and others in the extended family. In a reasonably healthy family, where parents have not sanctioned crippling competition and aggression among siblings, the children enjoy the benefits of the family love network. They learn to handle their natural aggressive and competitive impulses in healthy, creative, productive ways; and they learn negotiation, collaboration, and loyalty. They may even get to exercise some power.

Considered in this context, it's not so surprising after all that our sibling hypothesis — only children or firstborns in a family of girls — was not supported by our sample of political women. In fact, it would seem that birth order is less important than the presence of siblings, and the sibling experience is crucial to the development of WomanPower and women's leadership.

A Word About Husbands

Elaine Baxter, Iowa's secretary of state, told us that when she speaks to women's groups she is frequently asked, "Does your husband *allow* you to do these things?" She always replies, "Well, the secret is, you marry a man whose mother was in politics because he doesn't know that a woman isn't supposed to do these things."

The implication is that a politically active woman needs a husband who understands what she's about and is not threatened by her success. Over and over we heard the women in our sample say their husbands had picked up where their families of origin had left off, giving their wives the support and encouragement they needed to move forward. These women had selected a mate with that quality even if they had not been aware of it at the time.

As Congresswoman Pat Saiki remarked:

Especially if you're going into politics, you've got to have someone who is secure, independent, and not threatened about his own career. He's got to be absolutely sure about himself and not feel like he has to take a back seat to you. You can't survive in politics if you have to put up with your husband's disapproval. He will always feel left out.

Only two, or 8 percent, of our subjects, have never been married. A remarkably low 20 percent have been divorced, and 8 percent have been widowed. The remaining 64 percent are in first marriages, many of which are of thirty years' duration and more. Only 8 percent of those who have been married have no children. Family is obviously very important to these women. Their family ties contrast vividly with those of the women in *The Managerial Woman* who, if they married at all, did so later in life and never had children.

A number of women told us that it was their husbands who first gave them the idea of running for office. Congresswoman Olympia Snowe said that her first husband "originally broached to me the idea of running for public office, which I had not considered even though I had done other things for people." Her husband, who was a state legislator, chaired the local Republican city committee and urged her to run for the board of voter registration. She won handily and began her climb up the political ladder.

Congresswoman Nancy Johnson's husband talked her into running when she doubted her own abilities. Johnson said she had been thinking about running for the school board when she was invited to run for the town council instead. She told us what happened at home when she declined the invitation to run for town council:

> "I hear you're not going to run. Why not?" her husband asked that evening.
>
> "Well, I don't know anything about the council. I do know about the school board, but they don't have an opening now so I'm just going to wait," she responded.
>
> "Well, look who serves on our council," he said.

And after we thought about the incumbents on the common council, I said, "You're right. I can do that."

And she did.

Sometimes personal circumstances force a political husband and wife team to decide who continues and who gives up the political career. Congresswoman Barbara Kennelly and her husband had to make this decision when they were both state officeholders. Because their salaries as legislators weren't sufficient to support and educate a family, they decided that he would practice law full-time instead of part-time while she would continue in politics. "When I decided to run for Congress he was incredibly supportive," she told us proudly.

A Surprise Bonus from the Family

Finally, those strong messages about being loved and special have given these women one last boost: an ability to tolerate the absence of intimate relationships in their daily lives. Most politicians have a multitude of acquaintances, but they simply don't have the time to nurture intimate friendships. Fortunately, the women we studied have carried within them a sense of connection, first to their families of origin as they grew up and now to husbands, children, and surviving members of the extended family. So when Catherine Baker Knoll said, "Your best support team is your family," she may not have been aware of the breadth and depth of her statement.

5

Sandbox Dreams:
Can Little Girls Dream of
Greatness, Too?

When we asked U.S. Senator Barbara Mikulski if she ever dreamed when she was young about what she'd like to be, her response was surprisingly blunt: "I didn't sit around in my little sandbox in a Baltimore ethnic neighborhood saying, 'Oh, one day I'm going to be a U.S. senator.'"

She then added, "I also think that's characteristic of women." This observation underscores the fact that women seldom dream of what is possible for them to be in life.

Boys' Dreams of Greatness

Men, on the other hand, have always been encouraged to have sandbox dreams of doing great things for themselves and for the world at large. Not only do boys feel entitled to dream, they are expected to do so.

The following comments by three contemporary heroes, truly men of vision, illustrate how they came to live the dream. Robert Kennedy said, "Some men see things as they are and say why. I dream of things that never were and say, 'Why not?'" In 1961, President John F. Kennedy dreamed of conquering space and challenged America to put a man on the moon by the end of that decade. Martin Luther King, Jr., inspired a revolution when he said, "I have a dream."

Throughout their lives these contemporary heroes based the choices they made and the directions they took on their visions. They understood who they were, what they wanted to become, and how they wanted to turn their dreams into goals and accomplishments.

These men knew early that they were destined for greatness. Why did they dream of what they might want to be? Why did they feel entitled to dream of future greatness for themselves? Events in their early lives, family and social experiences, and cultural expectations for boys encouraged them to develop that sense of positive entitlement and to begin to think early about their future. Starting with the sandbox and even before, the world was open to them without limitations.

The two Kennedys and King dreamed of becoming, among other things, a congressman, a senator, a president, a minister. In both childhood and adolescence they rehearsed these roles. They tried out various identities. They experimented with leadership opportunities such as class president, captain of the debating team, and head of student government. Ultimately, after years of shaping and transforming the dream, they lived it.

These contemporary heroes grew up dreaming of role models they admired — visionaries such as FDR, Churchill, Schweitzer, Gandhi, Henry Ford, John D. Rockefeller. There was no shortage of heroes and leaders to dream about and to emulate, and all of them were male.

About the same time, our three contemporary heroes found additional male role models and mentors — fathers and uncles and ministers whose competence they admired — right on their own turf. These role models and mentors weren't inaccessible business, political, and movie star personalities. Instead, they already played an intimate part in the boys' daily lives. Bonding and love turned into identification as a way of feeling closer to these men.

Boys of earlier generations, when population centers were more concentrated, had greater opportunities to forge intimate relationships with heroes of their time. Famous role models often were more accessible than they are today. But whether a boy personally knows or simply dreams about famous role models, identifying with them makes him feel that he is entitled to be as great as they are. And the more role models there are, the more dreams and visions of future possibilities they inspire in their young admirers. In addition, the boy sees a relationship between the distant role models and the nearby realities whom he knows and trusts.

Young Men and "the Dream"

Because they can identify with both distant heroes and accessible mentor figures, men have been able to build a developmental stage of life that psychologist Daniel Levinson calls "the dream." Levinson says that men experience the dream in young adulthood (roughly ages seventeen to twenty-eight). The young man perceives the dream as a vague sense of the self in an adult world, something between a fantasy and a well thought out plan about what he will ultimately be.[1]

To bring the dream to life, the young adult uses his Creative Aggression to develop the goals, plans, and activities that will shape his dream. If, along the way, he also picks and chooses characteristics and identities from each parent and other people in his life whom he loves, respects, and admires — characteristics and identities that feel consistent with who he is and what his dream is all about — he will be following his passions and building a true, vital, and Competent Self. With a Competent Self, he will be able to make choices in his life that are consistent with the dream's personal road map. And when his life takes on a sense of purpose that directs him toward exciting, fulfilling goals, he begins to actually live the dream.

Such was the case for the prominent male politicians whose dreams were mentioned in Chapter 3. At age twelve many of them wanted to be professional athletes — the superstar, the powerful and wealthy center of attention. The specifics of the dream changed when they became adults, but the basic thrust remained: political superstar, the powerful (and often wealthy) center of attention. These men used prominent figures around them as role models to identify with and learn from, but the ultimate form of the dream was their own unique mix of ingredients. The dream could just as easily have been to be an outstanding computer programmer, a devoted husband and father, or a revered member of the community.

Sometimes the dream becomes problematic. If, for example, the dreamer lacks money or other such resources, has certain personality conflicts, is inhibited or passive, has problems with competition, or lacks certain skills, he may be unable to fulfill his dream. Instead, unfortunately, he can get sidetracked in a career that really doesn't interest him. If he shapes his life in ways that please his parents or other parental figures rather than himself, he'll build a false self. He will struggle throughout life to twist and distort himself in an effort to be compliant and to maintain the love and approval of the adults to whom he continues to feel he owes his survival. To accomplish this, he'll have to deny and alienate his true self and his true feelings. One way or another, those who betray the dream in young adulthood will pay the price later.

Girls' Two DreamTracks

Did the women we interviewed dream of doing great things? Did they use the dream to catapult themselves into the political arena? By and large, they did not. Most of the women in our study followed Barbara Mikulski's example: they didn't have sandbox dreams of greatness, as did the Kennedys and King. The women we talked with have lived sequential lives. They usually married and raised families or had other careers first, and they entered politics later in life.

Other prominent women who have been chronicled seem to have done the same. Mary Catharine Bateson in *Composing a Life* describes women who put life together sequentially or, as she describes it, piece life together as a crazy quilt. Among them are Johnnetta Cole, the first black woman president of Spelman College; Joan Erikson, an artist in her eighties and collaborator with her psychologist/psychoanalyst husband Erik Erikson; and Alice d'Entremont, an electrical engineer who worked on Skylab. For them, each DreamTrack became prominent in its own time. Along the way they came to forks in the road, as did the women we interviewed. At each fork they inquired, in Carol Gilligan's words, "whether it [would] be a good place from which to go on, as well as a good place to remain."[2]

Some stopping points were exciting, some were funny, and many were painful. For example, Gloria Molina, a member of the Los Angeles city council when we interviewed her and subsequently the first woman and first Latino member of the powerful Los Angeles County board of supervisors, remembered how her family was subjected to ongoing humiliation when she was a child:

> I didn't think there were really changes needed as much as I saw there were opportunities. I was poor, and it meant being denied.

It meant having to live in a Latino neighborhood because it was the only place open to us. Having to drive around looking for another place to rent, and when they saw so many kids we could hear, "Uh-uh, we don't take any more." I always saw these things as being denied, that things needed to be changed. What's wrong with having kids? I saw a lot of that. I guess I could see opportunities that could be created, and I think it comes from being denied so much and seeing my family be denied opportunities.

Socially and culturally, it's not hard to understand why women dream only vaguely of future eminence — or don't dream at all. Dreams are to a great extent built on images observed in the culture, taken inside, and embroidered with personal meaning until a unique and distinct visionary fabric is created. This process is harder if a girl has few if any role models on which to pattern her dream. And as we observed in Chapters 2 and 3, that is still the case for women today. The vision of women in high office is new. We have had a woman Supreme Court justice only since 1981. And after the 1990 elections, there were still only two women U.S. senators and three women governors.

Fortunately, women can have many dreams in this complex world. As it was for the women in our study and Bateson's, a life of sequential dreams is acceptable: You can have it all — you probably just can't have it all at the same time. One traditional, socially acceptable dream is to be a mother and raise a family. Another is to follow ambitions and pursue a career. A variation of the ambition DreamTrack involves becoming a leader, a visionary, an eminent and powerful person who makes great contributions to society and enjoys the public persona and the spotlight.

We believe that girls now can have two DreamTracks. They can blend aspects of both their nurturant and aggressive selves in the two tracks: a bride/mother dream and a parallel dream of ambition, purpose, power, Creative Aggression, and even eminence, focused on a career. These are normal, healthy Dream-Tracks for today's young woman.

All DreamTracks can lead to real rather than false selves. A woman's true self can be allied with dreams of ambition and career as well as marriage and family. Her true self is based on choices that make her feel real and vital. When Marjorie Lockwood abandoned her dream of being a globe-trotting fashion photographer for the life of a full-time housewife and mother to please her husband and mother, she abandoned her true self. She buried her true self in an effort to be a good girl and comply with the "demands" of her "parents" and keep this vital love connection intact. Thus she passed up the opportunity to reinforce her Competent Self by developing the kind of creative vision for her life that would have helped her feel fulfilled.

Managing DreamTracks

Women function well when one DreamTrack is in the foreground and the other in the background. The problem is their concern over managing how and when they will get to the other track. Mothers wonder about entering the job market behind their peers. Career women worry about their biological clocks running out. The women who try to do everything at once, to implement both DreamTracks at the same time, struggle with juggling the demands of both and frequently complain of being exhausted and depressed and having no time left for themselves. Most of the women we interviewed took care of the nurturant part of themselves first — they let that self be in the foreground — and kept the ambitious and Creatively Aggressive self in the background for years. Then, as family responsibilities changed, they shifted the ambitious self to the forefront. These women also experienced a conscious motivational drive to make society a better place — a visibly eminent "in the spotlight" career choice focused on making a contribution for the greater good of all.

We're not making the value judgment that women should abandon their traditional feminine dream in favor of the traditional masculine dream. Both dreams are valid. Nor are we advocating a particular pattern or sequence for managing your DreamTracks. Rather, we recognize that the choice is difficult and must suit the individual woman. Each dream represents a part of the Competent Self with both nurturant and aggressive components.

The nurturant elements dear to a woman's self are stimulated and expressed by taking care of others. For the political women in our study, nurturance is ignited by pressing social issues such as environmental protection, child welfare, or medical leave from the workplace. It follows that a number of the women we interviewed were attracted to political life because they knew they could deal most effectively with a heartfelt cause from a powerful policymaking position. The concern of Congresswoman Jolene Unsoeld to strike a balance in protecting the endangered species of the Northwest — the spotted owl as well as the lumbermen and their families — and Congresswoman Barbara Boxer's interest in reclaiming peace dividends from defense budgets and investing them in social programs are ways in which women address nurturant problems from a position of power.

Although most of the women we interviewed defined power as the ability to make people's lives better, it wasn't until much later in their political careers that they recognized another facet of power: the opportunity to implement their agendas. But before they felt safe enough to regard their WomanPower as a positive, helpful force, they first had to feel comfortable with their Creative Aggression. Senator Barbara Mikulski told us that she learned her ideas about public service from examples set by her family and learned to integrate public service and power from the nuns who taught her:

I learned from the Christopher movement when I was in high school in the fifties that through service you could change the world. No matter what that is, if you are a teacher, a mom, whatever, you can change the world because it's your world. You can have an influence on your sphere, your domain. It was better to light one little candle than to curse the darkness.

The idea of public service was so deeply ingrained in Mikulski that she considered entering a number of helping professions. First she thought about becoming a lawyer and then a newspaper reporter. And when she heard that women in some countries could not get medical treatment because the male physicians were not allowed to treat females, she considered becoming a medical missionary. Then she toyed with the idea of being a nun. All of these possibilities shaped her thinking; and by the time she entered college she had decided that social work focusing on community organizations was the best field for her.

After graduation, Mikulski went to work at a child welfare agency, where she gained firsthand experience with poverty-related problems. It was then that she realized she would rather try to change the system than spend her life attacking poverty all alone. She wanted to empower people, to create opportunities for them. At that point she considered getting a doctorate in community organization or social strategy.

During this time some residents of the neighborhood where her immigrant grandmother lived asked Mikulski to attend a community meeting. The meeting had been called to fight the construction of an expressway through the neighborhood. If the expressway were built, not only would the residents lose their homes, but the city refused to reimburse them for their losses. The neighbors were discouraged because the mayor and the machine politicians all supported the expressway. "You can't fight city hall," they said.

"Oh, we can fight it," Mikulski assured them as she organized a neighborhood campaign to defeat the project. And they succeeded in stopping the politicians and the builders from demolishing their homes and replacing them with an expressway. This watershed experience revealed to Mikulski an important true and Creatively Aggressive self that lay just beneath the surface ready to emerge.

In organizing the fight, Mikulski learned something about herself: "I realized that I didn't want to just be knocking on doors. I wanted to be opening doors," she said. "So I decided to run for the Baltimore city council." Everybody laughed at her. "No woman can do that," they said.

Undaunted, she built a volunteer organization with the help of her friends and defeated candidates of two political machines to win the seat. After several terms on the council, Mikulski was elected to Congress. And at age fifty-one she moved up to the U.S. Senate.

Changing the Feminine Legacy

Mikulski was a woman who was not completely satisfied with social work as her profession although serving others had been ingrained in her since childhood. Social work didn't provide enough sense of activism and power to please her. In contrast, public office gave her greater visibility and impact. As she has said, "Politics is social work with power." Would Barbara Mikulski's experience have been different had she been a man? Probably so.

And would the adolescent Mikulski, growing up in a Baltimore ethnic neighborhood today, dream of becoming a U.S. senator? Would she be able to have the dream in early adulthood, as men do? Perhaps not, because even today there are so few female role models and mentors for young women to emulate in their dreams and creative thought. Yet perhaps she *would* have the dream today because she would no longer be as vulnerable to society's cautioning voices. Instead, she would be able to hold on to her inner female experience learned in childhood — that morality is about connections, caretaking, and fairness — and feminine, caretaking concerns such as cleaning up the air we breathe and helping the homeless are indeed matters for serious dreaming, even when there is a threat of war.

We think that women have ambition and career dreams when they are young, but the desire for love, approval, and connections drives them underground. Other research supports our findings. Carol Gilligan's girls went underground with what they knew about themselves, telling themselves, "I no longer know what I knew, and the dreams don't come."[3] Likewise, a study commissioned by the American Association of University Women (AAUW) found that girls who stifle their DreamVoices in adolescence suffer a drop in self-esteem that boys do not experience.[4] When girls stifle their DreamVoices, they pay a high price in loss of self-esteem; the gender gap in self-esteem by age seventeen is quite wide.[5]

Once women are able to feel more comfortable with their Creative Aggression and desires for WomanPower, they will feel safe enough to dream earlier in life. Each generation of women will pass this newfound secret to dream on to their daughters. Eventually the feminine legacy will change from *re*pressing to *ex*pressing dreams. Women will be able to redirect their psychic energy from suppressing aggression to expressing aggression in a creative, not destructive, way. Then Levinson's dream will become a woman's story as well as a man's.

What Were Our Women's Dreams?

Given what we know about the female population, we wondered whether the women in our study had a dream either in
childhood or early adulthood. We asked them what they
wanted to be when they were children and whether they ever
dreamed about it.

Very few responded that they wanted to be elected to office,
be a corporate giant, or hold any other leadership role. Instead,
their answers ranged from a vague "rich and famous" and
"happy" to "a teacher," "dancer," "ballerina," "school nurse,"
"nurse." A few chose less traditional occupations, such as doctor, veterinarian, and test pilot, and there were a few who said
active Democrat, president or secretary of state, or congresswoman. One said she just wanted to make a difference.

Overall, only 8 percent of the women aspired to political
office when they were young, and 20 percent chose nontraditional occupations, including politics. The rest either didn't
respond or chose traditional feminine occupations such as
teacher, nurse, or social worker. Even those who chose traditional occupations were vague about their aspirations, with
many feeling they wanted to do good things on their way to
being wives and mothers. However, in contrast to many of their
contemporaries, the women in our study had something extra
inside them that allowed them to pursue high office, albeit
mostly later in life.

Political Women —
Building a Competent Self

We already know that for the most part the women we interviewed grew up in an atmosphere that equipped them to overcome the experiences that are usually perceived as obstacles to
women. They all talked of having a sense that (1) they were
loved and special; (2) they could do whatever they wanted to do
and had a desire to be in the spotlight; and (3) their autonomous
and independent behaviors reflected their true selves, making
them comfortable with their core feminine identity. How do
these elements contribute to a Competent Self?

Feeling Loved and Special

When we asked Suzie Azar, mayor of El Paso, how she knew
she was loved, she told us, "I always felt like my parents loved
me best, and that I was the cutest and the funniest and the
smartest. So I felt confident that I could be whatever I wanted
to be." She was telling us what we already know: feeling loved
and special was a crucial contribution to her developing competence and self-confidence. In fact, she's so confident that she
likes to fly F-15 airplanes in her spare time.

How does feeling loved and special help to build a Competent Self? As we said in Chapter 1, when children learn how to
get their mother's attention by crying, sucking, smiling, cling-
ing, and later by talking, they are learning the basics of effectiveness. They are also learning how to control their environment and their lives. They see that their actions are rewarded
by attention and love. They feel seen and heard, attended to,
loved, and cared for. As they continue to grow they also learn

that similar actions in the world can bring similar good results.
This sense of competence begins in infancy. Our earliest
experience of a Competent Self occurs when we realize that we
can have an effect on others. As we grow older, we simply cast
a wider net to include more "others" on whom we have that
impact.[6]

In other words, the actions we take and the consequences we
experience as a result of those actions help us become more
effective in dealing with our environment. Being effective is a
pleasurable feeling. Being effective feels powerful. *Feeling effective is a major, if not the most important, motivational
force in our lives.* Competence follows effective learning, exploration, and successful manipulation of the subject matter
we are learning. Our sense of personal competence is a powerful combination of all our feelings of success and all the interactions we have with others, as organized in our own unique
way. It is the subjective side of our actual competence that
others see every day.

Each positive human interaction includes both satisfaction
and a sense of social and personal competence. It fuels the
supportive internal dialogue that keeps us going through good
and bad times: "I am loved and appreciated. I am good. I am
worthwhile. I like myself. I am competent." This dialogue ultimately transforms into a sense of feeling worthwhile and then
condenses in our memory into ongoing rounds of internal applause that we can tap into at will.

Barbara Mikulski experienced it when she spearheaded the
neighborhood fight against the proposed expressway. It was her
first exposure to political activism on her own, and she found
it tremendously exciting. Mikulski's desire to make those people's lives better and her success at it illustrate how effectiveness motivated her to fight for people's rights. We can see how
her triumphant feelings fed her excitement at influencing both
the politicians and the residents. The success of the "people's

machine" that Mikulski put together gave the neighbors what they wanted; and, in return, she felt appreciated, which fulfilled a basic human need.

Fulfillment of the need to be loved and appreciated leads to a sense of social competence. It is the foundation for self-respect and security, ego strength and self-esteem. Feeling loved and appreciated, respected and secure maintains those rounds of essential internal applause in the theater of our mind. Inner voices echo fond memories of times past: a mother praising a daughter for helping needy senior citizens or for being the funniest child in the family. These sweet moments and the loving dialogue inside us become condensed memories and internal "comfort zones," as Pat Schroeder would say, that we can call upon in anxious or troubled times to soothe, comfort, and inspire us.

Doing Anything You Want, Including Claiming the Spotlight

"I was brought up to feel that I could do anything. I could fix anything," said Congresswoman Nita Lowey of New York. "All you have to do is set your mind to it. And I guess I really do believe I can do anything I want to, if I'm willing to work hard enough and set my mind to it, because I think success has to do with determination and hard work."

This statement was echoed over and over again by the women we interviewed. We believe it's because they were not raised to think they could have whatever they wanted simply because they were loved and special. That sort of message would have left them behind, at the starting gate, passively waiting for good fortune to smile on them. On the contrary, these women were raised to believe that hard work and persistence would pay off.

As Rhode Island Secretary of State Kathleen Connell put it, "Fundamentally, if you get out and work for something, you could get it."

A harder issue, according to Texan Ann Richards, "is knowing what you want. It's not *doing* it. Once you *know*, you can accomplish it because there are a lot of people who will help you do it."

Part of knowing what you want is understanding and accepting your limitations. This enables you to choose an achievable DreamTrack. For example, Louisiana Treasurer Mary Landrieu said she knew she'd never be a nuclear physicist although she was good at many other things. And, she added, "Given that you can accurately identify those real legitimate limits within what you can accomplish and what God has given you, I think there is no limit."

Clearly, being female did not present an obstacle to these women. Their mothers and fathers treated them as if they were competent and could achieve their goals. They were given a feeling of adequacy. Not only did those empowering messages enhance the development of their Competent Self, it enabled them to establish reachable goals and to persevere until they reached them. Then they could bask in the pleasure of accomplishment and use their success to carry them to their next goal.

How did the parents convey the message that their daughters so clearly received? Perhaps a parent literally said it. Congresswoman Jolene Unsoeld remembered her father telling her: "You can do anything in the world that you want to if you want to bad enough and put the effort in on it." Or these messages may represent a shorthand way for these women's memories to say:

I felt my best selves mirrored by my parents. I felt I had an effect on my parents and could get them to see and value me. I felt loved, appreciated, and admired. I could see their joy and pride in me in their eyes. If they feel that way about me, I must be lovable, admirable, confident, exciting, and competent.

For these women, such messages not only provided the basic elements of desire and ambition but went beyond that.

The women we studied went for high-visibility, "in the spotlight" careers. They chose careers in which public persona and visibility play a major part. Early parental values promoted lives of social service, but where did this need for the spotlight come from?

Do they need to feel the center of everybody's world as they felt the center of their parents' world? We think not. Their early experiences of feeling delighted in themselves as they were being mirrored and admired by their parents simply made them want to feel seen and be superstars in adult life. They "knew" and "know" from these experiences that they are admired and respected by others by virtue of the talent they possess and the contributions they make to society. These women claim the spotlight and recognition for their political leadership and policymaking talent rather like musicians, who get the spotlight and are respected for their musical ability. This is different from the self-centeredness of adults whose overindulgent parents set no limits and thus led them to believe that the world revolves around them.

These women's abilities to lead and to change society are the talent for which they are recognized. Their talent reflects the feelings of pleasure and effectiveness the women received from puberty onward from their parents — recognition for their independent opinions, autonomy, and leadership in the family growing up. So why give it up now? As we are growing up, it is crucial that parents, our only "public" for a while, mirror our need to be seen and valued.

These women had the kinds of mirroring experiences that

helped them to feel later that their Competent Self is a real and true self. Then, when the world became frustrating or depressing or frightening — or when failure entered their lives — they could look inside to find the good internal supplies left behind by their mirroring experiences. These experiences included a sense of feeling their parents were tuned in to them, understood them, and resonated with them, thus satisfying their needs often enough to make them feel loved, appreciated, and worthwhile. That sense of worth, like the internal applause, can be claimed and drawn on at will. It is inside of them and encourages and supports their efforts, helping them always to feel buffered against despair, to feel courageous and take risks, and to see the possibilities more often than the obstacles.

The need to feel you can do anything you want, to feel effective through experiences of Creative Aggression, and the need to feel seen and valued through mirroring experiences help us feel a sense of competence and WomanPower. The women we interviewed have found that, for them, public life is an arena through which to continue these enriching experiences in adult life, as well as a valid and socially useful way to express their needs to be in the spotlight.

Feminine Autonomous Political Behavior

Over the years it has been mistakenly assumed that politics, whether in the elective or corporate world, is masculine. That, in turn, has led to the widespread assumption that political role modeling by the father influences a daughter as much as it does a son. We disagree, and other research supports our view,[7] but the issue is more complicated than that.

We believe that a father's role modeling of political behavior influences his daughter only if at the same time the mother models, mirrors, and endorses autonomous sex roles and values. If the mother supports the father's use of leadership, power, and autonomy and the family reinforces these values, then it is more likely that the daughter will identify with them.

As we have said, most of the women we interviewed grew up hearing that they could do anything they wanted. In some cases, the father may have been the messenger and the role model of independent behavior. However, in almost all cases, the mothers modeled and endorsed Creative Aggression and WomanPower, thus validating the values of independence, autonomy, and success.

This maternal approval enabled these daughters to feel less conflicted about identifying with their fathers. They could go out into the world and put these values into action without feeling guilty. They were not torn between one message that urged them to press forward with their ambitions and dream and another that said, in effect, "nice girls don't do that."

Catherine Baker Knoll, treasurer of Pennsylvania, told of sitting around the dinner table with her mother, father, and nine siblings. She recalled her father saying, "'Remember, all of you girls are just as good as every boy at this table. You can do anything you want. Yes, you can do anything you want in life. Just put your mind to it, and there isn't any obstacle that you can't overcome.'"

Knoll clearly heard the message and incorporated it into her self-concept. As she told us, "I felt that I was a leader. I had so many encouraging words from family like, 'You could do this, you could do that, you try for this, try for that.' So I never stopped to think that I couldn't do something because if you can't do it one way, you improvise and find another way."

While Knoll's father was the ostensible role model for her political ambition, her mother modeled strength, feminine autonomy, independence, and loving nurturance. "My mother was very strong. My father often called her 'Little Dynamite.'

He would very often defer to her opinion. My parents were very supportive of each other, which was good." Knoll's mother may have been the power in her home as well as a powerful woman in her own right, but nonetheless she was still the woman behind the man. Her daughter has taken the feminine power in her family to the next logical step.

Congresswoman Pat Saiki of Hawaii remembers what it was like growing up in an Oriental culture. "You know, it's the boy child who is the most wanted, and my father had three girls. But he was very proud of his girls. He felt that each of us could do anything that we wanted to do."

What did she aspire to be when she grew up? "Successful. My mother let us know that there was never a choice about that. I always felt that my mother cared. My father wanted me to succeed; my mother cared about me as a person. I would tell my father about all of the successes I'd had. My mother would share in the things that were not quite as positive."

The "you can do anything" message is often delivered in subtle as well as obvious ways. Jo Ann Zimmerman, lieutenant governor of Iowa, told about feminine strengths she took in while growing up around strong women, who included her in everything.

Once, at her grandparents' farm, her grandmother asked her to come out and help kill the rats in the feedhouse. "All you have to do, Jo Ann, is shake a few of those sacks, and I'll kill them as they come out," said her grandmother. So, armed with brooms, the two of them flailed away at the rats.

It was a long time before Zimmerman realized that she was the only member of the family who helped her grandmother with that disagreeable task. While we can all laugh and say that she, too, could have refused to do it, we can also see her love and desire to please this idealized grandmother who could do anything, feared nothing, and automatically figured her grand-daughter was the same. This model of a stalwart, independent woman helped Zimmerman integrate her grandmother's values into her own self: "I guess you'd say I always went as far as I could until somebody said stop — and then I tried to figure out how to get around that," she told us.

We also looked at the strong relationship between the public role of the mother and the daughter's political and leadership activity. It is clear that the mothers of these women valued public life, accomplishment, hard work, aggression, independent thinking, opinion leadership, courage, integrity, and daring. All of these qualities are the elements of leadership.

How a mother lives her life and who and what she is are critical for determining if, when, and how a girl will strive toward leadership roles in corporate, academic, or elective politics. The way a mother demonstrates independence and leadership to her daughter influences how the daughter incorporates and uses those characteristics in her own life. This overturns the common belief that successful women primarily identify with their successful fathers. Through maternal role modeling, these daughters develop the expectations for careers, public roles, behaviors, and personal development that are generally associated with men.

Ruth Messinger, president of the borough of Manhattan, said there was never any question in her family about what she and her sister could do with their lives:

> Our upbringing, in terms of the message "You can do anything you want, you can be anything you want," was spectacular. We had three things going for us. One, my mother was a generation ahead of her time. Two, we had a father who in his own way was very proud of his wife and very invested in his three very smart women. Three, I had no brothers.
>
> I identified with my mother, who was the world's classic Superwoman. She had a full-time job in public relations. She did lots of volunteer work. She cooked. The only "anti-Superwoman" behavior on my mother's part was that she expected us to share in the cooking and to manage our own money and start

working early and be responsible for ourselves. That was the healthiest part of her, and it was a good way to engage with her.

The relationship between Barbara Boxer and her father would seem to confirm the old myth that the father/daughter bond is the critical factor in a woman's success. She said of her father, who was her vision of political behavior:

> I always went to ball games with him. He was interested in the stock market, and I became a stockbroker. He was interested in world affairs and politics, and we talked about those things. He went to law school and passed the bar at forty, and yet his family was his greatest pleasure.

However, to get the whole picture, we need to look further at her relationship with her mother and with her extended family. Boxer also told of feeling loved and special growing up. "I had a wonderful childhood, a very warm, loving family. Extended family, aunts and uncles. My mother was the youngest of six children, my dad was one of nine. All of them settled in New York, so it was always like Passover, with lots of family. It was a lot of warmth."

And then there was her mother, the capable and competent leader of her family, the strong woman who mirrored and endorsed her daughter's political behavior. Even some of Boxer's mother's offhand early comments stuck in her mind later, to serve as seeds of ambition. She always remembers her mother saying proudly, "You know, there's one *woman* in the U.S. Senate." That was more than thirty-five years ago. At a Los Angeles fundraiser in her 1992 campaign for the U.S. Senate, Boxer quoted her mother and added, "And now all these years later, there are still only two women in the Senate."

Thinking of running for the Senate, she had mused, "What's wrong with this picture, and what can I do about it?" One of her colleagues, Congressman George Miller of California, told her, "Barbara, the Senate needs a wake-up call, and you're the one who can do it." Boxer decided to change the statistics that had remained almost unchanged from that time so long ago when her mother had told her about the one lone woman senator. Together, Boxer's mother and father provided her with the essence of her autonomous, independent, and political behavior. Obviously, this confident, competent, aggressive woman from California is able to draw on the unlimited internal applause instilled in her by both parents when she was growing up in New York City.

Many of the women we interviewed credited their mothers, grandmothers, and other strong women in their lives with being their role models and chief influences. This intense connection to their mothers or mothering figures is perhaps the major key to their having two rather than one DreamTrack leading to eminent political life. However, without recognition of the legitimacy of two DreamTracks, girls can feel the pull to be like their enviable mothers fighting with their attraction to be like their more exciting fathers. A push and pull struggle ensues.

The path to eminent life is strewn with internal conflicts and obstacles — a crooked maze indeed. To ease this struggle we must change our way of raising daughters. Without realizing it, we often encourage our daughters to be clones of ourselves; unfortunately, cloning doesn't encourage autonomy. We must shift from embracing a model of rearing children who are exact replicas of their mother or father to one that includes permission to exercise self-definition. Then our daughters can choose elements from each, ultimately blending them into their own unique and satisfying Competent Self. We can move away from the need to make Creative Aggression a secret and hidden agenda for women to one of openly combining it with nurturance and WomanPower and removing the necessity for a girl in today's world to make a Hobson's choice.

Mixed Messages

We recently talked with several mothers whose daughters ranged in age from four to twelve. Each mother was successful in her chosen field: a literary agent, CEO, corporate vice president, and congresswoman. They told us that when they asked their daughters what they wanted to be, they were appalled at the answers. Two of the girls wanted to be brides, and two wanted to be wives and mothers. What, no career?

We wondered about the kinds of messages these highly achieving mothers were giving their daughters. There are two possibilities. Perhaps the daughters already have two Dream-Tracks, and now they're on the bride/mother DreamTrack of early childhood. This doesn't necessarily mean they won't learn leadership skills while they're on this track. Although they don't yet dream of greatness, little girls do absorb a sense of competence from their mothers and mothering figures while on the bride/mother DreamTrack, as did Jo Ann Zimmerman and Barbara Boxer. It is also possible, however, that they are getting a truly mixed message, one that says both "you can" and "you can't." This was the kind of mixed message described by several of the women we interviewed.

Iowa Secretary of State Elaine Baxter said it succinctly: "My father always spent a lot of time with me and encouraged me to get an education. No one in our family had ever been to college, but he very much wanted me to go." She remembered how he always encouraged her to do "something" with her life. And although he didn't specify what he meant by "something," he always pushed her to do well.

At the same time, though, he also prodded her in ways that she thinks now were inappropriate for her age, causing her pain and confusion. For example, when she was six or seven he would send her to visit her grandparents all by herself. To get there she had to take the streetcar downtown and then transfer to a train for a two-hour ride. She acutely remembered the mixed messages her parents gave her before those trips. While her mother cried, her father would say, "She can't be a baby all her life." The effect was that she was being told on the one hand to go out on her own, while on the other hand she was hearing that acting independently was bad and scary.

The mixed messages continued in high school. While her father constantly encouraged her to get the best education possible, her teachers were saying: "Don't exceed. Don't excel. You want boys to like you. Don't be the class brain." These were typical of the mixed messages that girls of her generation heard as they were growing up.

Mixed messages are confusing. Congresswoman and senatorial candidate Claudine Schneider of Rhode Island tells of the mixed messages she received from her parents:

> They wanted their son to go to college and become a professional. They wanted me to go to college so I could *marry* a professional. So their expectations of me were not particularly great. That was one message. The other message was, "You can do absolutely anything you want if you apply yourself." So that was the message I chose to adhere to.

The fewer mixed messages, primarily maternal, the daughter receives, the less conflicted she will feel later about her developing leadership capacities. A minimum of mixed messages will allow her to hear her DreamVoices saying that it's acceptable to dream of doing great things and then showing her how.

The daughter who feels conflicted and anxious about her competence will be inhibited in her capacity to dream because she unconsciously fears losing parental love or approval. The dream at this point will either die or become distorted. This is what happened to Marjorie Lockwood when she became head cheerleader and then felt consumed by guilt.

Congresswoman Nancy Johnson of Connecticut describes growing up hearing mixed messages even though her family deeply respected the achievements of their women:

> My mother was unusual for her time. She had a master's degree in history and was a successful teacher. She was a southerner with a gentle and soft touch. When her children were born she retired from work and became a full-time parent. It was a kind of mixed message.
>
> Because of my mother, my father had a tremendous respect for female accomplishment. But after marriage and children it was understood that your life went in a different direction. My parents never really bridged that gap in terms of relationship or in terms of seeing my mother valued. One of my father's best friends would say to her, "You know, it's wonderful — you're one of his least utilized resources."

Johnson's political record attests to the decision she made years ago to never allow herself to become an underutilized resource.

The Sexual Revolution and the Political Woman's World

Clearly, younger women who have enjoyed the freedoms won by the sexual revolution feel greater permission at an earlier point to pursue a visibly eminent career. The culture has begun to agree with parents who tell their daughters they can be whatever they want to be and, with integrity, follow their desire to be in the spotlight. In contrast, pre–sexual revolution women may have heard the same parental messages at a young age, but society didn't reinforce them; therefore, those earlier women were confronted with a far more difficult struggle in pursuit of their dreams of greatness.

For the most part, pre–sexual revolution women married and raised their children before becoming politicians whereas younger women, whose dreams were not as impeded by cultural prohibitions, sought political office at an earlier age.

This does not mean that we advocate raising your children in one way or another or that we are trading new dreams for old. Rather, we wish to reemphasize that there are now many possible dreams for women that can be uniquely woven into each woman's personal true and Competent Self.

A Pre–Sexual Revolution Woman
Lives Her Dreams

Nancy Pelosi, congresswoman from San Francisco, at first followed the traditional dream of a pre–sexual revolution woman. During the years she devoted to raising her family, which she found fulfilling, one creative self was in the foreground. Later, when her five children were more self-sufficient, another true self took over as she campaigned for and won political office. One example of her ability to change from one true self to another is her statement that she would give up her congressional seat at any time if remaining in office would jeopardize her family in any way.

A shy child, Pelosi had grown up watching her mother wholeheartedly support her father's political career. She admired the way her mother entertained almost around the clock, with people constantly streaming in and out of their home. But she also saw the emotional deprivation her mother experienced because her husband couldn't spend much time with the family.

From these early lessons, Pelosi knew she wanted to be politically active, but she didn't want to run for office herself until relatively recently. "I wanted to be involved in politics. The Democratic party was our life as a child," she told us. "But I didn't want to be the person on the front line who has no personal life."

Eventually, though, she found pleasure in combining both traditional and career roles. As planned, she became a very active Democrat and major fundraiser for the party. In fact, she was so successful at fundraising that in the mid-1980s the Democratic Senatorial Campaign Committee formally recognized her as the person most responsible for returning the Senate to the Democrats.

Pelosi was confronted with the opportunity to make a major role change when her mentor, Congresswoman Sala Burton of San Francisco, died in office in 1988. Shortly thereafter, with her husband's support, she decided to become a politician after all — and went on to win the special election for Burton's former seat.

Today, Congresswoman Pelosi fulfills her identification with her father as a member of the powerful Appropriations Committee, on which her father also served when he was a Maryland congressman before his years as mayor of Baltimore. And, obviously, Nancy Pelosi is using well the modeling, mirroring, and endorsement of competitive and political behavior with which her mother supplied her. The result is that she felt permission to be both a staunch party supporter and an independent woman, but she nevertheless is a woman of her time. She did not seem to feel the internal permission early on to become a politician, as did Mary Landrieu, whose story follows.

A Post–Sexual Revolution Woman
Lives Her Dreams

Thirty-three years old at the time of our interview, Mary Landrieu, treasurer of Louisiana, is clearly a post–sexual revolution woman who capitalized on the role modeling and values of her family.

Politics was very much a part of the Landrieu family's everyday life. Mary Landrieu's father, Moon, was mayor of New Orleans and later secretary of housing and urban development in the Carter administration. Her mother enjoyed being a supportive political wife. "In our house there was a strong, very clear drive that you were born to serve more than yourself, whether it was your community or family or both. Public service was very important," said Landrieu.

As a child, Landrieu wanted to be a nun because she so admired the nuns who taught in her school. Realizing her desire to grow up and get married, she transformed her dream into a career as a social worker. Clearly, she had heard her family's messages about serving others. After a religious experience in her late teens, she combined these choices and decided to be a full-time Christian worker. However, she was rejected when she applied for a position as a missionary, and she was devastated by the experience.

"I wondered what I should do with my life after that happened," she said. Like Nancy Pelosi, Landrieu never had thought of becoming a politician herself. The only political role she envisioned was as the wife of a politician, as her mother had been. However, after much soul-searching she decided to follow in her father's political footsteps. She successfully combined the current cultural endorsement of a career with her parents' support to enter public service.

Thus, Landrieu was able to turn bitter disappointment at her rejection as a full-time Christian worker into stunning political success. When she was elected to the state legislature at twenty-three, she was the youngest woman ever to have been elected in Louisiana. She felt alienated from her legislative peers because of both her gender and her youth, so she vowed to distinguish herself in office. She would show them! After seven years in the legislature, she felt ready to move up to higher office. This time with little money but lots of courage she took a well-calculated risk and ran a statewide race — and was elected state treasurer of Louisiana.

While circumstances prevented Landrieu from becoming a staffer with Campus Crusade for Christ, they also allowed her to serve as she serves best — as a highly visible public policy-maker. Perhaps in this way she feels closer to the good feelings inside of her provided by her mirroring experiences and the internal applause that tells her to "go for it." While she was trying to decide between public office and a career with a lower profile, it is likely that she fantasized about the constraints a nonpublic life would impose on her if she settled for a false and compliant self.

Finally, she discovered her own true self, which needed power and position so she could make a major difference in people's lives. She thereby fulfilled both her own and her parents' goals. Maybe Mary Landrieu has become a missionary in a way after all: thanks to her ground-breaking career path she has made it possible for women in Louisiana and throughout the country to dream more easily of political careers and leadership positions and to learn that they can have it all — ambition/career and bride/mother dreams. Mary Landrieu is now married and trying to balance family with thoughts of becoming Louisiana's governor. As we said, sequencing and Dream-Track management is very important.

Both Nancy Pelosi and Mary Landrieu successfully avoided the dangers of creating a false and compliant self. They heard DreamVoices that told them they were entitled to do whatever they wanted, including doing great things in life and going for the spotlight. Pelosi followed her generation's lead, raising her family first and seeking a public role later. Landrieu opted for the publicly visible route at a much younger age, as her generation is more apt to do.

Both women comfortably blended parental identifications into their own dreams. They became politicians like their fathers before them, and at the same time they took in their mother's personal messages, social and public roles as strong women, and mirroring and endorsement of autonomous and political behavior. Neither woman found it necessary to give up her feminine and nurturant self to be a politically successful and visibly eminent woman.

Endthoughts

We have found that women *can* dream of greatness. With a Competent Self, Creative Aggression, and WomanPower to help them feel effective and a cultural climate that endorses female leadership, women can be motivated to follow the ambition/career DreamTrack to career achievement, some following eminent and visible career paths. For some women, being in the spotlight in a high-visibility career reconnects them to the good feelings they had as children when they were admired and valued by their parents. At the same time, however, they can continue to follow their bride/mother DreamTrack, to integrate intimate lives with career ambitions. Each track includes nurturant and aggressive aspects of their Competent Self. Managing DreamTracks requires delicate balancing. Which track a woman follows at any given time varies with the twists and turns of her unique developmental pathway and the social and cultural messages of her time.

---------------   PROFILE   ---------------

Ann Richards
Taking the Risk in Texas,
Where Politics Is a Contact Sport

Risktaking is a critical factor of successful leadership. What better exemplifies risktaking than running for high elected office? Texas treasurer and now Governor Ann Richards serves as an example of how learning to take well-calculated risks early in life helps a woman to feel comfortable and excited about the necessary risktaking she faces later in life.

"Come January, you and I will meet on the Congress Avenue Bridge. Together, we will march up the avenue arm in arm and we will reclaim the capitol for the people of Texas." That was Ann Richards' campaign pledge as she ran for governor in 1990.

What a tremendous risk Richards was taking, giving up her position as state treasurer to run for governor. She explained it to us in very real terms:

> There is the risk that I will lose and will not have employment. I will be fifty-six years old, and it will be difficult to find a niche for me in which I can support myself. I have not been with the state long enough to have my retirement years vested. There are a lot of security risks at my age that will be difficult to resolve.
>
> I'm not sure how great the risk is, but I know that all of your personal life must be on hold during a campaign. You must give up literally everything that offers you social pleasure. If I should lose, will I have a hard time picking up a simpler life? The adjustment will be tough, I think. If I win, of course, it will mean that I will continue to lead this frenetic life.
>
> I think that relationships require nurturing, and I don't have

time to do that. I don't think my friends or my family will love me any less, but I think we will have taken an enormous number of years away from the nurturing of our relationship.

Richards put herself on the line when she announced her candidacy for governor. She knew that the opposition would play hardball — they always do in Texas, where politics has been called a contact sport. She knew that her opponents and the media would attack her alcoholism and her divorce. This is not the sort of history that plays well to the public, especially in a state where the "good ol' boys" had been in power for so many years. The campaign would be grueling, dirty, and hard on body and soul.

Richards was willing to take that risk because she understood human frailties and knew they can be overcome. We interviewed Ann Richards very shortly after her historic debate with Jim Mattox, her combative opponent in the primary for the 1990 gubernatorial race, during which she was asked by a reporter and refused to answer questions regarding her alcoholism. All of Texas and much of the country who remembered Richards' stirring keynote speech at the 1988 Democratic convention listened breathlessly and were shocked when she declined to answer. Most felt that the risk Richards took in not answering was one from which even her childhood secret weapon, Wonder Woman's magic lariat, could not rescue her. Everyone knows that in politics evasion is a mistake. We have only to look at Dukakis to know that his most critical mistakes, costing him the presidential election, came when he tried to avoid talking about his problems with the media, only to have them revealed by others later.

At a press conference the day after debating Mattox, Richards answered the unanswered question: "It is ten years," she said, "since I've had a mood-altering drug." People's reactions ranged from shock to disbelief. Richards' supporters thought she had blown it. They thought she panicked, miscalculated her risk, and just made a fatal if not *the* fatal mistake of her campaign. But Ann Richards knew better than everyone. In discussing the matter with us, she said:

> I've always learned more from my failures than from my successes. Ten years ago I joined the Alcoholics Anonymous recovery program to help me recover from the devastating effects of the disintegration of my thirty-year-old marriage, the greatest loss of my life. It is very hard for me to think of my alcoholism as a failure because to me it was and is a disease.
>
> I also found a wonderful counselor. And going to see her — that helped a lot, too. She helped me to learn to live alone, and it was a wonderful discovery.
>
> I gave the press that answer because it was the only one I could give. I believe in recovery, and I believe that as a role model I have the responsibility to let young people know that you can make a mistake and come back from it.

And she was right. She won the primary and went on to win the general election. But as Richard Shingles, a scholar at Virginia Polytechnic Institute who is studying gender and race in politics, said in *Time*, in Texas "it takes more for a man to be perceived as a bully than it takes for a woman to be perceived as a bitch."[1]

Richards has the capacity to turn failures into positives. That ability lessens the personal risk because even when she loses, she believes that good things can happen. She even turned her divorce into something positive:

> I think that the greatest loss, if it's described as failure, was the dissolution of my marriage. It is particularly traumatic when you've been married as long as I was and you are as old as I was when the divorce occurred. I dealt with it by telling myself that now I had an opportunity to do things that I would not have had an opportunity to do if I had stayed married. And I made that the case. One of the real joys for me was learning to live alone. I'd never lived alone in my entire life. I learned that I was good company, that I can entertain myself very well.

What happened when Richards was growing up that made her feel comfortable with risktaking? For one thing, she was an only child who was greatly loved by her grandparents and doting aunts.

Richards recalled that at age four or five, she would run away from home. "My mother was pretty restrictive when it came to the amount of time I was allowed to play. I knew that I was not supposed to leave the yard and go to a neighbor's house, but I was perfectly willing to do that although I knew that I would get caught and be switched for it." As early as that, she had determined she would rather face the consequences of her action than stick to the safe, easy way out.

Richards doesn't believe that her mother liked her to take risks. Her mother, however, had been strong enough to take risks when she was young, for after she graduated from high school she moved alone from the small community where she had grown up to the "big city" of Waco.[2] This was a particularly brave thing to do, Richards said, because her mother's family always lived close together, and when children grew up and got married they built their own homes in the same neighborhood.

Richards thinks her parents worried far more about risky activities that threatened her physical security than about her other adventures, such as running over to the neighbor's yard. Playing Wonder Woman must have thrown her parents into a frenzy: "I thought I was Wonder Woman. She had that magic lariat that she could throw out, and it would hold her up. I used to take a rope, throw it out, and jump off the garage." Richards also liked to climb trees and jump off barns. Fortunately for her parents — and herself — she shifted to less physical forms of risktaking when she was in school.

Money was short in her household, so even activities the family did for fun were also done seriously. For example, they didn't go fishing so much for sport as they did to get something to eat. Nevertheless, Richards enjoyed fishing with her father and said that "the greatest honor in the world" was being asked to bait his fishing hook.[3]

Richards, who showed an aptitude for public speaking in early girlhood, told us, "I think a lot of political life does revolve around your ability to express yourself on your feet." When she was no more than six she participated in "Expression," which was taught by a woman in the rural community where she lived at the time. "It was a kind of thing where you memorized little pieces and stood up and said them at a recital," Richards said. Her parents encouraged her and were very proud of her public speaking accomplishments.

Later, Richards became a champion debater and attended Baylor University on a debate scholarship. In debating someone wins and someone loses, but her parents accepted that risk because it didn't involve her physical safety. Indeed, Richards acknowledged feeling special to her mother when she won debate tournaments. She could sense her mother's approval because when she came home from tournaments, her mother cooked fried chicken and macaroni and cheese, Richards' favorite foods. This approval, demonstrated by her mother through her cooking even though she couldn't articulate it, made the risk worthwhile.

Despite all the risktaking activities Richards was involved in when she was growing up, she wishes she had learned then that it's all right to fail. It would have been a gift, she told us, and would have taught her that failures can be learning experiences. Had Ann Richards known that the risks she took were really experimenting with life, she would have understood that by definition experiments cannot fail. They may or may not work, but they cannot fail.

In the eleventh grade, Richards was chosen to attend Girls State, a national program sponsored by the American Legion Auxiliary, and her parents supported her decision to go. Girls Staters get a taste of the political process by campaigning for

and serving in mock political offices. Capitalizing on her talent
for public speaking, Richards went on to be one of the two girls
chosen that year to go to Girls Nation in Washington, D.C.
Being chosen to represent Texas was a particularly special
honor because of the large population of high school girls. Then
she was invited back as a counselor at Girls State for the following two years.

Marrying her high school sweetheart at nineteen and raising
four children, as Richards did, was not risktaking behavior in
the 1950s. It was the predictable life of the traditional woman
of that period, although Richards did finish college after her
marriage. Her husband, David, came from a politically active
family, and she joined him in Democratic political activities.
She soon began to volunteer in political campaigns, which
sharpened her grass-roots organizational skills and introduced
her to the issues and the people involved.

Richards got her first taste of public office when she served
on the local planning and zoning commission. During the same
period she was asked to manage Sarah Weddington's 1971 campaign for the Texas legislature. Richards' political skills must
have been recognized at that time because she didn't even
know Weddington, who had argued *Roe v. Wade* before the U.S.
Supreme Court. Weddington won the campaign, and a year
later Richards became her administrative assistant.

In the spring of 1975 the Democratic party asked David Richards to run for county commissioner. When he declined, the
party approached his wife. Until then she had never wanted to
serve in public office because "you couldn't make anyone
happy. At the end of a campaign I had always felt a tremendous
relief; I'd had the fun part, the figuring and conceiving and
strategizing" and had left the actual serving to someone else.
She became the second member of the Richards family to refuse to run — until her husband talked her into it. She won
that election, becoming the first woman to serve on the Travis

County commissioner's court, and with that began her climb up the political ladder.[4]

Richards speaks openly about her experiences as an alcoholic because she believes that her recovery has provided "probably the best program for living, for looking at life that I could ever have gotten. And because that was such a positive influence, I really can't look on it as a failure or disappointment. It was just a very difficult time," she said.

Richards achieved national prominence with her keynote address to the Democratic National Convention in 1988. Who can forget her, with her white hair and brilliant blue dress, speaking to the Democrats and to the nation. Her power, as well as her warmth and humor, captivated the country as she smiled wickedly and drawled, "After listening to George Bush all these years, I figured you needed to know what a real Texas accent sounds like."

And on January 15, 1991, Governor Ann Richards kept her campaign promise as she marched up Congress Avenue, followed by throngs of her supporters, to symbolically reclaim the capital for the people. It was a stirring, inspiring gesture by a woman who knows what's risky and what isn't.

6

Risktaking and Courage
The Confidence Factors in Leadership

In political life you run the risk of experiencing an assault
on your integrity and your persona. The question is
whether you've got the inner fortitude to withstand that
kind of attack and not be crumbled and destroyed by it.

— Jolene Unsoeld, Congresswoman,
Washington State

The word *risk* comes from the Greek "to sail around a cliff,"
which implies that we don't know what's around the bend.
While most of us don't expose ourselves to public scrutiny
daily, as Jolene Unsoeld does, or live on the edge of the cliff
wondering what dangers lie on the other side, we are all risktakers. Everyday living and functioning involve risk. We take
risks when we get out of bed, step into the shower, board the
bus or drive our cars to work, play sports, or go to the beach for
the weekend.

If we define risktaking as *taking a chance on life and living
it to the fullest,* then we are saying that risk involves searching
for opportunities to bring a greater sense of purpose plus more
joy, zest, and love into our lives. This sense of internal liveli-
ness enables us to accomplish tasks more easily and in the
process to feel more satisfied, more competent, and more confident and have greater self-esteem.

When Mary McCarthy, author of *The Group,* a groundbreak-

ing novel about women's lives, died, her friend Elizabeth Hard-
wick said, "A career of candor and dissent is not an easy one for
a woman." Running the risk of taking a stand, especially an
unpopular or difficult one, is hard for most people. It is especially hard for women, who for the most part have been brought
up to be nurturing and conciliatory and to avoid risks. Yet
having the vision to know what you want — and the courage
and confidence to take a stand — is fundamental to good leadership.

    Gloria Molina, former member of the Los Angeles city coun-
cil and now the only woman as well as the first and only Latino
to be elected to the powerful Los Angeles County board of
supervisors, told us about her experience of courage in leadership:

> Well, first of all, to get up every single day and be in this role and
> have people having these expectations of you. To have the cour-
> age to stand before them and say, "Place your trust in me, give
> me an opportunity to represent you, and I will go out and act on
> your behalf." It's a courageous thing to ask for. It's a courageous
> thing to go out there and now start doing it and be held account-
> able to it.
>
>   In addition, to stand up to those same people takes courage.
> They're not always right even though they voted you in. You
> have to stand up to them and say, "You're wrong" about this
> issue. And they get very angry. Their expectation is, "I want you
> to do what I wanted you to do, not what you want to do." So
> there are many courageous acts that you take on every single
> day. Plus the fact of just being in these roles. Being prepared on
> an issue. Having to have a camera shoved in your face and being
> asked your opinion and your comment on it, and hoping that
> you're going to sound articulate and have something to say
> about it. Being put on the spot when you're moving forward on a
> proposal and being sure that you have all the information so
> you're going to be prepared and look confident. All of those
> things are part of the courage that it takes to be in this role. So
> there are those courageous acts every day, I guess.

What a paradox this is for the woman leader. Using your Creative Aggression and WomanPower to be an effective leader means you must deviate from the passivity associated with traditional conceptions of femininity. It means that you run the risk of being seen as unfeminine, undesirable, and unlovable. Women leaders in all arenas struggle with this difficult dilemma. In *Campaigning in a Different Voice,* political analyst Celinda Lake reports that women candidates "must work harder on very limited resources to establish their positive credibility. They risk losing whichever way they move. Voters are uncomfortable with ambitious, tough, aggressive women; yet challengers cannot win if they are anything else."[1]

Elected women confirm this perception all the time. Evelyn Murphy, lieutenant governor of Massachusetts, observed:

> Are we all equal right now? The answer is no because there is still a strong bias that women can't handle major positions of power and leadership. It's true with all the women in major offices. I think if you haven't established that you can be tough, you can't get a major office, but beyond that I don't think people are yet expecting every woman to be Margaret Thatcher–like.

In reviewing Dianne Feinstein's 1990 gubernatorial campaign, her staff found that the hardest task they faced during the campaign was the need to establish Feinstein's credibility as a leader over and over and over again, despite her credentials as mayor of San Francisco and her charisma. Yet the public had no trouble seeing her mild-mannered Republican opponent, Pete Wilson, as a leader, for as a white male he fit the public's most comfortable leader image.

It is no different in corporate life than in elective office. In a study of executive women, researchers found that successful women executives were judged by a narrow band of acceptable behavior:

> They had to be seen as better than women as a group. But they couldn't go too far and forfeit all traces of femininity because

that would make them too alien to their superiors and colleagues. In essence their mission was to do what was expected
of them while doing enough of what was expected of them as
women to gain acceptance.

They were told, "Take risks, it's the only way to the top, but be
consistently outstanding."[2] However, to achieve the required
breadth of experience necessary to get to the top, these women
had to "take more and greater risks than men, or risk being
accused of being weak and too 'by the book.'"

As you can see, it is hard for women to risk freely and yet
walk a narrow line of acceptability. Ultimately, we must find a
way to change the situation. We look to those women who
have successfully navigated this tricky course as role models of
risktaking and leadership who can lead the way for the rest of
us. We cannot think of a group of women more willing to stand
up and be counted, to put themselves in the middle of this
conflicted psychological crossfire on a daily basis, than the
women leaders in high elective office whom we interviewed for
this book.

Gail Schoettler, treasurer of Colorado, described how she
experienced the risktaking balancing act:

> Well, absolutely you have to take risks. First of all, when you
> run for office you're putting yourself on the line. There's prob-
> ably no greater risk than being public about any potential failure
> or success. So there's the risk of failure in a very public way. The
> loss of privacy is a risk, although because you just expect it
> maybe it's not truly a risk. There is the risk that your children
> will be exposed to uncomfortable or unpleasant things. You're
> always criticized. The risk then is that the criticism will be
> unjust and unfair, which it often is. There's not a lot you can do
> about it. It's just part of the day.

For some of these women, the lucky ones, risktaking is an
intuitive skill they learned in early life. Later in this chapter
you will hear some of their stories; however, don't despair if

these stories don't describe you. Risktaking is also a skill that can be learned later, and we will offer some exercises and experiments to help you in Chapter 9. Not only is it learnable, but now there are identifiable women leaders who offer themselves as role models. The bonus we get at any age from adding stronger risktaking skills to our psychological and behavioral repertoire is feeling more motivated and effective.

When asked if she took risks in political office, California Congresswoman Nancy Pelosi shot back:

> Being an opinion leader and a policymaker is a risky business. Take risks? Of course! It's a risk business that we're in. You take a risk in everything you do, but you take a big risk when you run for office, especially if you're a woman. There will be attempts to trivialize everything that you do. That's a bad thing, but it happens. And I tell women who want to run, "You risk them trivializing you."

Lest we think that Nancy Pelosi stands alone in this feeling, Claudine Schneider, Republican congresswoman and senatorial candidate from Rhode Island, told of her struggles to be taken seriously. Schneider first gained visibility and political experience as an environmental activist. Her best-known accomplishment is seeing a vacuum and then filling it. When Schneider realized there were no law firms in Rhode Island devoted to environmental matters, she formed the Conservation Law Foundation, which specialized in representing the public interest. Instead of allowing herself to be overwhelmed by the organizational aspects of setting up a law firm, she faced the risk straight on: "Well, let's just do it." Later, as they encountered funding and related problems, she told her associates, "Don't worry. This will come. We will find the answer." And they did. That faith and trust, she believes, enables her to accomplish many of her objectives.

In 1978 the Republican party in Rhode Island was begging for candidates to run for office. As Congresswoman Schneider put it, they were imploring, "Hi, anybody out there want to run for office? We're desperate. Please apply." When her friends said, "This state is so corrupt. No one person can make a difference," Schneider decided to prove them wrong. She first asked her husband to run for governor, but he declined, saying his time would be better spent attacking environmental problems from the scientific perspective. "But you would be wonderful. I think you could get elected, and *you* should do it," he told his surprised wife.

"Well," she thought, "I'll do it." Although people kept telling her she didn't have a chance in the world, she decided to run for Congress for two reasons: to bring issues, especially environmental, to the public's attention and to attack the political apathy she had encountered with voters of her generation. But what a risk! Voter registration was fifteen to one Democratic, and no woman had ever run for major political office in Rhode Island. In addition, she was a thirty-one-year-old Republican who hadn't held any kind of office since college.

Schneider surprised a lot of people with her first campaign. Although she raised only $40,000, she got 48 percent of the vote — not enough to win, but an impressive showing for a newcomer. Afterward, Schneider decided that she had done well enough that she should run again. So in 1980, backed by a strong grass-roots campaign and a $365,000 war chest and armed with bumper stickers that said, "This time Claudine," Schneider won 56 percent of the vote. From then on, until her bid for the U.S. Senate in 1990, she was reelected to four more congressional terms with increasing margins (reaching 72 percent in her 1988 campaign).

Certainly, running for public office put Claudine Schneider and her self-esteem at risk. But what has all this to do with feeling trivial or trivialized? One would think a woman as confident as Schneider wouldn't give a second thought to the idea of feeling trivial. She wouldn't worry about feeling trivialized by anyone.

But let's revisit Schneider's early history, which we first talked about in Chapter 5. Remember the mixed messages she got from her parents? On the one hand they told her she could be anything she wanted to be; but on the other hand they encouraged her brother to get a college education so he could *be* a professional while they wanted her to go to college so she could *marry* a professional.

As a young girl she had dreamed of becoming a dancer or an artist. But when she told her parents, they said, "If you're going to be a dancer or an artist you'd have to move to New York to be the best. You just can't do that." Their desire to keep their daughter close to them is understandable, but what Schneider heard was a pushmi-pullyu mixed message. What effect did the mixed message have on Schneider's Competent Self, Creative Aggression, WomanPower, risktaking capabilities, and ultimate leadership capacity?

A dream that Schneider shared with us provides some of the answers to the question as well as some of the secrets of her power:

I dreamed I went to a bullfight with some friends. The bullfighter fought the bull for a while. Then, for some reason, he walked right out of the ring. The crowd yelled, "We need another bullfighter!" And they all looked at me. "You come down and fight the bull," they demanded.

"Now is that significant, or what?" Schneider asked us. "When that hit me, it was mind-boggling." The dream obviously was about selection by popular acclaim.

Everyone in the coliseum screamed, "You come and do it." And I thought, "No. Wait a minute. I don't know how to do this." But then I reconsidered: "I really love these bullfighter clothes. They ought to fit me. They're the fashion, you know. It's really me. Well, this is a challenge. Sure, I'll try it."

So I went down to the center of the ring and threw out the cape as though I knew exactly what I was doing. The bull came storming toward me. I could feel a little ripple of fear and excitement go through the crowd. Then all of a sudden the bull turned into a cartoon bull. He slammed on the brakes. He stood up on his two hind feet, put his hands on his hips, and started laughing hysterically. *"You're* going to fight *me!"* he sneered. I was so shocked. I thought, "Yes, I'm going to!" Then I woke up, laughing but determined.

Obviously, Claudine Schneider felt a calling to fight the bull in every sense of the word. She was ready to risk relinquishing control of old tried-and-true ways by giving up her safe role in the audience. Instead, she decided to "try on" the role of leader to see how it fit. She saw herself in heroic terms cutting through the bull — the graft — and restoring truth, integrity, and prosperity to the people of Rhode Island. Although she felt thrilled to be called to battle by the people, Schneider, who is, after all, the author of her dream, let us know that she also felt anxious or perhaps embarrassed by such a naked display of her desire for WomanPower.

Imagine thinking that she was the chosen one, that she was tough enough to kill the bull, that she would save the day for Rhode Island. Then, when she felt exposed, she quickly covered her excitement by turning the bull into a cartoon figure, diminishing its powers and making her feel safe and back in control. Unfortunately, in trivializing him, she also trivialized her own sense of WomanPower, as the bull in her dream scenario contemptuously snorted, *"You're* going to fight *me!"*

By the time Schneider had this dream, she had already built a strong enough Competent Self. Her confidence in her Creative Aggression, fueled by comforting memories of feeling admired and valued by parents and family, as represented by the admiring crowd, came through for her when she taunted the bull, saying, "Yes, I'm going to," and waking up laughing and determined.

While ambivalence and mixed feelings are part of our healthy selves, too many of them reinforce more mixed feelings about claiming our own sense of power and confidence than is helpful. These messages create pockets of anxiety that we cope with by various means, such as trivializing ourselves. They erode our feeling that we are competent and are entitled to dream of greatness. They make courage and risktaking that much more difficult to dream about, let alone put into action. And without dreams it is particularly hard for women to even become leaders.

Risktaking Begins Early

After analyzing a dream with such complicated psychological twists and turns, we cannot help but wonder when and where do trust, courage, and risktaking begin? And why do they flourish or flounder? Learning the answers will help us understand the roadblocks that inhibit our own risktaking. Then we can dismantle them by nurturing risktaking skills that we failed to develop earlier in life.

A study conducted with infants by Dr. Robert Emde at the University of Colorado Medical School demonstrates that the early seeds of risktaking and trust are sown by ten months. Taking their cue from the Greek term for *risk*, these researchers performed what they called "visual cliff experiments."[3] In such an experiment an infant is placed on one end of a large table, and Mommy stands at the other end. As the infant excitedly crawls across the table toward Mommy, she comes to the point where it looks as though the table has dropped away. The infant feels as though she has reached the edge of a cliff. At this point she looks toward her mother at the far end of the table as if to ask, "Should I keep going over the edge to reach you or should I back up to safety?"

If the mother mirrors her child's excitement and smiles as if to say, "Trust me. I welcome your desire to reconnect with me. Come to me, it's safe," and if the mother/infant bond has reached a point where the infant has learned to trust her mother, then she feels safe. She feels she has gathered enough "information" to decide whether or not to take a calculated risk. If she decides to do it, she relinquishes her controls, takes a leap of faith, and continues to crawl across the "cliff" to mother and safety, delighting in her mastery. However, if Mommy's face is expressionless, thereby not mirroring her child's excitement and sense of adventure, the infant feels endangered. She then freezes on the table because Mommy has signaled her not to take the risk of crossing the danger zone.

Obviously, the mother's capacity to risk and to enjoy feeling courageous influences any infant's experience of learning to trust, to risk and to happily venture over the cliff to a wider and unknown world. Fathers, siblings, and other authority figures also influence early training in risktaking. Fathers can serve as adventurous role models and mentors. However, since our beginning experiences in life are intimately entwined with trusting and loving our mother, the primary caregiver, it is in this relationship that we come to know the secrets of the feminine legacy. Maternal experiences thus play a much stronger role in coloring our capacity for trust, courage, and risktaking.

At the same time the infant is learning to trust her mother and to take risks, she is also learning to be wary with others. This is the age of stranger anxiety, when the infant typically recoils from strangers, whom she doesn't trust. By refusing to risk her safety with these unknown people, she is demonstrating an early ability to differentiate between safe and dangerous. Sometimes when we don't learn enough about well-calculated risktaking from mothers who are too anxious or not attuned to the interests of an adventurous child, we look to fathers and other maternal figures for encouragement to take risks. For those people who never found anyone to support the development of their risktaking, we will describe in Chapter 9 messages to give to yourself so that you can fill in what you missed.

From age four or five, Ann Richards of Texas remembers taking risks, as we saw in her story about venturing beyond her garden gate despite the price she knew she would pay for doing it. For adventure and excitement, Richards looked to her father, "who would take me fishing and other places and introduce me so I felt special." She also felt special with doting aunts and grandmothers who "thought I was clever and amusing and smart. I knew I was special because they got so excited when I came over. They loved me unconditionally." Richards used her "other" mothers to mirror her need to escape the narrow restrictions at home. With their help she could more easily follow her excitement and curiosity, explore the world, and go further than her parents had in life.

In addition to surrogate mothers, Ann Richards found a heroine in a fantasy, Wonder Woman, and her magic lariat. Richards' conviction that she was invincible and protected by a magic rope in early life has served her well as a secret of her power and leadership as well as the seeds of the risktaking necessary for courage and success in her political life. But perhaps her early need to risk and venture out, frustrated by maternal disapproval, has left her feeling anxious inside and "not sure I have felt lovable most of my life."

Obviously, this conflict — the quintessential woman leader's dilemma — pitting Richards' vitality, Creative Aggression, and willingness to grow and change against the desire to be a good girl and win her mother's love has left her more vulnerable to rejection and disapproval than she would prefer. She has had to learn that it is all right not to be loved by everyone. "I had to learn to separate personal slight and the idea that we could disagree on an issue and not be disagreeable friends," she said. Yet her vulnerability certainly has not kept her from risktaking and becoming a leader. (Richards's experiences are examined in more detail in the profile that precedes this chapter.)

Self-Trust, Courage, and Smart Risks

Mary Landrieu, treasurer of Louisiana, talked about courage and about trust:

> I have a good bit of courage, but I think that comes from having a good self-image and self-confidence, which I thank my parents for. I learned that I can trust myself, and that gives me the courage to do things I've never done before. If I did *this* and did it pretty well, I just assume that I can do *this* also. It's just a matter of taking one step at a time. Of course, you get shaky when you fail or when you've made a wrong decision because it diminishes your self-confidence. But most of the time I feel courageous and pretty strong.

When we hear a woman such as Mary Landrieu, who grew up in a political family and now holds high public office, talk so easily of courage, we wonder whether she was born with a flawless Competent Self. While we may admire her, we're also perhaps a bit envious and annoyed. Look at the role models she had, look at the advantages. Is that all it takes? Apparently not! Look at Nita Lowey, New York congresswoman, who also has great self-confidence, and she isn't part of a political dynasty. Lowey told us that risktaking came easily for her because as a child, "maybe I did take risks but because my parents gave me such confidence in myself it never seemed like a risk." With that kind of support, confident risktaking becomes intuitive, but it relies on planning and thoughtfulness, which these women do in calculating a potential risk and which all of us without early family support can learn to do.

When we asked New Jersey Congresswoman Marge Roukema about times in her early life when she took risks, she told us:

> I had been raised as a Roman Catholic although my parents were not practicing Roman Catholics. When I was sixteen and in high school I had a group of friends who were very religious. Today they would be called evangelical Christians. I really liked them, and something about their interest in religion attracted me. So I did something rather extraordinary: I left the Catholic church and converted to Protestantism. That was an act of defiance, in a sense, to my family because the rest of the family, aside from my mother and father, on both sides were devout Catholic. My parents weren't too happy about my conversion, but they didn't stand in my way. At times my mother thought I was "getting a little too religious" but she saw that it wasn't doing me any harm because I was a good student, and I'm still a good daughter. They gave me a lot of leeway and room.

The security of knowing that she was still acceptable to her parents and her trust in that self-knowledge gave Roukema the courage to risk moving away from their religion to one that she preferred. It's clear from their empathic reaction to her conversion that Roukema's family had fostered such independent opinions and self-trust from the beginning.

Ruth Messinger, president of the borough of Manhattan, told us about a risk she took during adolescence. It is particularly significant that she learned to see risks as challenges — despite the possibilities of being humiliated if she lost — at a time when feeling foolish in front of one's peers seems like the equivalent of death:

> When I was in high school I decided to go out for the basketball team. That was a big challenge. They wanted me to play because I was tall, but I had a reputation for being somewhat clumsy. We

had a gym teacher who acted like a marine drill sergeant, and for me it was a wonderful experience. You wanted to be on the team? You didn't have any choice. It was an honor system. There were about a hundred things that you had to be able to do, and the only way to do them was to go to the gym every day after lunch. You had to shoot ten baskets from a certain spot and record your score, and eventually you had to be able to do seven out of ten of all those different things. It was wonderful.

El Paso Mayor Suzie Azar also told us how early training can lead to smart risktaking in adult life:

I think I am wise enough to choose things that are doable. When I ran for city council there was no incumbent. When I ran for mayor there was no incumbent. I didn't take an odds-against-me risk. I think I took a smart risk. I announced early with all my campaigns, and nobody ever caught me. I learned a lot from defeat — first of all that I didn't like it, and second of all that you'd better get organized and let everybody know that this is what you want and this is what they want.

Azar takes the magic out of risktaking for us. She's clear on the step-by-step thinking process she goes through in analyzing the consequences of each risk, making a conscious decision to do it or not based on the possible outcomes of taking a calculated rather than an impulsive and hazardous risk. The fact that she's a licensed pilot and has done wing-walking exhibitions at air shows illustrates how confident she is about her ability to assess risks.

Nancy Johnson, congresswoman from Connecticut, got mixed parental messages that made her feel conflicted and anxious when taking the risks necessary to pursue her dream. Johnson remembers the time, when she was in the third grade, that her father asked all the kids to help reshingle the barn roof. She remembers how excited she was at being asked to work on this grown-up project, how she stood on the barn roof, queen of the mountain, proudly surveying the land below. Her mother looked terrified and yelled to her father, "What are you doing?

Your children will get killed!" "No, no, Gertrude," he said. "I've got a scaffolding. They're all right, look."

This experience and others like it peppered Johnson's childhood, blending over the years into a condensed memory of an exciting, adventuresome father who simply built scaffolding to support what he wanted to do. "I didn't grow up in a world with a lot of fears. I don't remember having any great sense of, 'Gee, I'd better not do that. I might get hurt.'" Johnson clearly incorporated into her Competent Self the "psychic scaffolding" her father had helped her to build. With a reliable internal structure in place, she knew she could trust herself to judge which risks were doable and which were not.

But another message, too, came from her father, and that message left her vulnerable:

> My father had such high standards he expected us to meet. The essence was always, Are you going to do well or not? So the fear of failure was very real although the fear of outside dangers wasn't. One of my dad's messages was "You can do anything you want to do," and the other was "You can't do anything well enough." Here my mother, who had done so much, was so competent, had a master's degree, had been a teacher, now was relegated to the life of an "underutilized resource."

Obviously, Congresswoman Johnson has continued to risk and to accomplish. But those early painful mixed messages have left her struggling courageously with her own sense of inadequacy as she moves forward.

What Landrieu, Lowey, Roukema, Messinger, Azar, and Johnson have said about risktaking being a learnable skill and outlet for Creative Aggression is summed up by Elaine Baxter, Iowa secretary of state. Baxter said of the calculated risks that look so easy from a distance:

> You can't win if you don't run. You have to reach a point where you're willing to risk defeat, and you're not going to risk defeat if you're going to stay right where you are. Then the risk is too big for you. But remember, unless you take a risk you can't win.

My husband sometimes says, "You're lucky, lucky." Maybe I am, *but I work very hard to be lucky.*

Mistakes and Setbacks — Learning Experiences

Risktaking means that we aren't always successful. Sometimes we make mistakes and are set back. How we handle the setbacks influences our willingness to risk again. Barbara Boxer, congresswoman from California and 1992 candidate for the U.S. Senate, told us how she has approached risktaking:

> I lost an election in 1972. It was a big ache because it was a very difficult year-long campaign. It was a year of my life. And never having held public office before, I wasn't really prepared for either the campaign or the loss. But it was a tremendously important experience that turned out to be a growth experience. It made me stronger and proved to me that I didn't have to be "someone" to be worthwhile.
>
> After I lost I went on to do some really interesting things. I became a newspaper reporter. I worked for a congressman. So it just showed that there's life after losing. That's a very important lesson to learn early because in this business there will be times to move up or out and times when you have to fold your cards. And if you don't know that you can survive that, it's very painful.
>
> I've seen people go through a lot of pain because they should have folded their cards but were afraid to because they didn't know if they could make it out of public life. When I lost, I faced the pain and the reality and found my strengths and weaknesses. It has really given me courage in my personal life to take risks. I decided to run for the Senate and give up the House, and whatever happens, I know I can handle it. It's not to be without pain, but you're going to survive, you know.

Jolene Unsoeld, congresswoman from Washington State, echoed and underlined Barbara Boxer's words:

> I say somewhat jokingly that it's true that you go home, you crawl back to your cave and lick your wounds for a few hours, then you start thinking about how you come back at it in a different way next time to make it work. So I almost cannot think of failures in isolation because they were just sort of parts of the route of a longer process.

Mistakes and setbacks, as we can see, are not only inevitable but necessary. Without the freedom to make mistakes and to learn from them, we cannot creatively savor life's possibilities and move forward. The women whom we studied told us consistently that the ability to trust in themselves, which grew out of early family support, gave them the self-confidence to cope with mistakes and setbacks in adult life. Betty Castor, Florida commissioner of education, said:

> There was always a kind of safety net for whatever I wanted to do. I never felt I'd be out on the streets. That's certainly been true in my political life. I never felt like the risk was irreversible or there wouldn't be something else I could do.

Castor now carries this "safety net" inside of her Competent Self. It is part of the sense of supportive internal applause that she can draw on when she has the impulse to try something new.

Castor feels sorry for the many women she knows who are afraid to take risks. She told us of one friend whose talents and background make her a perfect candidate for the school board but who won't run:

> To my way of thinking, it wouldn't be a risk at all. She's popular. Her husband has the money to support her. What could happen? She might lose. But she just won't do it. I find that a lot of people, especially women, have the attributes to become good

public officials, but they don't think that's something they could do.

Nancy Pelosi, congresswoman from California, told us why she has the courage to follow her impulses and take risks despite the possible consequences:

> One of the biggest risks is what the press will make of what you do. This is especially hard on someone who dislikes the public role. So the big risk is your reputation. You just have to say to yourself, "This may undo me, but it's what I believe in. And if I lose everything because of it, I did decide to run that risk." But you know what you're doing. You can't say, "Oh, my gosh, if I only had known."

Following Your Impulses

Poet and philosopher Ralph Waldo Emerson, the proponent of self-reliance, urged us to follow our "blessed impulse," that instinctual sense of what works best for us. That's another way of telling us to trust our inner DreamVoices, which lead us in productive and creative directions. These impulses, or visions, direct our risktaking. Both are built on self-trust and a comfortable sense of Creative Aggression, which empower and guide the calculated risktaking that helps us reach our goals. This is what Barbara Boxer meant when she said there are times when you have to move up or fold your cards. She added, "Take the risk and grow, or stagnate. Learn from your experiences. Take a chance on making a mistake, and come to know that there is life after losing."

As we can see, our women leaders endorse risktaking, with all its potential problems and the lessons that can be learned from it. They also believe in taking calculated rather than hazardous risks. They know that risktaking is a knowable skill with the following characteristics:

1. *Risktaking is a process aimed at change.* It is based on a decision to encounter and melt our resistance to change and to relinquish our controls over old ways and the myth that the future can be guaranteed. The decision to take risks is made in the face of potential consequences. It always involves giving up old and valued things, people, situations, feelings, or behaviors in favor of creating new solutions and situations. In other words, it means doing battle with our resistance to change. It means relinquishing our controls over what is comfortable and safe, loosening up, rearranging, and giving up or adding to old beliefs. You melt your resistance to change when you believe that you know what you're doing, that you're going to be all right, that if you fall on your face you can pick yourself up and start over — in essence, that the voluntary letting go can be reversed and our controls restored, at will, at any time.

We aren't advocating helpless submission. What we are advocating is development of the inner strength to make an informed choice between a risk and its consequences. Betty Castor, Florida commissioner of education, told us of one tough choice she made when she was in college:

> I headed up a student project to send books to Uganda. And as a consequence of that, I was selected to go to their independence celebration. I became an African expert. My parents thought I was a little strange. They just did not think that was a good idea. But I had made up my mind, so they said, "Okay, if that's what you want to do, guess you gotta do it." They had decided to trust me.

The risktaking process is a time of transition that can be likened to a state of mourning for that which we are giving up, a sense of loss in giving up the old ways, even when what we are giving up is a terrible job or a destructive relationship.

Anxiety often accompanies our sense of loss during transitions since we have not substituted comforting new objectives, behaviors, or relationships for the old. Sometimes we feel so anxious that we are tempted to give up and go back to the old ways. Our resistance to change always fights for its very life.

Risktaking is not only initiating change but also responding to and sticking with it. Taking a new job that is beyond your expertise suddenly feels possible when you think about taking a course or acquiring a mentor to fill in your knowledge gaps. This is a creative way to turn a scary situation into a risktaking success. Unique personal choices dictate both risks and reactions.

2. *A riskgoal is a vision we pursue through specific action.* Risktaking involves making a commitment to and taking a stand on an idea, and then following through with direct action. The ability to take the action depends on our faith in ourselves that, win or lose, we will land on our feet. It is truly a leap of faith. As we have said, the women we studied do this all the time when they stand up for the issues and causes they believe in.

Congresswoman Pat Schroeder did it when she decided to run for president. She did it again when she proposed the Family and Medical Leave Act, knowing that the process of getting the bill passed would be long, difficult, and frequently unpleasant. Congresswoman Nancy Pelosi did it when she proposed the Chinese Student Bill, which would have allowed Chinese students to remain in the United States following the Tienanmen Square massacre, despite opposition in the Senate and a potential presidential veto. Rosa Parks did it when she refused to give up her seat in the front of the bus in Alabama in 1955 and started the civil rights movement.

Anita Roddick, CEO of the Body Shop, did it in the corporate world when she founded an international chain of shops selling organic and natural skin products and cosmetics. Each Body Shop store reflects Roddick's altruistic and environmentally concerned philosophy by selling only biodegradable, environmentally sound products and using the store two months a year primarily for a "storefront" campaign dedicated to that cause. She treats her employees with the same respect she shows for the environment, giving them a half day off per week to work for a cause of their choosing. She also contributes millions of dollars a year in time, money, and services to charities. Roddick's business has grown phenomenally despite — or perhaps because of — the fact that she has successfully combined a nurturant philosophy, which flew in the face of supposedly good business strategies, with her own innovative, hard-nosed business sense.

Such stands forgo the status quo in favor of a leap of faith in the direction of the change, whether it be a lifestyle or financial change, building an organization, or creating an accepting environment for new ideas such as civil rights, corporate child care, or medical leave.

3. *Risktaking is a process of creating change by means of specific action aimed at a desired riskgoal with measurable effects.* Deciding to attend graduate school, get married, start a new business, become more confrontational, author a bill and shepherd it through the legislative process, ask for a raise, or become a better public speaker are examples of decisions we make because we want to attain specific riskgoals. During the process of risktaking, we actively take a leap of faith and follow it with experiences, encounters, and interactions with people, places, and situations in order to give meaning to and stimulate movement toward a particular riskgoal. We can monitor our feelings and actions during the process and assess the outcome when we reach the riskgoal. For example, you are either accepted into graduate school or not. If you become more confrontational, your relationships will perceptibly change. A piece of legislation either comes out of committee or doesn't. Your audience will let you know whether or not your efforts to improve your public speaking have paid off.

4. *Creative confusion fills the transitional space between old and new ways.* When we willfully change any part of ourselves, we are re-creating ourselves and our identities. As we decide to make a career change from manager to entrepreneur or from congresswoman to senator as Barbara Boxer, Pat Saiki, and Claudine Schneider did; to get a divorce; to give up the fast track to be a full-time mother; or to become more organized in our lives, a period of confusion and anxiety follows the decision. We enter a transitional space that often feels disorienting and unreal.

As we move from a vision to a leap of faith to direct action and experience the discomfort of creative confusion, we often find a core of strength in ourselves we never knew existed. During creative confusion we sort out options, calculate consequences, develop new skills, and make new choices. The process of solidifying new choices through new actions and behaviors is a measure of our motivation to overcome resistance to change and reach our riskgoal. It is a time that enables us to experience and nurture our risktaking, adventurous self and the behaviors that support the change. Like Ann Richards, we find the Wonder Woman within us, whose magic lariat supports us while we are trying out new choices and behaviors. Thus we transcend the transitional space by building bridges to new and exciting times.

5. *Risktaking and change make you feel different, but you will still be the same familiar you.* As the French say, *Plus ça change, plus c'est la même chose*: The more things change, the more they stay the same. The basis of a vital and dynamic self-identity is constant change. During the creative confusion of change our core self remains sufficiently recognizable that we can live in a way that pleases us. We are not disintegrating, even if it feels as if we are. We are re-creating ourselves, changing to meet new challenges while holding on to the old ways that still feel right to us.

Political Women
as Transformational Leaders

Not all risktakers are leaders. Not everybody wants to be a leader. However, all leaders are risktakers because they create new ideas and visions and have to convince others to follow them.

Barbara Boxer, California congresswoman and senatorial candidate, believes that being involved and putting forth your visions and ideas helps you build effective and humane leadership and power:

> More and more people look to me for ideas. I guess the ability to change people's lives and to have other people look to you for advice and assistance and leadership — I guess that's power.

As James O'Toole, executive director of the University of Southern California's Leadership Institute, says of leaders such as Barbara Boxer, "The true leader is a listener who listens to the ideas, needs, aspirations and wishes of the followers and then — within the context of his or her own well developed system of beliefs — responds to these in an appropriate fashion. That is why the leader must know his [or her] own mind. That is why leadership requires ideas."[4]

Being believers and experts in the art of risktaking makes the women we studied the kind of charismatic and courageous leaders that can be looked on as models of what has been called the "transformational leader."[5] They are leaders who motivate us to do more than we ever expected to do for the greater good. They exemplify WomanPower, which we have defined as power used to advance an agenda and make a difference in society. The women we studied are motivated by their desire to feel a strong sense of competence and confidence built on their feelings of being effective — that is, having an effect on others and having some control over changing their environment through persuasive influence, a narrow line to walk, indeed.

When asked about her ideas on leadership, Barbara Mikulski, Maryland senator, said:

> Leadership is creating a state of mind in others. The difference between being a leader and manager, all due respect to managers, is that leaders have to create states of mind. But a leader, first of all, has to have a clear state of mind, which is usually her own vision, which energizes her, motivates others, and then creates that state of mind in others. President Kennedy's legislative accomplishments were skimpy, but he created a state of mind in this country that endures long after his death.

Geraldine Ferraro, New York congresswoman, senatorial candidate, and the only female candidate for vice president so far, defined Mikulski as a transformational leader by Mikulski's own definition of leadership: "*Barbara Mikulski* didn't win because Maryland insisted on a woman candidate. She won because she built a reputation of achievement. She inspires people."[6]

Leading by Seduction

Finally! One of the banes of women's existence — being labeled seductive — is paying off in the workplace. Good leaders are charismatic and seductive. They seduce their followers in the best sense of the word. They inspire people to grab and follow their vision. They raise people's consciousness about issues of consequence. They inspire us to demand more of ourselves and others. They do this by showing us a better way and persuading us that it is indeed better.

Evelyn Murphy, lieutenant governor of Massachusetts, said:

> I have always thought I was persuasive with my colleagues at all
> ages. If I look back on my childhood I have a sense of running
> things, of always persuading the kids what we were going to
> play. I can't remember a time in which I wasn't running the
> show, from the earliest games through now. I always had the
> sense of leading and of getting colleagues to come along, do
> things that I wanted to do, play games I wanted to play — that's
> always been part of me as long as I can remember.

At the time we interviewed her, Evelyn Murphy was organizing the women of Massachusetts to help elect her governor,
educating them to a relatively new idea — that women can
help other women by raising money, a lot of it, and write bigger
checks than they ever thought they'd write to make it all
happen.

When we asked Murphy what achievement in her political
career she is most proud of, she told us it was blocking offshore
oil drilling in Massachusetts. This took place in the mid-1970s,
when she was secretary of environmental affairs, long before it
was popular to oppose offshore drilling. Murphy, the only major
public official to testify against the drilling, is proud that she
was the first high-ranking public official to take on and defeat a
major oil company. She showed people a better way.

Congresswoman Nancy Johnson told us:

> I was always a class leader. I always have been a leader; it's one
> of those things that's very easy for me. So in a sense I had ideas
> and always implemented them, and then I was automatically a
> leader.

Marge Roukema, congresswoman from New Jersey, has
grown much since those early days when she told her husband
she wanted to be president and then apologetically took her
words back. She has learned to take a tough stand and not back
down. She believes that leadership and power provide the vi-

sion to get things done, even when she has to take unpopular positions:

> There are times when you have to be an educator. When people don't understand, you have to educate them to the issue. That's leadership. Governance is leadership and moving the issues forward even when they're unpopular.

Roukema is a national leader on child support and pro-choice issues, both of which often are unpopular policies with many of her constituents.

Olympia Snowe, congresswoman and First Lady of Maine, talks about leadership as the willingness to move to the forefront on an important issue:

> In a 1982 interview right after the election, I was asked what my priority was for the next Congress. At that point I really was committed to working on issues that were important to women. So in January of '83 I organized Republican women. We had a press conference, went to the White House, and met with President Reagan on several occasions to develop an agenda. I just decided that it was important and that my role as a woman in Congress is to do something to help other women.

Snowe became Republican cochair of the Congressional Caucus on Women's Issues, which carries an agenda each year focused on a different issue that will make women's lives better. For example, in 1990 and 1991, Snowe was a major author of the Women's Health Equity Act, an omnibus bill that mandated, among other things, more federally funded research on women's health issues and Medicare funding for mammography. She and the other members of the Congressional Caucus on Women's Issues continue to champion health care in Congress.

Women as Natural Leaders
for Today's Society

We are living in a difficult time. The decline of America's economic and political power requires a new kind of leadership befitting an age of interdependent global enterprise, instant communication, and ecological limits. *Fortune* magazine describes some of the new management theories and practices that are emerging to meet the demands of today's world:

- Flexible networks will replace hierarchical organizations.
- Workers will be empowered to make decisions on their own.
- Group learning will replace orders from the top.
- Global thinking will replace national perspectives.
- Creativity and intuition will join quantitative analysis for informed decisionmaking.
- Love and caring will be legitimate workplace motivators.
- Mental and spiritual enhancement of participants will replace or augment the profit motive.[7]

These elements add up to more than progressive change. They add up to a major shift in the management and leadership policies of our nation. We are moving from a command and control style of leadership to a self-managed team approach emphasizing humanity, intimacy, interdependence, connectedness, collaboration, cooperation, caring, diversity, and a focus on human consciousness where money and profit are only a way to keep score. This leadership style will allow us to build in the integrity and courage necessary to maintain our ideals in the face of failures and setbacks and to risk proposing new and creative ideas regardless of their popularity.

As you know, the women we interviewed experienced leadership and power in WomanPower terms — helping to improve others' lives while making the women themselves natural transformational leaders for whom the new paradigm of leadership is also a natural. Women come to interdependent networking intuitively. It is a natural outgrowth of the intimacy and secret world of the mother-daughter bond, our nurturant selves, and our female experience. As the world embraces connectedness as a legitimate leadership force, women's natural leadership styles will become mainstream. Women will feel freer to risk since we will no longer be locked into a prescribed narrow band of acceptable behavior that is difficult to achieve and impossible to maintain.

Suzie Azar talked about the funny side of women's leadership as she described an experience she had while adjusting to being a powerful woman leader in a male bastion following her election as mayor of El Paso:

> As mayor, I find that I am surrounded by men continually although I have a number of good women department heads, and I'm going to get two more this year. You can see my sign up there: "A job worth fighting for is a woman firefighter." We don't have one in the El Paso fire department, but we will, I can assure you.
>
> My executive administrator, a woman, and I do a lot of things together. We women do a lot of leadership activity in city government, and I'm bringing other women along with me. So we go into the ladies' room together, and we talk about what happened in a meeting and we laugh because we're in the ladies' room. It's like a private women's spot — men could do that before in the men's room and now we women need our own spot.

Suzie Azar's experience reminds us of Barbara Mikulski's statement that the ultimate in power is to walk into the Senate gym and stop the locker room conversation cold. As Mikulski is only the second woman senator to be elected since 1987, women are virtually nonexistent in the Senate gym and are, we feel sure, not a comfortable presence there. But it's a beginning.

The results of Judy B. Rosener's 1990 research study of corporate women called "Ways Women Lead" reflect our findings on elected political women. The women Rosener interviewed

> described themselves in ways that characterize Transformational Leadership — getting subordinates to transform their own self-interest into the interest of the group through concern for a broader goal. Moreover, they ascribe their power to personal characteristics like charisma, interpersonal skills, hard work or personal contacts rather than organizational stature.[8]

As you can see, the issue is one of perception. Jolene Unsoeld, congresswoman from Washington State, lamented:

> The public does not know what the "proper" image of a woman with power is. Several years ago someone did an article on people, particularly women, in power. And inevitably the description of the women was "bitchy" — they had tantrums, they would have outbursts, displays of losing control. The men were described as "tough" and not tolerating dissent and this kind of thing. *So the activities being described were identical, but the perceptions were so different.* It is just assumed by men and many women that men are effective simply because they're men, but women, because they're female, are not effective. Women have to prove themselves all the time.

In 1990, the *Los Angeles Times* called the debate between California gubernatorial candidates Dianne Feinstein and Pete Wilson a draw — and then said that Wilson *looked* more like a governor. Research on women managers and leaders confirms Congresswoman Unsoeld's observations and personal experience in Congress. Experience and research are teaching us that women can be as good leaders as men. The only difference is in their styles, and in fact women's leadership styles are becoming part of the 1990s definition of leadership.[9]

We come full circle in proposing a solution to the women leaders' dilemma described at the beginning of this chapter: how to be a risktaking and courageous transformational and opinion leader and a feminine woman all at the same time. Fortunately, the solution is a great idea whose time has come. The 1990s are redefining leadership in covenantal terms to better fit today's world: "A covenant is a new reference point for what caring, purposeful, committed people can be in this institutional setting ... covenants bind people together and enable them to meet their corporate needs by meeting the needs of one another."[10] Leadership in covenantal terms is leadership in WomanPower terms — listening to what other people need and helping to make their lives better.

Those men and women who have the ability will use their creative visions, courage in hand, as springboards to take the calculated "smart" risks — in Suzie Azar's words — necessary to become effective transformational leaders. We will feel as comfortable and natural in our leadership roles as Elaine Baxter, Iowa secretary of state, who told us:

> I feel very comfortable where I am. I mean I don't feel at all that I don't belong here with the men. From the time I was that little girl, I was always dragged into things where little girls don't normally go, so I think it's absolutely normal that earlier today I was downstairs in the executive council, where the governor and the auditor and the treasurer, the secretary of agriculture, and I meet every week. And I chair it when the governor isn't there.
>
> I don't ever sit down and think, "What am I doing here?" or "I don't belong here." I've never felt that I am any less a leader. I think the disadvantages come in other people's perception of you. I think politics is a good thing for women to do. I felt this when I was on the city council, in the legislature, and as secretary of state. When I look ahead I wonder, "Well, could I be governor? Could I be senator?" I feel, "Sure I could be." I feel very comfortable with it.

PROFILE

Nancy Johnson
Figuring Out What to Do
with Her Life

Even when women have received the messages they need to build their own Leadership Equations, they have to pull the pieces together that create the dream, and thus a direction for their lives. How they do it is illustrated by Connecticut Congresswoman Nancy Johnson, who steered a steady course along life's path as she figured out what to do with her life.

Congresswoman Nancy Johnson of Connecticut grew up with all the essential ingredients to develop her personal Leadership Equation. Her loving parents taught her that she could do anything she wanted to do. Young Nancy found out that as long as she was willing to work, her parents were there to back her. For instance, her older sister wanted a horse badly. She became an excellent rider and barn hand, saved her money, found an appropriate horse, and got her father's backing to buy it. Nancy and her younger sister decided they would buy a horse as their involvement grew; they began boarding other people's horses and picking blueberries to pay for their own horse. Their father backed them by assuming risks they were oblivious to and solving periodic cash flow problems, though always with debt repayment plans attached. "Without his confidence in us, in something that he knew little about and that even aroused his childhood fears of riding, we could never have developed an involvement of such significance that taught us so much about economics and love."

On the feminine side, young Nancy was surrounded by

strong female role models who shared their secrets with her, taught her that women could be "movers and shakers," and gave her empowering messages. Her paternal grandmother, one of the first women graduates of John Marshall Law School and an early leader in the settlement house movement in Chicago, was also an activist in the League of Women Voters. Her mother had a master's degree in history from the University of Chicago and was a successful teacher before she married. While raising her four children, she, too, had juggled many balls — participating in the League of Women Voters and other community groups and always holding well-informed opinions on current events. Clearly, these mothering figures around Nancy modeled, mirrored, and endorsed autonomous, political, and independent behavior for her and her sisters.

This also made it easier for young Nancy to take risks and to, without guilt, identify with her father's and mother's more adventurous self, adding, as we pointed out in Chapter 4, the "psychological scaffolding" her father helped her build to support her Competent Self. This enabled her to feel safe and confident enough to be a risktaker knowing that regardless of the outcome, she would still be all right. Because this psychic scaffolding helped her to take physical as well as emotional risks, young Nancy was an adventurous child, sometimes with disastrous as well as funny consequences, such as falling out of trees and needing stitches after someone dropped a pointed metal clothesline on her head. Even after the accidents, however, she didn't sense, "Gee, I'd better not do that. I might get hurt." They were just part of growing up and taking chances.

Along with enabling messages, young Nancy also got subtle mixed messages during her early years, as we described in Chapter 4: that women may be intelligent, creative, and interesting but are still not equal to men and that although she could do anything she wanted to do, she couldn't do anything well enough.

Given these painful mixed messages, growing up in a family of modest means in an affluent neighborhood, and competing with children from highly achieving families didn't make it easy for young Nancy to build her self-esteem. She had her special talents and excelled in them, but she questioned her competence:

> The school we were in — everybody was smart. One of my best friends and next-door neighbor was Julio Fermi, Enrico Fermi's son. We all worked hard. And I did try, particularly in my later years in high school, to get A's rather than B's. I wanted to be in the top group. Well, I couldn't be at the top of the class in terms of grades. But I could be the best in leadership. I was the best in a lot of things. I was very good at sports. I was president of the girls' club, all those things.

In general terms, Johnson was a high achiever and went on to Radcliffe, where she majored in history. As she talked about her college years, her self-effacing manner and hesitant self-confidence in downplaying her academic successes reflected the mixed messages she had received. So we were amused when Johnson conceded that she really hadn't done too badly in college; after all, she admitted, she *had* graduated from Radcliffe with honors.

"And then I got married and had kids and did nothing," she told us. To Johnson, "nothing" meant "nothing" about her ambition/career track. But she certainly was doing something about fulfilling her nurturing self and her bride/mother track. But, never having really learned what was "good enough" as a child and not having society's benchmark of success — a paycheck — she kept doubting herself. As a young mother with a family, Johnson found the three or four years before she ran for office to be emotionally very tough:

> I couldn't figure out what to do with my life because I simply didn't have enough experience of the real world. I couldn't see

how the parenting and community activism, which I'd been
doing for years, related to the world of employment and a career.

In desperation, trying to find direction, Johnson decided to
work toward a law degree or a graduate degree in social work
and found a particularly interesting program that combined law
and social work. However, because of family illness that took
precedence, she missed the application deadlines and wasn't
admitted. But she was determined. "So I pushed myself through
it knowing the next year I would simply do it again, and then I
would do it right."

Clearly, Johnson was having trouble focusing and moving
forward. She knew she had to experiment, to put out feelers
and take some risks. Reaching out, she contacted the Radcliffe
career office. She was grateful for their help. The staff there
helped her translate her experiences into the kinds of jobs she
might enjoy and be qualified for. They helped her put together
a functional résumé, which stresses skills and highlights organizational and managerial talents honed in community activities, thus explaining the intermittent employment record that
many housewives and mothers have. For Johnson, developing
this résumé created her first vision of her professional self.
"That was a giant step forward in thinking about myself, where
I had been and what I had done and what I might be prepared to
accomplish," she said.

From there, Johnson's career moved from wife and mother to
"professional volunteer":

> When my kids were in school I had been very active in volunteer
> work — PTA, the church school, the church, the child guidance
> clinic board, art museum, symphony, library expansion fund
> drive. So when the school system began to get in deep trouble —
> there I was in the midst of school controversies — one of my
> friends, whose husband was the Republican town chairman,
> encouraged me to run for the school board. School board I could
> understand.

She was intrigued by that idea but, as we related in Chapter 4, was persuaded instead to run for town council after her husband pointed out the poor track record of the incumbents. She lost that election but learned a lot during the campaign and used the experience as a guideline:

> I learned why volunteer efforts in the city always failed to reach the black or minority community. I realized why we always failed to reach the Polish or Italian neighborhoods. And I really learned a lot about a city that I thought I knew a lot about. I enjoyed it thoroughly, and all those many political events I had attended with my father and mother came rolling back. I felt completely at home. I liked the issues and developed a strong interest in government. I began to see that all the community work that I'd been doing had really prepared me to be *making* public policy instead of trying to *implement* it as a volunteer in the nonprofit sector.

After the election, Johnson continued to attend town committee meetings "out of gratitude for having been given this opportunity." Then the Republicans asked her to run for the state senate, which she agreed to do, she says, for her own personal growth. She knew that the Republicans regarded her as a sacrificial lamb and expected her to lose the election:

> I was under no illusions about why they asked me to run. But here I was, having applied to school and not gotten in, having done the functional résumé and seeing what skills I had and what I didn't have, afraid to go back to school because my mind was so rusty. So here was a great opportunity to get my mind up and running. I'd have to learn something. I'd have to present it. I'd have to take a more professional role in the community. And I could see that that would move me a step forward. There would be certain things I could add to my functional résumé. And I'd certainly go back to school with a great deal more confidence. And furthermore, I might actually get up the courage to interview for jobs and maybe find a job that I liked more than going back to school.
>
> The Democratic party, which was very divided, had in the

primary defeated some of its old guard, so I was running against the last one. I beat him by about thirty votes out of thirty thousand, with the help of a lot of Democrats. The Democrats had been perfectly frank with me, saying, "We want you to beat this guy. We tried. We didn't succeed. We're going to help you. You get him out, and we'll get you out in two years. Just don't get too attached to the job."

So I won this sort of fluky election. The split in the Democrats mattered a lot, but I was also a very good candidate. I picked out issues that really mattered in people's lives and had four very good allies and worked my heart out.

Johnson loved being in the state legislature, she told us. It played to all her strengths and allowed her to be free in the summer and at Christmas. As a mother with a growing family, it was really an ideal profession for her. And to the benefit of the residents of her district, she made politics her career instead of going to graduate school.

Fortunately, Johnson had built her Competent Self early in life. She had indeed pulled the pieces together. The "psychological scaffolding" she had erected along with the "comfort zones" and the independent, autonomous, and political behavior modeled, mirrored, and endorsed by her mother and grandmother helped Johnson to look on the loss of her first election as a learning experience rather than a failure, or an identity crisis, and she tried again. Excitedly, Johnson realized she had found a DreamTrack that was actually better for her than a graduate degree would have been. Once again, she could hear Dream-Voices that she had incorporated long ago from her parents' and grandparents' experiences and she could be guided by them.

These voices may have been buried, but they were there waiting to be reclaimed and revived. They were part of the Competent Self that her family had fostered in her. They helped her to find her own path. Johnson put together the independence and teamwork, imagination, and interdependence that she had learned with her parents and siblings. She tapped into the class leader that she had always been in school, and integrated it into her evolving ambition/career DreamTrack, feeling comfortable with and excited by finally filling out her Leadership Equation.

When Johnson moved from the Connecticut senate to the U.S. Congress, she continued to concentrate on what she calls "nitty-gritty" issues, those bread-and-butter issues such as health care costs, the strength of the bearing industry trade issues, and social security benefits, all issues that affect her constituents' daily lives. And she feels that although she is in a powerful position, "No one in their right mind can long retain a sense of power in the face of the massive problems we have to deal with or the complexity of the legislative process in Washington." She has found a place for herself that draws on all her strengths — the body of experience she had developed in public education and community service, her leadership ability, her willingness to put her ideas before people, her independence, her capacity for risktaking, her competitiveness, and her concern for others.

Nancy Johnson has used her Creative Aggression and WomanPower to build and use her Leadership Equation. She has figured out what to do with her life. She has taken the secrets of her power and used them to put the pieces together for herself. Today, as she lives her Leadership Equation, she finds herself feeling fulfilled as she goes about her job of making society a better place to live.

7

The Secrets of Leadership:
Making the Pieces Fit

We can compare the three elements of each woman's personal Leadership Equation — Competent Self, Creative Aggression, and WomanPower — to the outside edge of a jigsaw puzzle. When the edges of the puzzle are put together, we have a picture-frame effect. This perimeter forms the basic structure and gives us some idea of how the finished product will look. But merely finishing the edges of the puzzle doesn't really give us the big picture. As with a real puzzle, we have to identify and insert all of the missing pieces before our task is finished.

In the case of the women we studied, as with the puzzle, we have identified some pieces and given you an idea of the basic shape of the Leadership Equation and what makes a woman into a leader. However, we have not yet explained how the women took in the early messages they received or how they transformed the secrets of power into their personal Leadership Equation, using it to take them to the top. We know that they had supportive parents and siblings. They felt loved and special. Their mothers and fathers told them they could do whatever they wanted. They learned to take risks. But we still want to know how they were able to pull it all together not having had a dream in young adulthood of where they were headed.

You Don't Have to Be a Lawyer

Don't take this the wrong way. It certainly doesn't hurt to be a lawyer. After all, law traditionally has been men's springboard into politics and other leadership positions. However, the women we interviewed followed a variety of paths into public office, many of which are particularly suited for today's woman.

Only one, Pat Schroeder, is an attorney. As we mentioned in her profile, she took time out from her legal career to "push peas" when her children were babies and to get involved in the community. Clearly, Congresswoman Schroeder's bride/mother DreamTrack was in the forefront then, although it switched places with her ambition/career DreamTrack when she decided to run for Congress.

Almost all of the other women we talked with had similar experiences. They followed the bride/mother DreamTrack through early adulthood until they felt ready to step out in the world. At that point they moved their ambition/career DreamTrack from the background into prominence, relegating the bride/mother DreamTrack into a secondary, but not forgotten, role. For some, like Congresswoman Nancy Johnson, it took exploration and several starts to find the ambition/career DreamTrack that worked for her. When you have not formulated the dream in your early twenties, it is harder to derive it later in life when factors such as age and family responsibilities color your fantasies.

However, as these women have demonstrated throughout their careers, it *is* possible to shift from the domestic DreamTrack to the professional pathway. If you didn't have the dream when you were younger, it's still possible to switch to the ambition/career track later in life. The women we studied did it and managed to learn a great many political skills as they were making the transition. Those skills are many of the missing pieces in the jigsaw puzzle we began to assemble in Chapter 4.

Education — the Single-Sex Factor

The women we interviewed were highly educated, and their education contributed to their readiness for leadership and power. All had attended college, and a number had advanced degrees, including one Ph.D. Not only were they well educated, but we discovered an interesting factor in their education: ten times the norm, or 44 percent, went to all-female elementary schools, high schools, and/or colleges. This confirmed the findings of previous researchers that a disproportionate number of women in politics and other high-powered careers have attended a single-sex school at some level.

The idea that grew out of the women's movement is that women need to attend coeducational schools from the earliest possible time to develop the competitive skills they will need as adults in male-dominated environments. The women we studied obviously had those skills, yet almost half of them attended single-sex rather than coeducational schools. How can this be?

We believe that the experience of attending all-female schools reinforced rather than contradicted the earlier parental messages that these women could do whatever they wanted. As Congresswoman Barbara Kennelly told us of her all-girls school, "There was no saying that you couldn't be first. Of *course* you could be first. And I think that going to a girls' school told me I could be anything I wanted to be."

Women's colleges have been found to be twice as likely as comparable coed schools to produce achievers. For example, the Washington-based Women's College Coalition found that all-female schools have produced one-third of the female board members of Fortune 1000 companies, one-fourth of the female board members of Fortune 500 companies, and half of the women in Congress.[1] This is all the more striking if you consider that only 4.5 percent of the women who have bachelor's degrees graduated from women's colleges.

We looked at the responses of the women in our sample in terms of how an all-female education helped them to develop the Competent Self, Creative Aggression, and WomanPower. Whether the women we studied went to all-girls or coed schools, they told us that their experience was that girls defer to boys in coed groups. In other words, girls are less comfortable with their aggression in coed groups. Here are some of the ways they expressed the idea:

- "I think that sex gets in the way in teen years. The kids are so busy showing off for each other that they're not directing their energies toward learning."
- "Boy, it was really clear at my school that it was wonderful to have a place where girls could go and be smart all day, every day, and not have to worry about anything else. Needless to say, it made socializing if you were not particularly attractive just appallingly difficult. But I still think it was worth it."
- "I did very well in a girls' school. You concentrate on all the things that make a difference to you."
- "As it was for many girls of our era, the message was 'Don't exceed. Don't excel. You want the boys to like you, not to be the class brain.'"

Nancy Pelosi, the only girl in a large family of boys, observed:

When boys came around, my friends would all of a sudden perk up, and their voices and their whole conversation would change.

I would think, "What's the big deal?" if two boys walked in. I
was used to ten boys around the house all the time.

Will this behavior disappear with the generation in which
most of these women were raised? Why do women receive less
attention in coed environments? Recent studies have shown
that the "chilly climate" for women in college classrooms is
still with us. In 1989 Harvard School of Education researcher
Catherine Krupnick studied Wheaton College two years after it
became coeducational; her study confirmed previous findings.
She had not expected to encounter a chilly climate for women
at Wheaton because half the faculty members were female and
the student body was still predominantly female. However, she
found that although the men made up only 10 percent of the
students in a class, they did 25 percent of the speaking. The
New York Times quoted Krupnick as saying that "college cata-
logues should carry a warning. The value you receive will depend on your sex."[2]

Women's schools provide leadership opportunities that
might not be otherwise available to women, for women *are* the
student government, the class leaders, the club presidents.
"Frankly, had I not gone to an all-girls school I'm not sure I
would have ever been a student body president or president
of the freshman class, which enabled me to be in a position
to develop my leadership skills," Louisiana's Mary Landrieu
told us.

Or as Barbara Mikulski put it, "We were taught how to be a
debater, to organize our thinking, to be a leader. Nobody said,
'Now when you get out there, you make him feel good — so he
can feel good that you won.'"

Women don't have the same opportunities at coeducational
schools to develop their political skills through involvement in
student government. Although they make up 53.5 percent of
all college undergraduates, women comprised only 40.4 percent
of college legislative bodies and 37.7 percent of the executive

boards at coeducational institutions in 1989. According to the Fund for the Feminist Majority, which surveyed campus leaders to get those figures, this is an increase of only 2.6 and 4.8 percent, respectively, over their 1988 survey.[3] The Feminist Majority found that liberal arts colleges were making the greatest strides toward equality in student government, and colleges and universities with religious affiliations were making the least progress. In fact, there wasn't one female president or treasurer at any religiously affiliated institution in 1989.

The downside risk of developing leadership skills in an all-female setting is the challenge of maintaining those skills in a mixed environment after college. This is particularly true in one that is heavily male, such as the executive, legislative, and judicial branches of government. Mary Landrieu said:

> By the time I got to the legislature, the shock of it — from the all-female world to an all-male world — was more than I could handle. I wasn't prepared for it even though in my family, which is half female and half male, I had a good relationship with my brothers; and my father and my uncles and my boyfriends and my male friends should have helped to make that adjustment. It was really hard for me.

Another advantage of single-sex education mentioned by the women we interviewed was the availability of role models. For several women who had attended Catholic all-girls schools, "The nuns were *it*. They certainly came across as strong women." Another noted, "I had women who were scholars, Ph.D.'s, and so on. So I saw women running hospitals — scholars, you know, who were doctoral candidates in history or who already had doctorates in chemistry." Like the women we interviewed, these strong role models weren't lacking in competitiveness. One woman remembered the nuns who told her debating team, "We're going to show you how to take on those Jesuit boys!"

We are not saying that coeducation precludes the development of Competent Self, Creative Aggression, and Woman-Power in women. Slightly more than half of the highly successful women we studied went to coed high schools and colleges. But the disproportionate number of women in our sample with a single-sex educational background still speaks loudly to the advantage of the protective environment of an all-female campus, where the vital components of the Leadership Equation can be developed, nurtured, and solidified before women encounter the prejudices and glass ceilings of male-dominated institutions.

From Bride/Mother to Politics
in the '70s and '80s

The value of a good education cannot be overemphasized, as the women we interviewed have demonstrated. But these women didn't become the leaders they are today only because of their education. What made the difference for them was the Leadership Equation: a Competent Self, which gives them the confidence that they can do as well as, if not better than, other officeholders; Creative Aggression, which enables them to feel comfortable while reaching for and wielding power; and WomanPower, which unites their interest in helping others with the power they need to make a difference.

In the following sections we illustrate how the women we interviewed integrated these factors into their personal circumstances and how that integration enabled them to successfully switch DreamTracks in midlife. We also talk about some of the political skills they learned along the way.

Entering Politics

Most of the women we interviewed entered politics at the local or state level and then moved up to higher office. The exceptions are Nancy Pelosi, who was elected to Congress after many years of organizing for the Democratic party, and Rebecca Vigil-Giron, a longtime activist in the Democratic party whose first campaign resulted in her election as secretary of state in New Mexico.

The women we interviewed were women of their time. Although they did not feel entitled to have a dream that they developed in their early twenties, many of them came into politics via leadership positions in environmental, public policy, education, and other organizations. Passionate causes ignited and excited them enough to develop a dream and an agenda to carry it out. After lobbying for their cause, these women came to realize that they could do more by being on the inside. Thus, their political dream grew. Their Competent Self, developed in childhood, provided the strength to risk going after the dream. Fostered by identification with their parents' autonomy and their mothers' mirroring and endorsement of that autonomy, their Creative Aggression provided the drive.

Because they were generally seeking office to advance an agenda, these women became exemplars of WomanPower, not perceiving power as a means to dominate others — not that they didn't enjoy the power they had — but as a way to get something done for the greater good.

Florida's Betty Castor acknowledged the role the League of Women Voters played in preparing her for politics. Already a member of the league in another state, she became engrossed in league activities after she moved to Florida: "While I was pregnant I was always president of League of Women Voters. It seems that every time I attended a league meeting I was pregnant or had babies with me." We surmise that many political women can identify with Castor. How many can remember trying to simultaneously entertain a squirming toddler and participate in a meeting or public hearing?

Not only can women learn about issues of concern to the community through involvement with community organizations, they also can develop networks of support to draw on when they seek leadership positions in the future. Education-related organizations are particularly productive training grounds for future elected officials. Congresswoman Marge Roukema and Ruth Messinger, president of the borough of Manhattan, both got their start in politics with election to the school board. Messinger told us:

> I ran for the local school board because I had helped to run an independent free school in this district and had fought with the local school board to get it funded. I had learned a lot about education and education politics. A friend of mine said, "You should stop complaining to the school board and just run for it." And I said, "I don't know anything about running for office." "No," he said, "but I do." And that's really what got me to run.

We were not surprised to learn that many of the women we studied entered politics after working in one of the traditional female careers: teaching, nursing, or social work. Iowa's Lieutenant Governor Jo Ann Zimmerman, one of the two nurses in our sample, believes that nursing experience is one of the best preparations for political life:

> It's a transferable skill. For instance, you might say to a diabetic, "Look, you've got a long-term disease, and you have to learn to live with it. Let's work together to develop a plan." You're selling a person on an idea. It becomes their plan, they buy into it and they do it. It's the same thing in a committee or in administration. You have to sell the people around you on an idea so they'll carry through. Same exact skill.

We can think of a number of other skills from traditional occupations that women can transfer to the political world. For example, from teaching comes the ability to organize, to speak before a group, to think on your feet, to maintain order in a group. Among other skills, social work teaches women how to work with people, how bureaucracies operate, how to get things done in spite of them, and how to operate within the rules and regulations imposed by government. Other important political skills — from budgeting to time management — can first be learned in nonpolitical fields ranging from marketing to full-time homemaking and then transferred to the leadership arena.

Most of the women we interviewed entered politics later in life, when their children were teenagers or older, although most began their community involvement when the children were much younger. They scheduled their own activities for the middle of the day so they could be home when the children went off to school in the morning and again in the afternoon when the kids came home. Thus they were able to participate in the adult world of ideas and challenges and to take the first tentative steps toward the ambition/career DreamTrack while the bride/mother DreamTrack still dominated their lives. Women with small children are not precluded from holding political office, but like any other balancing act between motherhood and career, juggling the two can make life very hectic and make mothers feel pretty frazzled.

Some positions, both elective and appointive, can fit into a young mother's schedule with no more difficulty than the church work, PTA activities, partisan political work, or other activities that young mothers have traditionally undertaken. In some cases, a young mother can balance the duties of local offices such as city council, county commission, school board, or airport authority board with the demands placed on her by her growing family. By holding local office, a woman can enhance her visibility while at the same time getting political on-the-job training that will serve her well later.

The real problem occurs with state or federal offices, which exact not only large blocks of time but also require at least partial residency in a state capital or Washington, D.C. However, Congresswoman Nancy Johnson found that being in the Connecticut senate was suitable to managing concurrent DreamTracks, highlighting her strengths and giving her the same vacation schedule as her children. And Pat Schroeder said that when her children were young she was the only member of Congress to come to work with diapers in her purse. She is an exceptional woman, with an exceptionally supportive husband and with children who seemed to thrive on their nontraditional lifestyle.

When women enter politics after their children are self-sufficient, they are very different from their male contemporaries, as Elaine Baxter, Iowa's secretary of state, observed:

> Women usually don't get elected to legislatures until they're in their forties or older, when their children are grown. Someone once said to me, "You know, there is really a great bunch of young secretaries of state now, and they're mainly women." And I said, "Wait a minute. We're not *all* young." In fact, the rest of them all were younger than I was. In politics, many women in their forties and fifties are new in their careers, and they approach the job with the enthusiasm of young men. These women are charged up and ready to go. You can't really compare them to men of the same age, who may be losing steam in their careers. There is room in life for people to emerge later on.

The energy and creativity, coupled with maturity and life experience, bring a unique perspective to government, as to any field that women enter later in life.

Some of the women we studied were first appointed to office and then decided they enjoyed public service so much they wanted to run for office. As Congresswoman Connie Morella told us:

I never fashioned myself as somebody who would want to be
elected to office. I think it was my generation, probably. Then in
1972 I was appointed to the first Montgomery County, Maryland, Commission for Women, which was quasi-governmental.
It was an appointment by our county executive with the approval of the county council. We had a budget in the magnitude
of a million dollars, and I was elected president. I testified particularly for women in housing, employment, credit, and education. We started the first affirmative action plans in our schools
and testified on three levels of government. Got appointments
on various commissions and boards for women; it previously
had not been that way. So that's when I thought, "I really think I
would like to be on the other side, where I would have more
influence to make some things happen." My springboard to office came through my involvement seeking equity for women
and minorities.

Running for office obviously requires a greater sense of competitiveness and risktaking than does being appointed. In the
latter case, the risk is only in the adequacy of the job you'll do
and not in whether you'll get the job. The faith that the Competent Self will withstand the possible loss of an election is
critical to making the shift from appointed to elected office.

One reason that the political entry points of women we
interviewed differ so much is that election laws vary dramati-
cally from office to office, city to city, and state to state. In
some jurisdictions, candidates only have to pay a filing fee to
get a position on the ballot. Other localities require office seekers to support their candidacy with a petition from a minimum
number of registered voters. In still other areas, candidates have
to be formally selected by a political party to get on the ballot.
Certainly the crazy-quilt pattern of election laws shaped how
the women we talked with entered politics and moved up the
ladder. But we also found that they had many similar experiences along the way. They wanted power so they could do
things for others. They thought they would exert more clout if
they had a vote on the board instead of having to lobby board

members. Their experiences differ in detail, but they all got a lot of in-service training that prepared them to excel in their present positions.

In Chapter 3 we talked about Jeane Kirkpatrick's categorization of women officeholders as either office seekers or ready recruits. We found striking examples of both categories among the women we interviewed. Among the Office Seekers were the following.

- Betty Castor, who decided to run for county commissioner when she was unable to find other candidates to do so and who won despite the fact that the eleven defeated candidates from the primary endorsed her opponent in the general election.
- Senator Barbara Mikulski, who, after helping her grandmothers' neighbors stop freeway construction through their neighborhood, ran for city council because she decided she'd rather be opening doors for people than knocking on doors as an organizer.
- Rebecca Vigil-Giron of New Mexico, who ran for secretary of state because of her interest in voter registration and won despite little name recognition, little money, and being only thirty years old.

Among the ready recruits, who didn't take the plunge until they had been nudged into it by someone else, were the following.

- Jo Ann Zimmerman, whose interest in issues led to party involvement and subsequently to office, after her friends shamed her into running: "Hey, Zimmerman," they said, "we've taken your resolutions up to the platform committee and you ought to be up here and be chair of this caucus because we're tired of doing the work for you."

- Maine's Olympia Snowe, whose first husband urged her to run for his seat in the legislature if anything should happen to him because "you have an opinion on everything."

That many women would not be office seekers is consistent with our contention that women do not have a leadership dream in early adulthood. Being an office seeker implies having a vision of what and where you want to be. A ready recruit may desire to see an agenda moved but may be less able to perceive the route to success or to see herself as its political champion, without the nudge. But even for these women to respond to the nudge, they had to have a Competent Self that would not be terrified of the possibility of failure and enough Creative Aggression to move ahead.

Learning Political Skills

Being in politics, Congresswoman Barbara Kennelly told us, is "like an old-fashioned carnival, where you put your head through the hole in a figure and everybody throws balls at you. We candidates put our names on a machine, and people close the curtain and either reject us or accept us."

In some states, partisan involvement is essential for women interested in running at any level. The experience of working as a party volunteer can provide valuable expertise to the budding political candidate. In addition to a firsthand introduction to the nuts and bolts of organizing and campaigning, a promising candidate can enhance her visibility by working for the party. After all, a person who is well known to the party's power brokers has a better chance for serious consideration when empty seats need to be filled or other opportunities materialize.

Sometimes, as this anecdote from Congresswoman Barbara Kennelly illustrates, it works with a little prodding:

> I went downtown one July day to see the person who was running the party in the city because there was a vacancy on the city council. I said I would like to be appointed to it. (I think sometimes when you get older, you lose some of this courage.) But he said, "No. We asked you to run for the school board, and you didn't. We've already picked somebody for this vacancy." I said, "Well, that's all right. I'll enter the primary in September." (I don't think I ever would have, but I said it to him.) And the next thing you know — there were two vacancies — two of us went to the council that August. And I loved it. It was like I'd died and gone to heaven.

The value of hands-on training in someone else's campaign pays off in many ways, including improving self-confidence. Iowa Secretary of State Elaine Baxter told us how that happened after she had built an enviable reputation as a party volunteer:

> In 1968 our candidate for Congress asked me to coordinate his campaign. I accepted although I didn't really know what I was saying yes to. When he came to town, I would set up press interviews and events. He would talk to me about them and would ask me questions such as "Who do you think I need to see?" That seems funny now, but a man running for Congress had never asked me before, "Who do *you* think I should be talking to? What do *you* think I should say when we go down to the newspaper office?"
>
> My youngest child at that time was just three years old, so I was still a mother at home with children. Even though I was a political activist and a volunteer worker in my community, I was still very much at home. I remember often being on the phone with people from his office on issues as well as the logistics of the campaign. But in my life, which was somewhat circumscribed at that time, this was the outside world coming in. This was people calling *long-distance*! Things like that don't happen when you're a housewife — you're talking to children all the time. And from that point on, I started doing more for candidates at a more responsible level.

Then I started to think, "You're a real workaholic. And if you're a workaholic, why aren't you doing some of this for yourself? If you can work this hard to help get someone else elected, what could you do if you went out and worked on your own?"

Working on a campaign also eventually led to ready recruit Mary Landrieu's position as treasurer of Louisiana. At a crucial turning point in her life, she was encouraged by her father to volunteer in a friend's campaign:

> After I was there a few weeks, I realized, "This is where you need to be." And then campaign workers came up to me and said, "Mary, we've been observing that you're very good at this and you're very enthusiastic. Have you ever thought of running yourself instead of working for other people?"

Not long afterward, at age twenty-three, Landrieu became the youngest woman ever elected to the legislature in her state.

Anyone who chooses to live in the public arena has to be able to withstand the pressures and personal attacks that come with the territory. Talking about some of the brutal campaigns waged against women toward the end of the 1980s, Gail Schoettler of Colorado observed, "If you can't take it and fight it, you can't beat it. It's really brutal. It's not as though you can say, 'This is not a personal attack.' Of course it's a personal attack." A Competent Self is the key to survival in such situations because when you are secure in who you are, the barbs, innuendos, and even lies, although experienced as hurtful, are recognized for what they are and not absorbed by the self as if they were painfully true.

A related problem, especially for women, is learning not to respond emotionally to attacks because emotional responses by women are frequently ridiculed or used as examples of women's inability to handle real pressure. It was a skill that Betty Castor had to learn:

I have dealt with it by trying to argue for subjects in a nonpassionate way, trying to be nonemotional in expressing conflict. That has been extremely important. I learned those lessons, I think, very early. There is a way to do that, and often I think people especially have held women to a different standard, so we've had to be very, very cautious. When I have been involved with debates and differences of opinion, although inside I felt great intensity I've tried to control that by saying to myself, "Control this anger" and "Control this response — don't let it get away from you."

Similarly, when the issue is an emotional one, the emotions need to be restrained. As Congresswoman Nancy Pelosi observed:

There are certain times where you can say from the heart something that is emotional, but you cannot resort to emotion every time you get up to speak or else they'll just think that your brain is not in charge. Because however motivated you are or however emotional you are about it, you must have a perspective on it.

Politics should be a constant learning experience, not only about conduct and strategy but also about the unending variety of issues that must be addressed. Sometimes the issues may be decidedly unglamorous, such as the intricacies of financing and operating a sewage treatment plant, but the women we talked with told us how stimulated they were by learning so much about so many subjects. Kathleen Connell, Rhode Island secretary of state, cautioned against getting bogged down in women's issues only. Always doing one's homework is the best protection against developing a reputation as a one-issue officeholder, a political lightweight.

Political women must often take pains to learn the same political skills that men learn routinely as they are growing up, often through competitive sports and other organizational experiences. Mayor Suzie Azar remembers how learning to compromise made her a more effective leader:

I recognized that I didn't know how to negotiate. I like being absolutely right one hundred percent, and I didn't know how to back down off a position and reach a compromise and still feel like I had won. It was like you asked for something and didn't get exactly that, so you went away mad without ever thinking that you could go back with a counteroffer.

However, Congresswoman Marge Roukema cautioned against jeopardizing one's fundamental beliefs over the need to compromise:

> If you're a politician, there are certain parameters in which you must work, and you can modify positions. Indeed, you sometimes learn as you go along. I mean, you better! In public life if you don't, there's something wrong with you. But there are certain fundamentals which shouldn't be swayed by the climate or the public opinion of the day, whether it's reflected in polls or whatever.

Learning how to build coalitions and how to network are other skills that women frequently don't learn growing up. Consequently, it is often hard for them to understand that networking with the members of a board to line up their support before a formal vote can pay off. Congresswoman Nancy Pelosi compares coalitions to a kaleidoscope. The combinations of supporters and opponents change with each movement. Being able to accept that — in other words, "agreeing to disagree" — and still be friends is another skill women often have to learn for themselves.

We must say that Jo Ann Zimmerman of Iowa came up with a most inspired way to build bridges to political cohorts who clearly were not pleased with her election. She built upon her woman's sense of the value of connectedness:

> When I was elected lieutenant governor I won against a popular senator and one who wasn't so popular — and then they had to work with me. Now, I know the value of nonverbal messages. I know if I touch you and look right straight at you that our

relationship is different forevermore. Not everybody understands that. So as I traveled around the state I asked to stay in
the homes of some legislators I thought might be difficult to
work with. And as a result, I didn't have the problem that some
of the previous lieutenant governors had had in the past, partly
because I had worked with these people and pulled them into
my election instead of shutting them out.

Making the effort to learn the written and unwritten rules of
the particular decision-making body and playing by those rules
is a valuable skill. As Ann Richards of Texas told us:

> I think it's tough for women to be confronted with the classic
> male managerial fashion of drawing a line in the dirt with a
> sword. The question is how a woman accommodates her natural
> instincts and sociological training with the reality of the male
> style. There are good points to both methodologies. And those of
> us who are going to be very good are going to learn to use them
> both.

As we discussed in Chapter 6, smart risktaking involves
knowing how to pick your battles. Another part of risktaking
is being strong enough to stand up for your beliefs and to face
irate fellow legislators or constituents if need be. According to
Congresswoman Nancy Pelosi:

> If you're going to throw a punch in politics, you better be pre-
> pared to take a punch. So if you go out slugging for your issue,
> you can just count on getting slugged back very hard. You must
> be prepared to be tough — expect the punch and take it with
> grace so everybody knows that you can throw one and that
> you're a pro. I always thought I was really raised to be a peace-
> maker but trained to fight in case I had to.

Kathleen Connell, Rhode Island secretary of state, told how
she developed toughness as she progressed from community
activist to elected official:

> I think I came into it so gradually I must have gotten a tough
> hide over the years. It was devastating to me the first time I

realized people I didn't even know absolutely hated me personally. People I'd never met and never had anything to do with
hated me over a school bond issue or a school budget issue. The
vehemence of some of the feelings was really quite shocking to
me. But once you go through it once you just say, "Hey, it's part
of political life."

Being unable to roll with the punches makes the job that
much harder. Problems come in shades of gray, and so do their
solutions. Few issues in our pluralistic society appear magi-
cally in black and white. Whether assisted by a large staff, a
small one, or none at all, the officeholder must ultimately
make the tough decisions and cast those controversial votes. It
can be very lonely in office, especially for the thin-skinned who
agonize over which position to take and then have difficulty
standing up to the heat it generates.

Congresswoman Barbara Boxer believes it's important to
speak up when you feel strongly about the issues, whether or
not you're on the losing side. What if you speak up for issues
you support, get in there and slug it out politically, and still
lose most of the time? Do you tell yourself, "This, too, will
pass," and hope for the best? Do you decide that one vote just
doesn't make any difference and give up? This is how Barbara
Boxer handled it:

> When I got on the board of supervisors I was in the minority in a
> 3–2 vote on practically everything — sometimes even 4–1 —
> and yet I appreciated the fact that this was a role I would just
> have to play until things changed. And sure enough, two years
> later someone got elected on a platform that I believed in, and
> we had a 3–2 our way for the next four years. So I think the
> lessons in life, to be able to cope with adversity and not feel I
> had to go along just because the majority wanted to go a certain
> way, have served me well.

Congresswoman Marge Roukema, among others, pointed out
the need to be tenacious instead of giving up easily: "You have

to be competitive to win an election or be able to serve well and be an advocate and a fighter for your constituency. You also have to be tenacious. If you can't get it done one way, you have to be willing to try another." Gail Schoettler of Colorado combines tenacity with willingness to accept partial victories: "If you don't get it one way, you figure another way to do it. With legislation, if I fail with the big package, what I do the next year is go back with a piece until eventually we get the deal or close to it. You just keep working."

We believe it's significant that some of the women we talked with viewed losing an election as "almost winning." What appears on the surface to be a Pollyanna-like way of looking at things is really a way of identifying the opportunities that presented themselves. The first time out, most of the women were virtually unknown in the political realm. Yet they made a credible showing, learned the basics of running a campaign, put together a campaign organization, and met a lot of people in the process. After losing her first election, Marge Roukema ran again because she "didn't want to spend the rest of my life wondering 'what if?'" And as we said in Chapter 6, Congresswoman Claudine Schneider viewed her narrow loss as a win and went on to win a seat in Congress and reelections by ever-increasing margins.

What they are telling us is, "I do not lose the person who I am, even when I lose." They are not devastated. Upset, absolutely — but able to recover, as one would from an illness or the death of a loved one, and go on. Catherine Baker Knoll, treasurer of Pennsylvania, was frank about how she felt after losing:

> You first have a good cry because you worked hard and you expected that you were going to win. Then you just look in the mirror and say, "Well, it's not the end of the world. You still have your family and you have your husband, who's been very supportive, and you ran a good show and you did a good job — unfortunately the public didn't really realize that they should have voted for you, so it's their loss."

I had an aunt who would say: "I don't want you feeling sorry
for yourself. You know, there are other things in life. You'll win
four years from now. It's just unfortunate we have a setback, but
it's not the end of the world." She said that to me when she was
ninety-one. That's remarkable, isn't it? I think about her so
often. When I'm worrying about some of the problems I've had
with this office, I wonder, "Now what would she say?" She'd say,
"You can do it. Don't worry about it."

Evelyn Murphy of Massachusetts told us how unprepared
she was for losing early in her career: "That was a major setback, and I walked into it without hedging my bets. That is,
the day after an election I woke up in debt, broke, no future,
zero plans, not quite knowing what I was going to do next, and
feeling lousy about the whole thing. I found it emotionally very
wrenching." But upset as she was, Murphy did not withdraw
from politics or life. She recovered and ran again.

To take some of the pain out of losing, Nancy Pelosi would
give candidates this advice:

> Have your values in order so that winning or losing an election
> is not the end of the world. What's important is who you are as a
> person and why you want to be in office and whether the issue
> is served. And from the standpoint of your private life, when
> after all is said and done, that's the only thing that's important.

Along the same line, Kathleen Connell of Rhode Island told us:

> I've always said it's no disgrace to lose because you've given
> people a choice, and there's always going to be a winner and a
> loser in these things. It doesn't make you any different as
> a person than you were before you started. Now when you
> get a little further along in politics you see a lot of people,
> particularly men, with their whole identity tied up in that title.
> To lose it is devastating. I would never want to be so tied up in
> that title.

Just before the 1990 general election Rebecca Vigil-Giron,
New Mexico secretary of state, said about losing: "There's al-

ways the next day. The sun shines and life goes on, and you have to go on with it." Then, several weeks later, shortly after she had lost her bid for Congress, she told us optimistically, "I have to think of ways to make it better. It wasn't my time, but I'll win next time."

All of these women were able to bounce back after losing. Clearly, they all felt good enough about themselves — had that sense of uninterrupted internal applause — to view defeat not as an obstacle but as an opportunity for the future.

Women who have made it in politics are a growing cadre of role models for those women coming up the ladder behind them. As more and more are elected, they will help young women to formulate a dream of a political career to which they can bring their values and agendas. As Nancy Pelosi said:

> Ninety-eight percent of politics is rough-and-tumble, hard-hitting, fighting, maneuvering kind of work. The other two percent of it is "Here are the women in Congress. Isn't it wonderful that we have some. Wouldn't it be better if we had more?"

When Political Women Become Leaders

In sum, perhaps the most important lesson we can all learn from the political women we interviewed is that leadership is learned and develops over time. We learned that leaders do not spring forth like Athena, fully grown, from Zeus's head. The seeds are planted in early life in a warm, loving, intact family, which nurtures and supports a girl's knowledge about herself and the elements she needs to build a Competent Self, WomanPower, Creative Aggression, and, ultimately, her Leadership Equation. Then, gradually, she puts the pieces together.

Conventional wisdom says that unlike men, women do not generally dream of greatness in early life. We have seen that women do have dreams, but they have multiple DreamTracks starting with the bride/mother DreamTrack, adding the ambition/career DreamTrack and including dreams of greatness later. Even if, as so often happens, a girl suppresses her aggressive, dreaming self and it goes underground in early teens, it does not go away forever. It is there to be uncovered and reclaimed when the DreamVoices of her ambition/career DreamTrack begin to speak and demand to be heard. By then, she is capable of risktaking because her Competent Self is sturdy. She knows she can survive the losses and mistakes that are inevitable to risktaking and that everyone experiences and learns from along the way. These experiments do not destroy a girl or woman who has built a Competent Self. Her core strength enables her to feel safe enough to have dreams, to develop visions, to take a well-calculated leap of faith, and to put her ideas into action. She is then ready to truly be a leader by sharing her dreams and her vision with others and empowering them to do and be their best.

Vicki Reynolds, mayor of Beverly Hills, talks about leadership: "It's the personal commitment to stepping out and speaking out for what you believe and helping others to know what needs to be done. It's really putting yourself out there."

Whether in the corporate world, the academic world, school systems, professions, or other career arenas, women now have the opportunity to gather skills and to learn leadership if they wish to. Over time, they can put together their own unique DreamTracks and Leadership Equations. They can make use of their growing WomanPower, the caring power that aims to empower others, not destroy them. WomanPower also helps women leaders to advance their own agendas and, in doing so, infuse the work environment with the traditional female values of humanity, intimacy, and interaction, values that enhance the workplace for men and women alike and meet the challenge of working effectively in this diverse and interdependent world.

Giving every woman an equal chance to be the best leader she can be is still a long way off. In politics and in the workplace we are far from the critical mass of women and like-thinking men necessary to tilt the scales toward the kind of wholesale acceptance necessary to foster and develop the transformational, nurturant leadership style that is so natural to women. But every woman we add to elective office, to corporate management, to school and hospital administration, and to other positions of leadership and power moves us in the right direction. It moves us toward a day when WomanPower is the norm and young girls are able to have and hold dreams of greatness as they look to the woman leaders around them as models of what they, too, can be.

8

Empowering Messages to Give
Your Daughters

We have gathered far more from our research than just interesting, quotable anecdotes from twenty-five prominent political women. We know that the parents of these women passed on the secrets of leadership to their daughters through the intimacy and shared private moments of both the mother-daughter relationship and those father-daughter relationships that included intimacy. These parents translated their secrets into empowering messages that they sent to their daughters, enabling them to develop into leaders. Although the content and style of the messages and secrets varied with each family, every set of parents shared enough intimate secrets and the empowering messages that flowed from them to fill their daughter's personal Leadership Equation: Leadership = Competent Self + Creative Aggression + WomanPower.

We believe that the most important contribution to come out of our research is the identification and analysis of the secrets of leadership and of the enabling messages derived from them that these women received. Now, mothers who recognize these messages and the sense of connectedness that reinforces them can hand them down to their daughters. Furthermore, we believe it's still possible for women who didn't receive such messages and feminine secrets of leadership during their own childhood to compensate for them. As we will explain in this and the next chapter, both young girls and adult women can take in these messages to fill their own Leadership Equations.

As we have learned, girls have two parallel DreamTracks, the traditional bride/mother DreamTrack and the ambition/career DreamTrack, each of which is built by the many messages that flow back and forth between parent and child during the growing years. Every new mother, regardless of her achievement orientation, transmits shared feminine secrets in the form of traditional messages to her daughter through the sensual, interpersonal, psychological, and emotional bonding process. The daughter takes in these messages and organizes her personality accordingly. This is called the "reproduction of mothering."[1] We have only to watch the mutual delight of a mother and infant to see maternal power and influence in action. It is as natural as the sunrise. It doesn't have to be taught. These unspoken messages and shared secrets are an integral part of mother-daughter connectedness.

This connectedness enables girls (and women) to identify and empathize with each other. As we illustrated earlier with examples from Carol Gilligan's research, the female need for connectedness is the reason that women, unlike men, define themselves through relationships. It should be obvious, then, why little girls dream of being brides and mommies no matter what other role model their modern mother presents. Wife and mother are connected roles that fit with the child's experience of her mother. They are some of the secrets and unspoken messages that mothers hand down to their daughters.

The messages of the traditional DreamTrack are there, solidly. We don't have to think about how we will convey them to our daughters. However, the messages of the ambition/career DreamTrack are not inherent in traditional mothering or fathering. Those are the secrets and messages we need to think about and make a conscious, deliberate effort to convey if we are to help our daughters dream of greatness.

Suppressive Secrets and
Unspoken Parental Messages

Let's first review the powerful shared secrets and unspoken messages that can suppress a young girl's aggression and ambition. These ancient suppressive secrets and insidious messages are still transmitted from parent to daughter and reinforce the stereotypical female role, despite the changes wrought by the sexual revolution and the overt encouragement to achieve that so many of today's mothers give their daughters. For underneath a mother's desire for her daughter's autonomy and success still lurks the feminine legacy equating desirability and lovability with passivity. In addition, a parallel societal message teaches us that feminine voices speak about caring and connection. Since these are labeled unimportant values, they are not voices on which to build dreams of greatness.

Parents must look inside themselves to see if they are holding on to old messages and values. If so, they are either giving their daughters a clear message that women can be only wives and mothers or an ambivalent message that says one thing — "You can do whatever you want" — while carrying with it an unspoken contradiction — "Don't make people not love you."

The freer the mother is to build and blend old and new more achievement-oriented values, the freer her daughter will feel. These values include the freedom to become a leader in a feminine way that espouses caretaking and connectedness, which as we said in Chapter 6 is the new leadership style of the '90s for men and women alike.

Today's mother needs to develop early unambivalent messages to her daughter encouraging her to create herself and to become her own person. These empowering messages need to include the ideas that girls are entitled to dream of greatness, that nurturance and aggression are both legitimate parts of our feminine and cohesive Competent Self, and that feeling forced

to choose one self over another is not necessary. As Congresswoman Pat Saiki put it, if children are given that kind of confidence "they can fly with it."

Empowering Messages to Give Your Daughters

These are five basic secrets of leadership and enabling messages
every girl should receive:

1. You are loved and special.
2. You can do anything you want.
3. You can take risks.
4. You can use and enjoy your Creative Aggression.
5. You are entitled to dream of greatness.

It is especially important that these empowering messages
be reiterated loudly and firmly during adolescence, when girls
feel such pressure to acquiesce to the boys around them in order
to maintain their relationships and loving connections to the
important people in their world. Hearing these messages then
is crucial if young girls are to hold on to their preadolescent
independence rather than letting it slip underground, as so
often happens, when society pressures them to be feminine and
desirable in old, prescribed ways.

It is also critical that daughters not be expected to be clones
of either parent. Instead, they should be free to choose elements
from each parent, as well as from others whom they respect. A
clone of a parent is not an autonomous individual. Ruth Messinger, Manhattan borough president, told how she recognized
the need to become her own person rather than a carbon copy
of her mother:

What was there for me to do given that my mother had done it all? She was a very strong and important influence on all of my growing up. I then went through a period where I tried to rede-fine how I was not my mother, having spent my entire adoles-cence assuming that I would be her. What more could you ask for than somebody who was a serious professional, an active community person, a wife with a solid marriage, a good cook, and a great mother? So how could you want to be anything except just duplicate that?

It was vital for Messinger to redefine herself in her own terms to choose her own DreamTracks.

Message 1: You Are Loved and Special

The bedrock of a solid sense of self is a feeling of being loved and special. As a parent, how can you convey this message to your child? The idea is not to assume that a child automatically knows it. Parents must actively and repeatedly convey the sense that their daughters are loved and special.

First, say it. Say it a lot. You can't say it too often. The words "I love you" are powerful, and too many people are shy and stingy with them.

Next, demonstrate it physically. Hugs and kisses are another commodity you can't oversupply. Asked why her grandmother kisses her so much, a two-year-old who replies "Because she loves me so-o-o much" already has that sense of being loved. She will carry that with her wherever she is. Physical affection conveys love.

Every child has some characteristic that is unique. She may be the oldest, youngest, happiest, sweetest, smartest, most ar-tistic, best soccer player, and so on. Find the superlative — and then verbalize it. No matter how many children you have, it's possible to find something special about each one.

In the interest of fairness, some parents make the mistake of trying to do exactly the same things with and for all their children. Unfortunately, that diminishes each child's sense of specialness because it conveys the message that all of the siblings are alike. A better plan is to allot equal individual time to each child but to use it differently, depending on the child's interests and talents. Catherine Baker Knoll was one of nine children, but her father took her to political events, giving her a unique place with him built on special-interest times together.

Some parents are afraid that if they or other family members are too complimentary the children will become insufferable brats. In our experience, that occurs only when parents, instead of discriminating between acceptable and unacceptable behavior, dote on everything the child does. That is *not* what we are advocating. Children should be corrected and taught the right way to behave. What you want to convey is the message "I don't accept that behavior. You may not hit other children" or "You may not take things that don't belong to you." But these and all similar examples should also incorporate the message "I love you even when you misbehave" to let the child know she is still loved and special.

Love should never be withdrawn as a punishment or held out as a reward for compliance. Parental love must be unconditional. This generates the internal feeling of being lovable, which in turn enables the child to take risks and to weather the consequences.

Keep in mind that the goal is to foster development of the internal applause that your daughter will eventually carry within her wherever she goes.

Message 2: You Can Do Anything You Want

This is an enabling message. It implies that a child can achieve what she sets her mind to, not that she will be given whatever she wishes for just because she is who she is. Congresswoman Jolene Unsoeld described it as making children "believe in themselves and their power to achieve."

It is crucial to treat sons and daughters alike and not to expect more from boys than girls. Congresswoman Nancy Johnson told us how she felt when her husband never asked their daughters to mow the lawn: "Well, I had been asked to mow the lawn. So I knew if they weren't asked to mow the lawn they'd never believe in themselves. I mean, that was a kind of way of building permanent inequality."

Daughters need to be encouraged to be persistent and to take some risks. On the playground, in school, and at home, they need to hear "You can do it." "Try it." "Don't give up." Mothers must mirror their daughters' pleasure in physical, academic, and interpersonal success: another secret in helping a daughter to build her sense of her Competent Self.

The story of three-year-old Barbara Gallagher walking down the street with her mother illustrates the point. Barbara ran to the top of a steep concrete incline. Her mother didn't tell her she couldn't run up the incline, so she did, without fear. She got to the top of the incline and then, hands on hips, queen of the hill, she shouted to her mother to look and see what she had accomplished. Her mother turned from the parking meter she was feeding in front of the bank and saw Barbara standing proudly at the top of the incline. "That's terrific, Barbara," she said. "That's my strong girl. You look great up there and so proud of yourself." Barbara looked delighted and indeed proud. She wasn't told "Get down, you can't do that!" The message from her mother was "You *can* do that. Of course you can do anything you want. Women can do these exciting things."

Barbara held out her arms and shouted, "You come up here, too, Mommy!" Mrs. Gallagher climbed up the incline, hands outstretched, smiling broadly. When she got to the top, mother and daughter clasped hands and walked into the bank. At that moment they were sharing a private and special moment of pride and joy together that legitimized as feminine Barbara's developing strength and risktaking capacities.

Daughters must be listened to so they learn that their views are important. We know there are times when it is difficult to pay attention to what children have to say. Their language may not be precise or their reasoning that of an adult. But the parent who listens, with interest, is telling the child that what she thinks about and does has value. And this encourages her to keep thinking and doing. As Congresswoman Pat Schroeder put it: "You have to make girls feel that their opinions count and that they're just as worthwhile as a brother or whoever they tend to compete with. It is important to give them a kind of solid sense that who they are and what they think about counts, from the littlest on."

Message 3: You Can Take Risks

The ability and willingness to take risks is vital to independent behavior. The timid nonrisktaker is locked into doing what she has been taught, in the same safe manner all the time. She is a conformist. The creative, original, and adventuresome risktaker, however, courageously moves out in the world on her own.

To be comfortable with risktaking behavior, little girls need to know that they will still be loved if they fail or if they do something different from what Mom and Dad do. That is why Message 1, that you are loved and special, is so critical.

As we have said before, by *risk* we don't mean dangerous

activity, although what is perceived as dangerous for girls is often different than for boys. Tree climbing and bicycle riding are examples — and climbing steep inclines as Barbara Gallagher did. We do mean taking chances to do new, innovative things where the outcome is not guaranteed. We mean stretching to do something difficult when success not only isn't assured but is doubtful at best. This is particularly true in politics, as Iowa's Elaine Baxter pointed out: "Unless you take a risk, you can't win."

Encouraging girls to participate in individual and team competitive sports gives them the opportunity to experience both winning and losing. They learn that losing at an activity does not result in a loss of self. No one likes to lose. It may hurt a great deal. But the experience of winning and losing teaches girls to savor the win and to pick themselves up and try again when they lose.

Louisiana Treasurer Mary Landrieu feels strongly about the lessons that competition can teach a young girl. When we asked for her suggestions about raising a daughter for a career in politics, she responded jokingly, "Tell her to play football!" On a more serious note she added, "Let her play football, soccer, baseball, and anything that would be in a competitive group." She regrets that even today girls do not participate in organized sports as much as boys do.

Perhaps if the media paid as much attention to women's sports as they do to men's, more girls would want to participate. The widespread community interest that girls' and women's basketball and soccer create in parts of the Midwest is a start. But until that kind of interest occurs throughout the country — and in more sports — girls will have to rely on parental encouragement and mothers' role modeling to learn those valuable lessons.

Colorado Treasurer Gail Schoettler described what she did with her daughter and two sons to encourage them to develop independence:

They started going to an outdoor camp when they were about eight for either four or five weeks in the summer. They learned how to take care of themselves and their group in the wilderness no matter what happened — rain, thunder, lightning, snow, whatever. They learned to be very independent, very resourceful, and very able to react in a crisis or an emergency to take care of somebody else or themselves. As a result they are all very independent, self-reliant, and self-confident.

It is sometimes difficult to let children go. Many parents feel the urge to shelter their children from frustration and failure. But by letting them go, letting them practice taking risks, parents enable their children to learn what the political women learned: to choose their risks well, to pick their battles.

New Mexico Secretary of State Rebecca Vigil-Giron gave this advice for parents:

> Let them go. If they want to be involved in a school activity, let them do it (a legitimate school activity, of course). If they want to be in the school play, encourage them. If they want to be in student government, let them do it. If they want to go on a field trip, let them do it if they are well supervised. Children need to learn about themselves by learning from other people. This brings out the best and the worst in them. Then hopefully they can get rid of the worst part by being exposed to other people.

Message 4: You Can Use and Enjoy Creative Aggression

Remember that when we speak of Creative Aggression, we are talking about behaving in a forthright, firm manner to achieve an objective. We are talking about setting a riskgoal and not being afraid to go after it.

To instill that quality in your daughter, you will first need to listen carefully to how she states her goals; you will need to share with her those secret, private moments when communication between mother and daughter is the most clear and the most effective. Then you will have created the emotionally open climate in which you can hear her goals expressed. They may be expressed in the form of wishes: "I wish I could play the clarinet" or "I wish I could go to camp next year." They may be envious comments about a peer or sibling: "Mark can ride a two-wheeler already" or "Caryn always gets good grades."

When you hear the riskgoal, encourage your daughter to go for it. Help her develop a strategy and plan to achieve it. Let her know that you think she can achieve it if she works hard and that it won't happen by magic if she sits passively by and watches others. Encourage her activity by your interest and support, such as those quiet looks between you as she, beaming with pride and pleasure, plays her clarinet in the school orchestra and you, mirroring her pride, beam back at her from the first row. These times become the secret and very special moments between parent and child that later transform into the rounds of internal applause so crucial to success and self-confidence.

From your daughter's babyhood, a good rule of thumb is not to do for her what she can do for herself. Thus, when she can feed or dress herself, clean her room, or do her own homework, she should be encouraged to do it herself.

In Chapter 2 we discussed developing a sense of power: "I am. I can. I will," in Althea Horner's words.[2] "I am" implies "I have an identity." "I can" suggests mastery. "I will" describes the intention to take certain action. It is the latter that is a key component of Creative Aggression. And you as a parent can influence its development by those secret moments when you applaud independent behavior and mirror your satisfaction to your daughter.

Girls of previous generations, like Congresswoman Claudine Schneider, were encouraged to marry well to be assured of a comfortable, secure life. "Marry a doctor" is one such message that is heard even today. "Marry well and be passive." We still hear it. That feeling hasn't gone away.

We believe that today's girls need to learn, from childhood, to depend on their own initiative and drive to provide for their future. They can rely on their Creative Aggression when they move out into the world. Mothers who are themselves strong and independent provide the role models that the women we interviewed described so eloquently.

By both your words and your behavior, be sure to send your daughter, overtly and through intimacy, those secret experiences that are the real glue of mother-daughter relationships, messages that it's not only acceptable but also desirable to rely on and enjoy her Creative Aggression to get her where she wants to be.

Message 5: You Are Entitled to Dream of Greatness

We have talked at length about how little girls don't dream of greatness. Society still doesn't encourage them to do so, and there still are too few role models of female leadership.

Therefore, parents have to help their little girls to dream. They can suggest some potential dreams of power and greatness. And certainly they can respond with pleasure and praise to a daughter's expression of her dreams. The little girl who wishes to be president of the United States, or CEO of a large corporation, or superintendent of schools should never be told, "Don't be silly," nor should her parents' unspoken messages convey that she is. Remember how Congresswoman Marge Roukema took back her wish to be president? We hope that upcoming generations need not do that.

"Bring your child up with expectations that are limitless," suggested Congresswoman Claudine Schneider. Note that we are talking about the *child's* expectations for herself, not the parents' expectations for her. The difference is that if the parental expectations are limitless, the child feels as if she can never measure up. Then, instead of developing a Competent Self, she will always feel inadequate.

Another facet of the message is that both the bride/mother and ambition/career DreamTracks are valuable and important. The career woman and mother who registers dismay when her daughter speaks of growing up to be a mommy is devaluing that portion of her daughter and herself. The housewife and mother who appears threatened by her daughter's ambitions may stifle the development of that dream in her child. Prior to the sexual revolution, women who chose careers opted out of marriage and family. Today's women work hard to have both.

Girls need to hear how women manage the two DreamTracks because there are a number of ways that work. Congresswoman Nita Lowey said, "When you discover who you are and what you want out of life, the trick is to prioritize, to set your goals and go for it." You can help your daughter think through her priorities. If she reads the autobiographies of women like Pat Schroeder, Ann Richards, Bella Abzug, and Geraldine Ferraro, she will see how these remarkable women managed their two DreamTracks.

As we have pointed out, most of the pre–sexual revolution women whom we studied put the traditional DreamTrack first, whereas younger women frequently hold that one in abeyance. Some women are on both DreamTracks simultaneously. This is the most difficult and demanding course to choose because of the amount of time and energy each track requires. Sequencing is easier. Share *your* secrets, both of connectedness and leadership. Talk to your daughter about how you are managing your DreamTracks and expose her to friends and relatives who have chosen different courses. Let her know that there is no one correct path.

As Ann Richards of Texas suggested:

> Allow your children to follow their hearts. I think it is a mistake for us to predetermine what we think our kids want to be or what *we* want them to be. I would encourage parents to give their children opportunities to do anything they want to do, to not be discouraging.

Three Special Messages for Political Careers

With those five messages as part of her being, your daughter will grow up with the ability to be a leader in whatever field she chooses. But what special messages might she need if she is to express her capacity for leadership in the realm of elective politics?

Most of the women we interviewed did not believe that children should be raised to be politicians per se. In fact, several of the women strongly opposed raising daughters for political careers. For example, New Jersey Congresswoman Marge Roukema said:

> Quite frankly, whether male or female — and this is not a daughter or son issue — I would hope that people would not raise them to be politicians. I hope they would raise their children to be something else, and if they found that they liked public service along the way they would apply those talents, whether they are in business or medicine or social work or education, to the political sphere. I find that you can apply your other skills to politics rather quickly. I think the people who consider themselves professional politicians are very myopic. They're more intent on being part of the party apparatus than they are in public service and being legislators.
>
> Therefore — I hope I'm not shocking you — I really wouldn't ever raise a child or encourage a grandchild to be a politician. I'd want them to know themselves, get a broad education, develop, and become adept in some other field and apply that to politics, to the field of public service.

California Congresswoman Barbara Boxer would concur:

> I think anyone who goes into politics or life wanting power is not a good person. Power comes to you if your life works out that way. You don't go into something because you want power. I think if you do, you're not going about your life right. I never said word one to my children about power. I talked to them about caring, about true friendship, about leadership, about following it through, about goals, and then I lived my life. My husband and I have lived those values.

Notice that neither Roukema nor Boxer suggested pushing power messages to instill ambition and dreams of greatness in their children. With those precautions in mind, let's consider several messages that enhance the likelihood of a daughter choosing a political career at some time in her life:

1. Political behavior is a natural part of life.
2. Give something back to society.
3. Any career can lead to politics.

Political Message 1: Political Behavior Is a Natural Part of Life

Girls who grow up in families where politics is discussed, where public service is looked on as valuable, and where voting is considered an essential right and responsibility are likely to consider politics interesting and important.

Take your daughter along to the polls. Let her play with the model voting machine and enter the voting booth with you if that is permitted in your state. When you vote in primaries as well as general elections, in local as well as national elections, you are conveying a message about your positive attitude toward the election process. The more involved you become, as a member or worker for a political party or particular candidate, the more you are modeling political behavior for your daughter. Even little children can do some of the tasks in a campaign. El Paso Mayor Suzie Azar told us that her children have been involved in campaigns since they were five or six years old.

Your involvement in community organizations that hold elections and in boards that make decisions gives your daughter an opportunity to learn about political behavior from a close vantage point. It is important that you talk to her about what you're doing and take her with you when possible.

Even TV viewing, so often condemned, can be a learning activity if the family watches the news and other programs that deal with political issues. A family discussion of what you've seen says that politics is important.

Finally, when your daughters talk about their school politics, support their involvement in leadership and school government. Firsthand experience is a wonderful teacher. Ann Richards told us of going to Girls State and Girls Nation when she was in high school.

> Both projects set up a mock government in which you run for office and in some sense perform in office during the limited time that you are there. I remember hearing the men who spoke to us, the attorney general and the governor, and thinking what a terribly exciting and wonderful life that must be. So if there were any seeds at all for my political career, I think that those are probably the ones.

Political Message 2: Give Something Back to Society

We frequently forget that a career in politics is a career in public service. It is a career devoted to the welfare of others, to making life better for the community, the state, the country. It may appear glamorous, but as we learned from our interviewees, it is demanding and time-consuming and leaves little time for other interests and relationships. Therefore, to choose it as a career, a woman has to believe in the concept of giving something back to society.

For your daughter to hear this message, she will need to be taught to be unselfish and to share with others. If you have more than one child, that part of the message is conveyed naturally in day-to-day living. If your daughter is an only child, she will need to learn about sharing and unselfishness with her peers, and you will need to remind her.

You will also need to be careful not to overindulge your daughter. She doesn't need everything she asks for, every toy she sees on TV. When the "no" is not as a punishment but as a way of conveying "You have enough already," she learns to be satisfied with what she has rather than developing an insatiable appetite. Further, if charitable activity begins very early, the message of sharing becomes clear. Giving some Halloween candy to children in hospitals or some toys to poor families at Christmas is a way to help children live the message.

And you will need to tell your daughter, as she gets older, that being in government is a way to share her life and energies with others. Ruth Messinger learned early about social service and then translated that into politics:

> The entire orientation of my original family is around social service. It's obviously not the entire orientation, but that is the dominant message. You're supposed to be doing something for people who are less well off. You're supposed to be giving something back. And that is overwhelmingly true about my grandparents, my parents, myself, and my sister. I think it was often used to define our family even against others in the extended family. It was a very strong impulse. And that's the background as opposed to politics.

Messinger was involved in social action from adolescence, gradually beginning to lobby people whom she thought should be able to make changes. Then, she decided, she could be one of those people.

Political Message 3: Any Career Can Lead to Politics

As we talked about in Chapter 6, you can enter politics from any previous career. So as your daughter gets older and starts making her career plans, point out to her that the women in politics came from a variety of career paths.

The important message is that if there is something going on in society that really is important to you, think about a political career as a way to make a difference with that issue. It is lawmakers who determine what will be done about abortion, the environment, family leave, and issues we can't even anticipate. The young women who have received the five basic messages contained in the secrets of leadership will have the Leadership Equation available to them and will, with this additional message, consider the political option as a way to make a difference.

A Word to Fathers

We spoke in Chapter 4 about nontraditional fathers, those who facilitate the development of daughters who feel entitled to develop their leadership potential. Two important facets of your behavior will enhance that probability: your behavior toward your wife and your behavior toward your daughter.

The women in our study told us that their fathers treated their mothers as equals. If you respect your wife's ideas and input, beginning when your daughter is young, then your daughter will learn that women are valued for more than just their traditional nuturant behavior. If you treat your wife as subservient to you (and she accepts that), then your daughter will learn that it is appropriate for women to defer to men, and perhaps to other women as well.

The way you behave toward your daughter will obviously have a major impact on her development. If you are too protective or much more responsive to her passive than to her independent behavior, you will be perpetuating the message that males love only dependent females and that being creatively aggressive will put her at risk for ever getting married and having a family.

Spend some secret moments together, some private time without the other children along, doing things with your daughter, really interacting with her. You can even play ball with her. Take her to your workplace. Expose her to the same things to which you expose her brother. Be like Catherine Baker Knoll's dad, who said, "Remember, all of you girls are just as good as every boy at this table You can do anything you want."

The more that you yourself blur the line between "woman's work" and "man's work," the more you will be showing your daughter that either sex can do almost everything. You should be involved in child care, for instance, and not just refer to it as "babysitting." The sitter substitutes for the parents. You aren't a substitute. You are very much a parent, too.

Not only do daughters gain when their fathers are more involved with them, but the fathers reap a reward themselves, in the relationship that develops. Shared experiences lead to a sense of loving connectedness and pride that comes with such good and intimate relationships.

Endthought

Parenting is a difficult task. No one is trained for it. Fortunately, you're not expected to be perfect at it. But in the presence of love, children can tolerate their parents' mistakes and still grow up to be strong, psychologically healthy people. Daughters who have received the secrets of leadership and the empowering messages that flow from them that we've spoken of here will have the bonus of feeling comfortable with the competent, aggressive, powerful parts of themselves. As more women are raised this way, we can look forward to seeing more and more women as leaders in all areas of life, including politics, bringing women's unique perspective to bear on our world.

――――――――――― PROFILE ―――――――――――

Olympia Snowe
Determining Her Own Life

As all too many of us know, not everyone has the good fortune to have a life that runs smoothly. Does that mean that there is no chance for you to develop your Leadership Equation and achieve your dream? Not at all. Maine Congresswoman and First Lady Olympia Snowe turned adversity and hardship into stunning success, as her life story so aptly demonstrates.

It is important to hear the right kinds of general and political messages during childhood and adolescence, but what happens if those messages are interrupted while the girl is very young? Can she still develop enough Creative Aggression, Competent Self, and WomanPower to help her succeed as a leader?

We believe she can *if* she takes in enough messages to generate the constant internal applause that keeps her on the leadership track. The most extraordinary example of this capacity among the women we interviewed is Congresswoman Olympia Snowe, who was elected to her seventh term in Congress in 1990. She represents Maine's second congressional district, geographically the largest congressional district east of the Mississippi River.

Snowe spent her early childhood in Augusta, the state capital, where her Greek-American parents, George and Georgia Bouchles, operated a restaurant. She was only eight years old when her mother, who had been ill for a long time, died of breast cancer. The following year her father, who was considerably older than her mother, died from heart disease.

Despite their early deaths, her parents gave her a firm foundation on which to build her life. Snowe remembers that as long as her mother was alive she, her older brother, and her parents were always close. She felt loved very much by both parents.

From her first days in politics Congresswoman Snowe established an enviable record of public service, of helping others. As a young girl she had demonstrated an unusual concern for other people, which developed as a result of her parents' illnesses. For example, in a letter to a friend, who later passed it on to Congresswoman Snowe, Mrs. Bouchles told what happened on the day when she was on her way to the hospital. Young Olympia was crying as the two stood together in the pouring rain. Then the shy, serious girl looked up and said reassuringly, "Don't worry, Mom. I'll take care of you."

Another time when her mother was in the hospital, Snowe decided to help with the wash:

> I took all of the clothes we had to wash and threw them in the bathtub, filled it up with soap, washed them all, and then hung them outside. I don't think my father was wild about the idea when he came home because I'm sure I never got the soap out.

Snowe recalled trying to help her father and always worrying about him. She told us that she will always remember the day when she was getting ready to go on an outing with some neighbors. But after watching her father mop the floor she got so worried she went next door and told her friends, "I can't go because I don't think my father's feeling well."

Not only did Olympia care for her parents, but from a young age she also worried about others. One day, at about age three or four, she was sitting with a friend on some concrete culverts in a vacant lot next to her father's restaurant. She remembers holding on to her own pocketbook as well as her friend's little red pocketbook and rolling down the culverts. "Well, there were bees there and I got stung top to bottom. I remember dropping the pocketbook, screaming, and running to my father's restaurant. He stripped me down in front of the restaurant, made mud, and plastered me with it. The whole time I worried because I had left my friend's red pocketbook behind. I was horrified since it was *her* pocketbook." Even when Snowe was suffering, she thought of somebody else.

When Snowe's mother died, her father, overwhelmed by having two children to raise, a job to do, and poor health, sent her off to St. Basil's Academy, a Greek Orthodox boarding school in Garrison, New York. Snowe lived at St. Basil's during the school year but came home on vacations to be with her father and brother. At first her father hired a couple to drive her to St. Basil's but at about age eleven she began taking the train back and forth by herself. For her this meant a long ride from Maine to Grand Central Station in New York City and then a change of trains at Grand Central to reach Garrison.

After her father's death Snowe continued to live at St. Basil's during the school year, and her brother lived with their aunt and uncle. But the aunt and uncle, who had five children of their own, could not take in both Snowe and her brother. So when she came back to Maine for the first Christmas after her father's death, her brother was sent off to live with one of their father's grown children from a previous marriage.

Snowe vividly remembers what happened the day she came home on holiday:

> I can remember exactly where my brother was standing and where I was standing when I came in and he was leaving. It is etched in my mind forever. I'll never forget the look on his face as he was leaving.

When we asked how she handled this painful living arrangement, she told us:

> I had the support of my aunt and uncle and five cousins. Obviously they were struggling to make do. My uncle was a barber

and my aunt worked in a textile mill. But I had the support of people I knew and loved. And I was comfortable when I was away at school. I had my niche.

Her niche was being a leader at St. Basil's, where she headed her dormitory and did well in her studies. At thirteen one of her earliest political activities was running Republicans for Nixon at St. Basil's, although she said she wished John Kennedy had been a Republican "because he was so young and handsome and charismatic. I couldn't believe that he was a Democrat." Thanks to her efforts, Nixon won the straw poll at St. Basil's.

Congresswoman Snowe's early interest in politics may be related to what she observed in her father's restaurant, just down the road from the state legislature. Political figures often ate there. Her mother also had strong associations with people in state government. Perhaps Olympia Snowe's political activity is a way to stay connected to her parents.

Politics is consistent with her dream as a young girl that she would do something in the realm of public service. "I never really thought about actual public office," she told us. "I don't think in my generation girls ever talked about running for office even though U.S. Senator Margaret Chase Smith was from Maine."

With both parents gone, Snowe knew she needed to develop a sense of independence to survive. When we asked how she took risks as a child, she told us this story:

I was with a younger girl in Grand Central one day, going home for the Christmas holidays, when a policeman stopped me. He thought I was running away from school. I told him that I was taking a train home — I even gave him the time of the train — and explained that I was putting the other girl on the train to Chicago. The policeman couldn't believe it. "Well, you have to come with me," he said. "You better not make me miss my train for home," I replied. He called my home and the school, and they

told him everything was fine, so off he went. He was amazed. I
think I developed a great deal of independence at that point. So I
guess in that way I was a risktaker. It didn't bother me.

About the same time, she developed an interest in her sur-
roundings as a way of dealing with being out in the world on
her own. "I wasn't going to let my environment get me down
because things were difficult," she said. "In spite of my circumstances I was committed to the idea that I would be able to
make something of myself, that I would do something worthwhile — it would just be a matter of time."

She attended high school in Auburn, Maine, and remembers
being very unhappy then. Fresh from the all-girl environment
at St. Basil's, she felt like an outsider among students who had
gone all through school together. She didn't do as well academ-
ically as she had at St. Basil's because of her difficulty in adjusting: "I couldn't concentrate, and it affected my self-esteem. But
I kept telling myself it would be all right. I was a survivor, so I
worked through it." Notice that in the absence of parents,
young Olympia learned to soothe herself and to give herself
positive messages.

In comparison to high school, going away to the University
of Maine in Orono seemed easy and familiar. Olympia majored
in political science and loved it. Shortly after graduation she
married Peter Snowe, who was active in Republican politics,
and he soon got her involved in the party. Then, because of her
strong interest in politics, he talked her into running for a
vacant seat on the local board of voter registration, which she
won. It was her first political office.

Snowe was proud of her husband, who had been elected to
the Maine house of representatives, but she also liked having
her own identity. She demonstrated this one day at a board of
voter registration meeting. The woman seated next to her said,
"Olympia, tell them who your husband is." Snowe replied,
"That's my husband. That's not me."

In 1973, four months into his first term in the state legislature, Peter Snowe was killed in a car accident. Congresswoman Snowe tells how she dealt with his death and how that has affected her relationships with people:

> Taking care of everybody was my way of getting it out and dealing with it, but most other people would rather not talk about it. I'm more of an expressive person. That's how I handled death in my life. When my first husband died, I knew exactly what I had to do to overcome this enormous hurdle. You're never sure when you're faced with that kind of calamity whether or not you're going to survive.

Snowe was elected to her husband's unexpired term in the legislature in 1973 and was reelected for a full two-year term in 1974. In 1976 she moved up to the Maine senate, where she was particularly known for her interest in health care issues.

In 1978, at the age of thirty-one, Olympia Snowe was elected to the U.S. Congress. She had the double distinction of being both the first Greek-American woman and the youngest Republican woman elected to the U.S. House of Representatives. She has served on a variety of committees in the House, including the Congressional Caucus on Women's Issues, which she and Pat Schroeder cochair.

In 1989, she married John McKernan, Jr., governor of Maine, whom she met years ago when they were both serving in Maine's house of representatives. Now Snowe is both a congresswoman and First Lady, and her husband is the first governor ever to have married a member of Congress.

The hardships she has endured have shaped her life and character. Snowe believes that one outgrowth from her past is her sensitivity. "That's what helps me do my job because I really can identify with other people's hardships." She prefers to negotiate rather than argue, although what she ultimately does depends on how strongly she feels about an issue.

When she announced her candidacy for reelection in 1990

she reiterated her wish to do things for others: "Out of my experiences in life has grown a conviction that no pursuit is as valuable, or worthier, than the simple idea of helping others — of enabling individuals to improve their lives, to soften the hardest days and brighten the darkest."

Congresswoman Olympia Snowe has turned her adversities into her strength. She talks openly about her problems and knows that expressing them is a way of dealing with them. She says she didn't want to end up being a bitter person or an angry person or a chip-on-the-shoulder person. As she puts it, "I have determined my own life."

9

If Your Parents Weren't Perfect,
or Even Good Enough . . .
Messages to Give to Yourself

I have determined my own life.
— Olympia Snowe, Maine Congresswoman, Maine First
Lady

What in the early experiences of Olympia Snowe and the other women we studied enabled them to put the pieces together so successfully? What is the genesis of a woman's power? What allows one woman to feel entitled to dream of greatness, to steer her life on a leadership course, while another woman stays on the traditional road or the followers' path? What are the secrets of women's leadership? These are the questions we have answered in this book. The answers have led us to develop a psychology of women's leadership so that you can use it to develop and integrate power and leadership into your Competent Self.

At a lecture in New York, congresswoman, vice presidential, and 1992 senatorial candidate Geraldine Ferraro spoke of women and politics. Ferraro, who redefined the possibilities for American women in politics, who helped us rediscover what has always been there — that politics and political behavior are feminine as well as masculine — said, "Some leaders are born women."[1] She's right. That means 52 percent of the American population are potential leaders. Whether or not we live out that potential depends on what hand we are dealt in life, what messages we are given by parents and grandparents, extended family, teachers, mentors, and others who have been meaningful in our lives, what secrets they share with us. Whether we fall short of or reach our potential also depends on how we respond to those messages, what we do with them, and what choices we make.

Becoming a leader can mean many things: we can be a leader of ourselves by practicing ongoing self-definition, a leader of our families, a leader of causes, and a leader of others. Today, women have many opportunities to become, as we said in Chapter 6, "a leader of leaders," a transformational, interactive, and nurturant leader in the leadership style of the 1990s that is so well suited to women. The choice is determined by our dreams. Our dreams can take us in one direction or another, toward either the bride/mother DreamTrack or the ambition/career DreamTrack. Some of us do it all, though not usually at once.

It must have been both heartening and discouraging for you to learn that many of the early experiences of the women we interviewed revolved around parents who were supportive, in general, of their growing daughters' political behavior and the development of their Creative Aggression and WomanPower. It may have seemed to you that many of our women had the perfect parents. Certainly, Barbara Gallagher, whom we created, was raised by "Brady Bunch" ideal parents. We hope we made it clear that the real women whom we interviewed had parents who were not perfect. However, they were good enough so that their daughters had the strength to struggle with the pain of the mixed messages they received as well as the disappointments, loss of parents, and other less than optimal early experiences and to triumph over them.

But what if your parents, like those of Marjorie Lockwood, the unsuccessful political woman we created, were not good enough? Marjorie, you may recall, had a somewhat self-centered, traditional, uninvolved father who wanted her to be a superstar but did not show her the way and a shy, frightened mother who was neither a good role model nor a mirror of her husband's autonomy. Mrs. Lockwood was unable to foster a sense of Creative Aggression and WomanPower in Marjorie since she was so frightened of her own aggression. The Lockwoods were not evil and malicious. They simply did not have what it takes to be good enough parents, and Marjorie suffered the consequences.

And what if your parents were even less than adequate, perhaps neglectful, abusive, or alcoholic? Does that mean that you cannot build your own Leadership Equation? Not at all. You can uncover and reclaim those crucial missing elements in yourself, such as aggression and risktaking, which, as threats to traditional feminine desirability and acceptability, were stuffed into an emotional closet long ago. Like plants in the dark, they lagged far behind your other growth and maturation, thus remaining small, ineffective, and minimally useful to you. They may even have made life difficult for you by causing anxiety or depression every time they and their offshoots — your hidden sense of inadequacy and helplessness — were threatened with exposure.

What did Olympia Snowe do differently from Marjorie Lockwood? What messages did Snowe give to herself to fill in her Leadership Equation and Competent Self, to generate those constant rounds of internal applause? What suggestions do Olympia Snowe, Ann Richards, Pat Schroeder, Nancy Johnson — the women whose profiles appear in this book — or the other women we interviewed have to help you put the pieces together for yourself? We've sifted through their ideas and added some of our own exercises and experiments for you to try if your parents weren't good enough to help you fill in your Leadership Equation. These exercises and experiments will also help you strengthen your Competent Self and Creative Aggression and find your own secrets of leadership and power.

We've put the answers in the form of messages to give to yourself, and we've framed our suggestions, exercises, and experiments by the five messages that we discovered are the *secrets of leadership* of the political leaders in this book. These five messages represent the common denominators among the women leaders we studied. They are the critical elements in the structure of these women's Leadership Equation.

We recognize that it is harder to develop a skill or a strength as an adult that ordinarily should have unfolded in childhood. Just think of learning languages as an example. When language is developing in toddlers, they can learn several at a time, quickly and easily, but adult immigrants struggle valiantly to learn the single language of their newly adopted country. Our recognition of how difficult it is to develop emotionally and psychologically as an adult is one of the reasons that we suggest that you think of your efforts to change as experiments; by definition, an experiment cannot fail. It either works or it doesn't.

The messages we'll discuss are the same as those we suggested you give to your daughters because they provide the basic elements of your personal Leadership Equation. To repeat, those messages are the following:

1. You are loved and special.
2. You can do anything you want to do.
3. You are entitled to dream of greatness.
4. You can use and enjoy your Creative Aggression.
5. You can be courageous and take risks.

Message 1:
You Are Loved and Special

At this point we imagine that you are staring incredulously at the page and saying, "Who are you kidding? If I didn't get it then, there sure ain't no way to get it now." Humor us! Suspend your disbelief for just a moment, give us a break, and read on.

Getting it now takes feeling loved and special over and over and over again.

Exercises to Feel Loved

Help yourself to know you're loved every day. You can't hug and kiss yourself as you would your daughter, but you can give yourself hug-and-kiss equivalents by doing something that makes you feel good, anything from a bubble bath to signing up for a health spa or talking to a friend who is a good listener.

These are "just because you're you" rewards — unconditional love equivalents. Self-esteem begins in infancy with enjoying the sensual pleasures of your body as your mother loves and cares for you and glows with pleasure at how you look, feel, and respond to her caretaking. After a while these experiences become condensed memories and internal "comfort zones." So one way to call on these condensed memories and to tap into and use these early, soothing comfort zones and bolster your self-esteem is by reconnecting to and pampering your body and yourself.

Exercises to Feel Special

Help yourself to know you're special. Remember that Suzie
Azar's mother thought that her daughter was the funniest and
smartest child in the family and that that identity of being the
child with the "mostest" helped Azar to feel very special as
well as very loved. You need to become aware of *your* specialness and reaffirm it very, very often. Find your smartest, funniest, "best-est" qualities. Most of us are sufficiently subject to
and sensitive to lots of criticism that comes our way. Begin to
rebalance the scale on the side of good feelings and enhancing
self-esteem by using self-affirmations to make yourself aware
of the "best-est" characteristics about yourself. You need to
hear and "see" them over and over and over again, until you
believe them — for real.

There are several ways to make this happen. Practice putting
affirmations into your life.[2] Find a time in the day when you
can relax for fifteen to thirty minutes. Find a comfortable chair,
lounge, or bed, and lie back and close your eyes. Visualize
yourself in the following situations:

- Satisfactorily completing a project or closing a deal on which
  you've been working hard
- Winning in a sport or other game you play
- Successfully starting a new friendship or love relationship
- Relaxing on a well-deserved vacation you've always wanted
  to take
- Being articulate and informed at a gathering of people on a
  subject that has always intimidated you — the economy, the
  stock market, politics

Linger on each visualization for two or three minutes. Savor
it. Try to enjoy your feelings of satisfaction. When you are
comfortable with the visualizations, say them to yourself in

front of the mirror, and try to enjoy how you look as you say them. Say the following affirmations in front of your mirror in these ways: (1) as they are written; (2) changing *I* to *you* and imagining someone close to you saying these things to you lovingly, supportively; (3) changing *I* to *you* and imagining someone you admire a great deal saying these things encouragingly to you.

Affirmations

I _____name_____ know that I am a good _____career/job/profession_____ . I feel especially good about _____ , and I was especially proud of

_____ .

I _____ know that I am a good _____wife/husband/etc._____ . I feel especially good when _____

_____ .

I _____ know that I am a good _____mother/father/daughter/son/etc._____ . I feel especially good when _____ .

I _____ know that I am a creative person. I feel especially creative when _____

_____ .

I appreciate my own creativity, talents, and capabilities.

Experiment

Enroll in a course or seminar you've been wanting to take. Try one that is low risk to you so that you will feel more able to participate and to brag. In addition to learning new information, use it as a laboratory to sharpen your self-observation skills.

See if your feelings about yourself change between the beginning and the end of the class. Do you feel others in the class mirror the good feelings about yourself that you hear and see coming back from your own mirror? Do your levels of activity, spontaneity, comfort, and participation increase over time? This is also your chance to see how much you can enjoy the spotlight that is a part of everyday leadership and life, from talking to clients and colleagues to participating in committee meetings, to teaching, to making presentations at seminars, to negotiating a deal.

Message 2:
You Can Do Anything You Want to Do

Once you are convinced, relatively speaking, that you are loved and special, it is, as you may recall from Chapter 5, a hop, skip, and a jump to connecting to your feelings of effectiveness and competence and a sense that you can do anything you want to do. With the preceding exercises, you have already begun to bolster your self-esteem by giving yourself "just because you're you" unconditional love messages and rewards. You are also working on continually reinforcing how you see yourself as special.

Suggestions

Now that you have identified your own ways of getting in touch with feeling loved and special, it is important to figure out which people of those around you feel that way about you. Then you can set up an interactive feedback system by which they and you know that each of you needs to feel heard and understood, loved and cared for.

Not only will this help you reinforce feeling loved and special, but setting up a feedback network will help you feel effective and in control of your environment in the most positive way. It's not that you will never hear criticism or feel hurt. But by virtue of your wise choices, your carefully chosen network will reinforce your feelings that you have had good judgment, and your self-trust and confidence will increase. The empathic connection between you and your network will help you feel good about the positive things you hear about yourself and buffer you against the critical. Choosing carefully, you will also change the balance of more good, less critical in your favor. You will "feel your specialness"; your autonomous, independent, and political behavior; your Competent Self; your Woman-Power; and your Creative Aggression mirrored and endorsed by those who count. Don't worry. This network will not serve as a destructive hideaway from the world. Instead, as with the single-sex educational experiences of many of the women we interviewed, your network will provide a protective environment in which you can feel safer, experiment, and take risks. This will help you to feel that you can do whatever you want to do.

In time you will have created a situation that allows you to hear ongoing rounds of internal applause. The dialogue that accompanies this applause is reaffirming. It says, "I am loved and appreciated. I am good. I am worthwhile. I like myself. I am effective. I am competent. If they think I am capable, then I am. I can do anything I want to do." Lest you think you are being defined by another, remember that you made it all happen in the first place. And, after all, children who have learned to do whatever they want learned it from other people's reactions to them.

Congresswoman Connie Morella of Maryland said that her earliest memory is of being in a kindergarten play about the wedding of Jack and Jill. "They had a little bride and groom and a wedding party, and I sang the song to bring Jack and Jill and the other characters together. I have no singing voice, but it didn't matter. I remember the teacher would say, 'Oh, listen to Constance now. She's telling you to come forward.' I must have been a ham at the time . . . 'Listen to Constance' . . . a touch of the extrovert even then."

Although she couldn't sing very well, Morella's extroversion, hamminess, authority, and sense of leadership led her teacher to tell the other children to "listen to Constance." How important and powerful she must have felt. How proud and excited. Her teacher had mirrored and endorsed her and given her permission to enjoy her leadership capabilities. Morella is forever grateful to the admirable and enviable role model who taught her that envy fosters dreams, visions, and ambition and who helped her "know" she could do whatever she wanted to do.

Exercise

To help yourself learn that you can do whatever you want, think of a subject that has always interested you — and perhaps one that is usually labeled a man's topic — the economy, the space program, the stock market, politics. Educate yourself about the subject. Visualize yourself holding forth to a small group of friends or colleagues, at least half of whom are from your network. Imagine yourself being informative, articulate, and witty. If the visualization breaks down for any reason, back up and start again.

Try to emulate someone whose conversational style you admire. Choose only the aspects of her (or his) personality that you can reasonably approximate. Start with those and add to them gradually. Don't make the goal impossible to reach. Try your visualization again, pared down to the doable. Don't try to be anxiety- or resistance-free; it's impossible to do something new without experiencing these feelings. Just breathe deeply a few times and try to keep these feelings and blocks to change down to a manageable roar. It's also impossible to do something new smoothly and perfectly. Expect imperfect and even sloppy performances at first. They never look as bad as you feel they do.

Experiment

Pick a real gathering that is very low-risk to start. Now is your chance. Using the new information you've learned about your subject, chime in. Record in a simple journal your feelings about your participation in the conversation. Record what others say and what you think they're thinking about you. In the future, as you get more practiced, see if your feelings and thoughts about what others think about you match what they actually say. Remember, some anxiety and resistance is natural. Forget about smooth. As most people who enter the New York marathon tell themselves, just try to stay in the race — clumsy, anxious, sweaty palms, and all — and you will have won. This is an experiment you will need to do over and over again. Repetition and success wear resistance down. Good luck!

Message 3:
You Are Entitled to Dream of Greatness

As you may recall from Chapter 5, we learned that women by and large do not share men's sense of positive entitlement to dream in early adulthood of doing great things. We also learned that men use their dreams as visions on which to build their futures. As we analyzed the data from the women we studied, we realized that, even in today's world, women do dream as young girls and then suppress those dreams in an effort to remain desirable and acceptable. Unlike men, women have two DreamTracks, the bride/mother DreamTrack and the ambition/career DreamTrack, which can include "being in the spotlight" dreams of eminence and greatness while making major contributions to society. Women can go in one direction or the other, or both, but usually not both at once. On the way from bride/mother to ambition/career, women often get lost. Because sequencing DreamTracks is easier than trying to have it all at once, sequencing management is an important skill to learn.

As girls, we unfortunately learn that the nurturant base of the bride/mother DreamTrack is not the stuff of greatness. We also learn that the world we hear about from those DreamVoices, the importance and value of feminine caretaking and connectedness, is not the kind of world valued by our society. So we stifle our DreamVoices. Why bother to build dreams on the unimportant? Other research supports our findings. Remember Carol Gilligan's girls who went underground with their dreams and forthrightness at age eleven and the girls in the AAUW study who did not feel "smart enough" or "good enough" to have and to try to achieve great career dreams?

Let's add to the possible explanations for girls' dreams going underground with a word about envy. Envy, like women's aggression, has had a bad rap for a long time as a negative and even evil feeling. Not so! It is a DreamVoice. How can we dream if we don't look out into the world and identify what we find enviable and say, "I want that" or "I want to be that" or "Now I know what I want." Envy precedes visions and points to goals to shoot for and actions to get you there, where none existed before. The AAUW study, which overturns the popular notion that an adolescent's peers are the most important influences in his or her life, informs us that adult family members and educators are the chief influences. As the adult world affirms the "greater value" of what more boys can do (such as math and science), we are mirroring boys' greater self-esteem and pleasure in themselves and their achievements. Conversely, by devaluing girls' more nurturant talents, we withdraw the mirror, and girls lose confidence in themselves and what they can do.

So look around you for women you want to be like in politics, in corporate leadership, at your job, in your community. Make them into your multiple role models and mentors, near and far. Take from each person those attributes and characteristics you admire. Play with them for yourself, discarding those that don't work and keeping those that do, in part or in whole. Don't worry, you're looking for building blocks, not clones. Let yourself imagine yourself being like them. Although it is often uncomfortable and even painful, honor your envy, embrace it, use it to grow.

As adults, we can make use of the visualizations we have been practicing and the images of women we admire to help give our dreams and visions some shape and substance. Suzie Azar, mayor of El Paso, has what she calls "blue feather" dreams. She came up with the blue feather idea after reading Richard Bach's *Illusions: the Adventures of a Reluctant Messiah:*

> I always visualize myself in whatever activity or role I want to try on. I always have to think it, and therefore have the confidence that "Yes, of course you can be that." My first blue feather dream was to become a private pilot, which was very expensive for me. I was working and had two children, and I paid one hundred dollars or more a week for flying lessons. That is not lunch money. That is an extraordinarily crazy amount to spend on just a sport. But in order to do it I had to come up with the

money and the stamina and the time and the perseverance. But I visualized it, that I was going to be a private pilot. The first private pilot in my whole family.

And the first woman mayor. I could see the headlines. I wanted for four years to be on the front page of the *El Paso Times* above the fold. I had made it below the fold in black and white twice, once for almost being arrested by a slumlord and calling the police and the other time for winning my second election. But getting to be mayor was part of that, seeing myself on top of the fold, making the headline. So visualization and having a dream are essential. As you start any kind of project, see it through to the end, visualize it, and then all the ideas rush into your brain of how you will make that dream happen. Then, if I can just get everything done that I think of, it works.

I did the same thing with swimming. I didn't learn to swim until I was ten, which was late for Michiganders, who usually learn by five or six. Swimming became a big deal to me. I visualized what I was going to do, not to only be able to stay in the deep end, but to be able to swim well. And not only did I become a good swimmer, I joined a swim club and got involved in synchronized and competitive swimming.

Suggestion

Learn from Suzie Azar. Make a list of past and present dreams, no matter how fantastic. Choose a dream, a vision of something you want to do, from your list. Keep the first one simple and doable. If you can't think of a dream, use your network — old, close friends will have heard the DreamVoices you've expressed over the years although you haven't heard them yourself.

Do some research. Jot down in your journal some of the steps it will take to give your dream some shape and substance. For example, if your dream is to be a local tournament tennis player, your list should start out with getting into shape by walking, biking (stationary or for real), going to a gym, or doing an exercise videotape at home. Tennis lessons help a lot. You can often find inexpensive but good ones available at local parks. It's also a great place to meet partners and new people. Or you can go the Cadillac route and take private lessons, or anything in between. If you don't have partners to play with, don't worry; your teacher will find you some at your level. She or he will also put together tournaments where you can compete with people at your level. As you can see, success at this dream of greatness is almost guaranteed.

Experiment

Choose a dream of your own to put into action. Look over the list of dreams you've created for yourself. Ask yourself which feels most achievable and satisfying. Start with a small dream. Set out a plan to achieve it, following the step-by-step pattern that we showed you in the tennis example. Take one step at a time, and praise yourself as you accomplish each one. The internal applause will help you move closer to your dream. And when you've achieved a small dream, you will know that it is all right to dream of greater things. Your dreams will motivate and energize you.

The women we interviewed began to dream of politics. Your dreams of greatness will be suited to you and will motivate and energize you. As Victor Hugo said, "There is nothing like dream to create the future."

Message 4:
You Can Use and Enjoy Your Creative Aggression

At a Los Angeles fundraiser for her 1992 reelection bid, Barbara Mikulski, knowing she had been targeted for defeat by the Republican party, said, "I love being a senator. Every morning I wake up and say, 'What can I do to make this country a better place to live?'" This is her way of expressing the Creative Aggression and WomanPower she uses so effectively every day.

Creative Aggression is defined in Chapter 1 as taking initiative; leading others; speaking out and expressing autonomous opinions; setting goals and making efforts and plans that carry them out; insisting on your rights; and defending yourself when challenged.

It is impossible to use and enjoy your Creative Aggression if you do not experience desire and ambition. Including yourself and your desire and ambition in the Leadership Equation, as a legitimate part of femininity, is what makes the equation work. If you define femininity in the traditional way as "selfless," you are in a bind. Then you cannot include yourself and self-care in the equation. You cannot then hear your DreamVoices and "know" what you want and need. Unfortunately, depression and a sense of alienation often follow such oppressive decisions. To make the point even more strongly, we offer this Victorian poem, which tells us the story of the "selfless" traditional woman:

> There was a young man loved a maid.
> Who taunted him "Are you afraid,"
> She asked, "to bring me today
> Your mother's head on a tray?"

He went and slew his mother dead,
Tore from her breast her heart so red,
Then towards his lady love he raced,
But tripped and fell in all his haste.

As the heart rolled on the ground
It gave forth a plaintive sound.
And it spoke in accents mild
"Did you hurt yourself, my child?"

— "The Severed Heart," J. Echergray[3]

It is also impossible to use your Creative Aggression if you are uncomfortable with your own anger. Therefore, it is critical that you convert anger into Creative Aggression. Difficulty in handling anger is a nearly universal problem. It is particularly hard for women, who even today are socialized to be more passive and submissive than men. Women do not learn to manage their anger, to hold on to their sense of self when angry, and to define clear messages about what they really want.

In addition, women are not always prepared to handle the intense and often volatile negative reactions that we all provoke when we begin to define ourselves, set limits, and assert our opinions. We are often afraid that being clear on our sense of "I" — who and what we are and what we want and need — will threaten or even destroy a relationship. This is a fear rooted in early childhood where children, especially girls, were expected to keep their anger or disagreement to themselves to please their parents. Stating independent and autonomous opinions often brought on those sometimes paralyzing and frightening separation anxiety feelings, which made the child feel terribly alone. Most children, then, quickly learn to utter words of conciliation to restore the connection and feel safe and loved again and not alone. So instead of using anger as an opportunity to think more clearly, our fears often fuzz over our personal clarity. We get intimidated by the intensity of our feelings and turn into the nice lady who makes peace: "I can't think when someone is angry with me" or "I just want to smooth things over and make peace."

Let's put these concepts into a reality experience. Have you ever had a review or evaluation that was less glowing than you expected, thus putting your pride, confidence, bonus, and raise at risk? You feel invalidated and get furious. But when you try to confront your boss she says, "Well, you're not quite perform-ing as sharply as we expected you to, and a couple of people feel you're not enough of a team player." This makes you feel unap-preciated, hurt, angry, and defensive. Tears jump to the edges of your eyes. Here you thought you were doing great. You always thought you got along well with everyone. And you expected a big bonus to help out with the bills. After all, being a single mother of a seven- and a nine-year-old makes life very expen-sive. The real-life consequences of your disappointing review make it all that much worse, and your anger melts into more defensiveness.

You tell your boss how surprised and disappointed you are about your performance rating and why you were counting so much on this raise. She becomes sympathetic and reiterates her faith in your potential. Then she offers to help you structure some goals that will enhance your performance for the next review.

After you have left her office you realize that you don't really know what it is about your performance that is not "sharp" or who has been complaining about you and why. Here you had struggled to stand up for yourself, and now you feel angry, disappointed, and ashamed of your wimping out. You feel foggy-headed and inarticulate. Perhaps you would have gotten more concrete answers if you had asked clear and concise ques-tions, but you feared that doing so would make your boss uncomfortable — which would have left you feeling terribly alone, the feeling you had worked so hard to avoid. Besides, you feel intimidated by your boss. So instead of making yourself clear, you make peace, reinstating the connection and the status quo and apologizing for your initial disagreement. Also, maybe in your anger you want to make your boss feel guilty for making you feel so bad — a better move, you think, than making direct statements that might bring on her anger or make you feel alone.

This is the unconscious at work, denying anger, frightened that clear thinking means trouble because it might highlight your differences with your boss (parents). Then you would feel pressured to fight for your rights and might make other people angry, becoming the target of some real "terrifying anger" yourself that would provoke those awful separation anxiety feelings again. Or you become afraid that those mythical people who think you are not a good team player may have some real authority. They could get angry at you and make your life a living hell. They could even get you fired. Your anxiety escalates as your mind races through the possible destruction your anger may bring. Fears of destruction or that terrible sense of disconnection and aloneness turn your anger into hurt, tears, and peacemaking.

After a couple of days, you become caught up in your work again and forget about your anger. As a matter of fact, when you think of the meeting with your boss, you don't even feel angry about it anymore. It just doesn't seem to be important. Yet you have been treated unfairly and protected another person at your own expense. And the truth is that of course you're still angry.

An Experiment to Manage Your Anger Differently

Changing anger patterns is hard work.[4] It takes time and repetition. You can begin by observing your own anger patterns. Do you turn anger to hurt, tears, and peacemaking as we just described? Do you emotionally cut off and distance yourself? Do you become helpless or overorganized and bossy? How do you interact with those around you when tempers flare? Do you insist on talking it out and get hurt when others need space? Do you tend to blame others?

Decide to do something different with your anger. Make a plan that will break your usual pattern the next time you encounter angry feelings, yours or someone else's. Count on your resistance to step in and raise your anxiety and throw up blocks. But if you hold firm to your plan and work on melting your resistance, using your anger as an aid to expressing your feelings and needs, you can change the internal and interpersonal feelings surrounding how you handle relationships, especially where negative feelings are concerned. Only then can you really see the patterns and the changes you need to make. Once you consciously begin to discern a pattern, you can then make changes within these existing patterns and structures.

As for most women, it's hard to hold on to your anger. Yet denial of it and giving yourself up in the process, as in "The Severed Heart," has negative consequences. As we saw in the preceding example, the real-life consequences of giving up your anger and yourself are great. In addition, you may feel tired, bored, unenthusiastic, or even depressed. You may find that you can't concentrate as well or that you become forgetful. You may be abrupt and snappish with others. These are some of the uncontrollable emotional results of putting your energies into suppressing your anger. As your angry feelings demand to be heard — just as your Competent Self, WomanPower, and Creative Aggression demand that you stand up, be counted, and be taken seriously — you hear a tape start up in your head: *women are not supposed to be that aggressive.* You mind says "Oops!" and resolves the conflict between expression and suppression of anger as it is apt to do through physical symptoms and emotional discomfort. You and your physical and mental health demand that you feel entitled to be taken seriously and to challenge your boss or others when you feel you are right.

But remember, as in any risktaking venture where you try something new, you will have to hang in and accommodate the anxiety of fear, confusion, and change. If you do, soon you'll break the poor anger patterns that have not been serving you well, and you'll rearrange old and new behaviors into a unique new way of handling anger between you and another person. Then the anxiety will dissipate as you create a bridge from the old to the new. This new attitude of tolerating — even valuing — the struggle with creative conflicts rather than ducking them can serve as a signal to you that new, positive feelings and attitudes are already beginning, replacing fear and anxiety about expressing your aggression and anger. You can now build on them as well as enjoy the experience of these new glowing feelings. You have transformed the self-defeating effects of your inhibited aggression and anger into new patterns of expressing your aggression creatively and your angry feelings more directly and effectively. You have re-created yourself in this context. Repetition and monitoring will help you to solidify your gains and integrate the new behavior and the new feelings. In all, you have summoned up your courage, envisioned a change, developed a strategy and a plan to implement it, and taken a leap of faith — that well-calculated risk — to achieve it. And you succeeded. Congratulations on a job well done.

Message 5:
You Can Be Courageous and Take Risks

At the same lecture at which she told us that "some leaders are born women," Geraldine Ferraro said, "If you don't run, you can't win. If you lose, go out and beat 'em the next time." Ferraro is obviously a courageous risktaker, as she demonstrated in the 1980s and again in her 1992 campaign for U.S. senator from New York.

Taking our lead from Ferraro and the women we interviewed, we defined risktaking in Chapter 6 as *taking a chance on life and living it to the fullest.* This means departing from the status quo, taking a deep breath, and stepping out into space to find new adventures and bring creative changes into your life. Risking is also bringing together synergistically, as if $1 + 1 = 50$ and not 2, your sense of positive entitlement to your slice of life's pie and all of the skills that you've learned from the other messages. By putting them all together, you are ready to move toward directed and creative action in whatever sphere you have chosen for yourself.

Now that you're a little more comfortable with the ideas of feeling loved and special, the knowledge of feeling you can do whatever you want to do, the notion of feeling entitled to dream of greatness, and using and enjoying your Creative Aggression to help make your dreams come true, you are ready to put the pieces of your Leadership Equation together and to take risks. We've been a bit sneaky, if you hadn't noticed, and included small steps in risktaking all the way through this chapter. We believe Aristotle's statement that "we are what we repeatedly do. Excellence, then, is not an act, but a habit." Now that you have practiced many aspects of risktaking, you have a more solid foundation under you and know that you'll still be loved and considered special by the important people in your life even if you take risks to be and do something different and separate from your parents, siblings, spouse, mate, bosses, friends, or colleagues — or if you fail.

Feeling loved and special cannot be contingent on being a clone of these meaningful people in your life or on always succeeding. If that's what's required to maintain their love and caring, you've got a problem — because then there is no place for your risktaking, your autonomy, your independence, your Competent Self, your WomanPower, or your Creative Aggression. If that's the case, you may need to rethink your definition of love and caring lest, without realizing it, your independence and autonomy have all gotten lost in trading dreams for security. It is not easy to hold on to your dreams. It does take courage.

We think that you can be courageous and take risks, learn to handle the anxiety of creative confusion with much, much practice, and, when you're ready, take a leap of faith such as Suzie Azar did and "learn to swim in the deep end." Otherwise, as Geraldine Ferraro said, "You *can't* win if you don't run." *But* there must also be room for your experiment not to work, so that if you run and you lose, you can go out and beat 'em the next time — or not, if you so choose.

How to Do It

Using Chapter 6 as our reference point, let's review the characteristics of the risktaking process by creating an acronym for greater ease in holding only these concepts in our heads. This acronym, MARSI, describes the *stages of change in risktaking that help us get from desire to vision to riskgoal, passing through five transitional stages:*

M = Melting your resistance as you trust yourself, your vision, and your riskgoal, relinquish your controls, and take a well-calculated leap of faith

A = Accommodating the anxiety of creative confusion as you sort out old structures and new possibilities

R = Re-creating a new core Competent Self as you combine the old and the new into unique new structures and selves

S = Solidifying and reinforcing new structures and behaviors

I = Integrating new structures and behaviors into a new core Competent Self

As you can see in Message 4, we have already offered the ideas included in MARSI without formally introducing the acronym. An experiment to use your Creative Aggression and change your anger patterns is certainly risky enough to make good use of the MARSI concepts. It will also give you an opportunity to familiarize yourself with the risktaking process as well as to practice thinking about the five transitional stages of change as you go through them.

We can't repeat too often that, in any change you make, your resistance fights like a tiger to put up blocks to change. So be prepared to be courageous and tenacious about moving forward. Try to remember (in the heat of the moment, rational thinking won't work all the time) that your frightened and confused feelings are part of melting your resistance — which is fighting for its very life — and accommodating the anxiety of creative confusion. If you persist in courageously moving toward your goal, reinforcing the changes in an uneven jagged line of two steps forward and one step backward, you will work through the anxiety and the confusion and be ready to solidify and integrate your gains.

Suggestions for Choosing a Riskgoal

To learn about and integrate the essence of this message, we suggest choosing a concrete riskgoal. Think about a riskgoal here that can add to your life experiences and help you tap into and reinforce all the vital centers inside of you that fuel the elements of your Leadership Equation. For example, start out with a riskgoal that is specific but more experimental and less risky than a job change:

• Participate in a group devoted to some cause you consider worthwhile. Consider leadership in the group down the line.
• Participate in competitive sports. This has been men's practice arena for centuries for learning about Creative Aggression, its strengths and limits, the rules to play by, and the consequences of being aggressive. Now it's our turn to take advantage of this learning and playing field.
• Speak out more at work, before the town council, at school board meetings, and socially, using your feedback network for role models.
• Run for a local government position in your community.
• Seek out membership or leadership on an important committee where you work.

Getting better and more active at any of the above will help you feel more competent and effective. Remember Althea Horner's recipe for power:

• I am = I have a self, an identity.
• I can = mastery of skills and the environment.
• I will = the intention to take certain action.[5]

In other words, power over yourself means a sense of self-recognition, a sense of mastery, and the ability to make things happen, allowing you to feel effective and powerful in the world around you.

Take stock of your needs and wishes. Decide what needs to change. Help get yourself started by thinking about your wishes and needs in terms of the past, present, and future, using images for each wish as much as possible.[6] For example, if you want to try for a promotion, imagine yourself in the job, in the place of the person who is in that position now, or in a new position that you hope will be created for you. Imagine yourself doing the job in the office now designated for that position as you see it or redesign it in your mind. Linger on each image for a while. What feelings does it bring up? Mentally or in writing, record the feelings that the images evoke. Don't edit your thoughts. Put down everything that comes to mind. Make as long a list as you can and when you run out of ideas — stop for a few minutes, walk around — sit down and add some more to your list. You might want to put each item on an index card so you can shuffle and reshuffle them later on.

Here's a way to think about each of your time categories.

Past lingering wishes. Is there anything that you've always wanted to do but never have — such as a career move, personality change, or hobby? If it's something that has kept hanging around in the corner of your mind for years, put it on your wish list or on a card under this category. Perhaps you've always wanted to open an art gallery and give up being an executive, or the reverse, or become a therapist and give up the law, or reduce what has always been too many crises in your life to a more "peace of mind" pace. Write down that lingering wish here, starting with the phrase "I have always wanted _____ ."

Present. What desires, wishes, and needs currently preoccupy your thoughts? What ambitions and goals nag at your brain most recently? Perhaps you've always wanted to tame that quickly flaring temper of yours so that you can stop apologizing to everyone all the time. Maybe you want to find a haven from the rat race and dream of taking up the violin and playing in a string quartet. Or go in the opposite direction and get in touch with your wish to rev up your career and try for a promotion. Put down these present and perhaps recent thoughts here, starting with the phrase "Now I want to" or "Now I can see myself _____ ."

Future. These are the "gleam in the eye" wishes and wants, the potential and the possibilities that occur to you when you say, "If only I could" or "Someday. . . ." It could be anything, from wanting to become CEO of your corporation to leaving the corporation and opening a bed and breakfast to taking up tournament bridge. Put those thoughts down here, starting with the phrase "I can see myself down the line" or "Two or three (or five or ten) years from now, I would like to _____ ."

Now *prioritize your lists.* Lay your cards out under each category and survey your lists. Think of your life *right now.* Rate your choices A, B, or C:

A = I want to and think I can do this *now.*
B = I think I want this and think I can do this — but it isn't as tempting as the items on the A list.
C = I want to do this one day, I think.

Quickly rate each choice until you have your top ten A's in a high-priority pile. Those that you linger over, put aside into a B possibilities pile. If you can't find enough A items for your high-priority list, choose some items from the B possibilities pile that appeal to you and add them to your A list until you have ten high-priority picks.

Then convert your top ten picks into "I want" goal statements. Put your goal statements onto separate cards. Imagine an image and a feeling for each card. Sit in a comfortable chair or lie down, breathe deeply, close your eyes, and let yourself relax. Imagine yourself working for that promotion and then getting it. What feelings and images come up? Which ones feel good — satisfying, exciting, frightening, frustrating? Where are the blocks when no images come at all?

When you know what you want, the next step is to go after it, not sit back passively and wait for it to happen.

An Experiment in Risktaking

Now that you have identified your own riskgoal, you need to set out a plan to achieve it. As you did before in thinking about your dreams, create a step-by-step plan to follow.

Hang on to the feelings that you are loved and special. Remind yourself that you can do anything you want to do. Don't forget that you are entitled to dream of greatness. And use your Creative Aggression to move you toward your riskgoal. If you don't achieve it immediately, try to find out what you've learned from the experience that you can use the next time you try this or some other riskgoal. And when you do achieve it, the experience will have given you the chance to integrate a new element into your personal Leadership Equation.

One Further Risk to Consider

As you near the end of this book, we imagine you are saying, "What now? I've read the book, I've tried out some of the suggestions, exercises, and experiments, and it still isn't enough. I can't seem to make the changes that I want to make for myself, by myself." That doesn't make you a failure. It just may be the time to seek professional help. When you feel you've tried everything you can and still don't feel that you're able to make the kinds of changes that you want to make in yourself and in your life on your own, professional help may be the answer for you. Several of the women we interviewed, including Ann Richards, acknowledge that they have been helped by therapy at some time in their life.

Although entering therapy may feel like a great risk, therapy really can be helpful. It can help you deal with the resistances to change we've mentioned so often. Therapy can help you look at yourself and your life through a new lens, which will help you focus and point you in a new direction. Therapy can shift the balance in favor of your growth and development so that you can achieve a sense of fulfillment and your personal Leadership Equation. And that, after all, is the ultimate goal of having shared with you the secrets of leadership and power of the twenty-five wonderful and dynamite political women who shared them with us.

Epilogue

We opened this book with a controversy between our psychological perspective and the perspective of the women in Women Executives in State Government with whom we first discussed this book — Evelyn Murphy, Gail Schoettler, and others. We asked them how they overcame the obstacles to get where they are. They looked at us incredulously and asked, "What obstacles?" They finally convinced us of the wisdom of their view and we approached our interviewing with their credo in mind, seeing the possibilities rather than the obstacles. It's not that there are no obstacles to women's success in our culture, but the psychological "comfort zones" provided by these women's early lives buffered them from the impact of the obstacles.

This difference allows these women to confront the usual obstacles in a problem-solving way, to move around or through them quickly and easily. If they are blocked or stopped, such as by losing an election, they are, as we all would be, upset, angry, and even distraught. However, they generally view this upset as adversity — to be learned from — moving onward and upward quickly, bruises and all. We were able to observe firsthand how these women lived this out.

All of the interviewing for this book was completed before the general election in 1990, which was supposed to be the Year of the Woman. That did not turn out to be the case. As we reported in Chapter 3, the number of women in Congress and in governorships did not change. However, the proportion of women in state legislatures, which increases approximately 1 percent per year, reached about 18 percent as a result of the 1990 elections.[1]

In general, the women we interviewed fared well. Congresswomen who ran for reelection retained their seats. Unfortunately, the two who sought to move up to the Senate, Claudine Schneider of Rhode Island and Pat Saiki of Hawaii, were defeated.

Those women who ran for reelection to executive positions in state government retained their offices, with the exception of Jo Ann Zimmerman of Iowa. A change in the Iowa constitution required Lieutenant Governor Zimmerman to run on a team ticket. This ticket was defeated by the incumbent governor.

Several women ran for a different office in state government than they held at the time of the interviews. Rebecca Vigil-Giron, who under New Mexico law could not succeed herself as secretary of state, was defeated in her run for Congress. Evelyn Murphy lost her bid to move from lieutenant governor to governor of Massachusetts. And Ann Richards successfully moved up from state treasurer to governor of Texas.

Murphy and Richards provide us with sterling examples of how to handle defeat and victory. Murphy, who wrote to us after the election, demonstrates that there is life after losing. She told us how she plans to live and enjoy the vitality of her Leadership Equation after losing her election. Her letter indicates that her Competent Self is intact, and she is enthusiastically turning her Creative Aggression and WomanPower into exciting new directions. She is, as always, ready to take another risk in another arena:

I'm slow at responding to your letter of late November but I'm finally free of state government and ready for my next adventure! . . . Ann Lewis and I are writing a book on the eight women who were on the ballot for governor in 1990. . . . I am weighing several offers now and should know soon what career path I'll take next. Whatever it is, I intend to help get more women elected governor in the coming election years.

Governor Richards' inaugural address tells us how she will live her Leadership Equation in her new position of power. She expresses her sense of WomanPower in the clarity of her agenda and in her thrust toward helping others. She, too, perceives no obstacles in her path.

Those of us who heard the governor deliver her address know that she deviated from her prepared remarks at the outset and spoke from her heart of her loving connections to her family, her mentor, and the people who were gathered on the capitol lawn to witness the event. Then she began her prepared remarks. Even in these excerpts we could hear her Competent Self in the background. We could hear her DreamVoices as her Creative Aggression came to life for us to know:

Today is a day of celebration.

Today, we marched up Congress Avenue and said that we were reclaiming the capitol for the people of Texas.

Today the headline has been written . . . but the pages that follow are blank.

Tomorrow we begin filling in the pages, writing line by line the story that will be told long after the joy of this day is forgotten.

Like the Reverend Martin Luther King, Jr., who was born on this day, we have come this far on the strength of a dream.

Our challenge is to transform that dream into reality . . . to fill the pages of history with the story of Texans who came into office envisioning a new era of greatness . . . and breathed life into that vision.

Today, we have a vision of a Texas where opportunity knows no race or color or gender — a glimpse of the possibilities that can be when the barriers fall and the doors of government swing open. . . .

Today, we have a vision of a Texas where the government treats every citizen with respect and dignity and honesty . . . where consumers are protected . . . where business is nurtured and valued . . . where good jobs are plentiful . . . where those in need find compassion and help . . . where every decision is measured against a high standard of ethics and true commitment to the public trust. . . .

Years ago, John Kennedy said that "Life isn't fair." Life is not fair . . . but government must be.

And if tomorrow, we begin with the understanding that government must stop telling people what they want . . . and start listening to the people and hearing what the people need, we will make government mean something good in people's lives.

Nothing is more fundamentally important to me than the understanding that this administration exists to *serve* the taxpayers.

As Ruth Mandel of CAWP pointed out, the 1992 elections have a plot complicated by redistricting and reapportionment. The good news is that reapportionment creates many open seats. This gives women a chance to run without the uphill battle of trying to unseat an incumbent. The bad news is that reapportionment often reshapes the electoral map in such a way as to cause some good women legislators to lose their seats.[2]

As you may remember, CAWP calculated that it will take women 410 years before they are represented in Congress in the same proportion as they exist in the population — or even 64 more years before half of state legislators are women.[3] We hope it doesn't take that long. As men have studied presidents and generals as models of leadership from which to build their own Leadership Equation, women now have and can study a growing cadre of models of the ways women lead. These women can show the way for all leaders, men or women, who want to lead in the new, more collaborative, interpersonal style of the '90s.

We hope that with women's growing activism and more women leaders stepping forward to run, we can fast-forward the clock. We also hope that the *women in power* whom we have studied and their peers in government will have taught us the *secrets of leadership* that all women can use, including the importance of taking a leap of faith and looking for the possibilities rather than the obstacles. Finally, we hope that women in elective positions can serve as models of women's leadership in and for all arenas of life.

Afterword

Geraldine Ferraro

In reading the experiences shared by the various public officials profiled in *Women in Power: Secrets of Leadership,* I found myself nodding in agreement. Of course I have been loved and made to feel special as a child, and my mother, a widow, had told me I could be anything I wanted to be. I learned very young that to move out of the South Bronx, both literally and emotionally, I would have to take risks. I also knew that no one was going to give me a ticket to a better life; I had to earn it.

I can still hear my mother's voice encouraging me when I would run into an obstacle — "Remember, Gerry, your name. It's root is *ferro,* which means iron. You can bend it but you can't break it."

The most interesting thing about *Women in Power* is that those secrets of leadership can be taught. And if they're taught early enough, they can result in greater representation of women in political office and leadership.

That's important not only because role models are essential for little girls but because women in positions of power can change the attitudes of little boys and ultimately of society as a whole.

On a trip to London a few years ago, I was told the following story. A woman parliamentarian overheard two children playing "grownup." The little boy turned to the little girl and said, "I want to be the prime minister." The little girl responded,

"You can't, you're a boy."

I'm sure Margaret Thatcher's decade as prime minister of England has influenced the attitude of an entire generation of young boys who have grown up knowing her leadership. If a woman can be prime minister, is there any job a woman cannot do?

And beyond role models and changing attitudes is the fact that women political leaders bring a different perspective to solving the problems that face us as a global society. According to Carol Gilligan, women speak *In a Different Voice.* Instead of engaging in confrontation, women are more apt to negotiate. Instead of dealing in win-lose terms, women are more apt to see the gray area in between. Instead of thinking only of today, women are more apt to think in terms of the needs of generations to come.

And it is the women elected officials who seem to speak up loudest on issues that affect women. Just take a look at the legislative records of a few people profiled in *Women in Power.* Senator Barbara Mikulski authored the Spousal Impoverishment Act. Congresswoman Pat Schroeder has been an effective voice for women in the military. Barbara Kennelly has addressed the issues of day care and pension equity. Marge Roukema has spoken up on health care.

Now, would those issues have been addressed if those women were not in Congress? I'm not quite sure. In the same way Agent Orange legislation was introduced by a Vietnam veteran, sanctions against South Africa by the Black Caucus, legislation to compensate Japanese-Americans by two Japanese-American congressmen, so too do women legislators understand and speak out on issues that are of particular concern to women. We each bring our individual experiences to the legislative bodies in which we serve. Those legislatures, to operate effectively, should reflect and represent our very diverse population.

Finally, I don't quite share the pessimism of CAWP that it

will take 410 years before we are 51 percent of the Congress. It's not that I have better information. They're academics who study statistics. I'm a politician who acts on gut. But I believe that if we get more women to run, more women to take the risks, then we will address legislatively the rules that afford protection for incumbents and the political playing field will become fairer. When that happens women will be elected in record numbers. I'm looking forward to it!

Appendix

Notes

Index

Appendix

PERSONAL DATA QUESTIONNAIRE

1. Name: _____

2. Address: _____

3. Date of birth: _____

4. Siblings: Number of female: _____ Number of male: _____

5. Your birth order position in family:

   1 _____ 2 _____ 3 _____ 4 _____ 5 _____

6. Father's occupation: _____

7. Mother's occupation: _____

8. Family socioeconomic status:

   _____ lower class

   _____ lower middle class

   _____ middle class

   _____ upper middle class

   _____ upper class

9. Were your parents living during your entire childhood?

   Yes _____ No _____

   If no, which parent(s) died? _____

   How old were you? _____

10. Rate yourself as a student: Excellent   Good   Fair   Poor

    Elementary school   _____   _____   _____   _____

    Junior high   _____   _____   _____   _____

    High school   _____   _____   _____   _____

    College   _____   _____   _____   _____

    Graduate school   _____   _____   _____   _____

11. Extracurricular activities:

Elementary school: _____

_____

Junior high: _____

_____

High school: _____

_____

College: _____

_____

Graduate school: _____

_____

12. Who were your heroes/heroines growing up? (You may include fantasy, radio, movie, TV, book, or comic book figures.) _____

_____

_____

_____

13. Who were your role models growing up? _____

_____

_____

14. As a child, what did you aspire to be? _____

_____

_____

15. Educational history (include college and beyond):

    Institution   *Degree*   *Date granted*   *Major*

_____

_____

_____

16. Marital status: M _____   S _____   W _____   D _____

17. Date(s) of marriage(s): _____

18. Children: Number female: _____   Ages: _____

     Number male: _____   Ages: _____

19. Present position in government:

     Title: _____

     Responsibilities: _____

     _____

     _____

20. What do you like most about your position? _____

     _____

     _____

     _____

     _____

21. What do you like least about your position? _____

     _____

     _____

     _____

22. What aspects of political life, either in office or on the campaign trail, do you find most stressful? _____

     _____

     _____

     _____

23. How do you cope with these stressors? _____

     _____

     _____

_____

_____

24. Previous experiences in government (voluntary, appointed, or elected):
   Position   *Dates held*

_____

_____

_____

_____

25. Other occupational experience:
   Position   *Dates held*

_____

_____

_____

_____

26. Who were your mentors?
   Name   *Position or relationship to you*

_____

_____

_____

27. Would you encourage a daughter to seek a career in politics?
   Yes ___   No ___
   Explain briefly: _____

_____

_____

_____

28. Future political aspirations: _____

_____

_____

_____

STRUCTURED INTERVIEW

1. a. We are interested in how you got to the political position that you're in, particularly in what in your early life experiences got you here. How *did* you get here?

   b. Did you ever have a dream about what you'd like to be? If so, what?

   Now, in the interest of time, I'm going to ask you somewhat more structured questions.

2. In the light of our interest in the effect of your early experience on what you are today, could you tell me about your earliest memory?

   When you answer the rest of the questions, please think of yourself at ages 5, 11, 16, and leaving home.

3. I want to ask you some questions about times in your life that you felt loved.

   a. By whom did you feel loved, and how did you know?

   b. To whom did you feel you were special, and how was it conveyed?

4. a. Tell me about your mother.

   b. Tell me about your father.

5. Many people believe that in political life you have to take risks. Do you see it that way? What are the risks now?

6. Many people believe that it takes courage to be in political life. Do you see yourself as a courageous woman?

7. a. Everyone experiences setbacks or failure at some time in life. Can you describe examples in your early and later life and how you dealt with them?

   b. Do you believe you can do anything you want? If not, what can't you do, and does that interfere with your life?

8. There are typically a whole range of actions, experiences, and feelings which have been harder for women to deal with than men, for instance, such things as conflict, anger, hurting others, competition, and jealousy. What kinds of experiences have you had with these feelings as you grew up?

9. You have chosen to be in politics, which most people see as a powerful leadership position.

   a. What does power mean to you?

b. What does leadership mean to you?

c. Reflect their definition. Can you tell me about some instances in which you behaved that way growing up.

Questions if time permits:

10. What advice would you give parents regarding raising their daughters for careers in politics?

11. Is there anything you haven't spoken about which you think would contribute to my understanding of how you got where you are?

Use for 6 interviews only:

12. What is it like to be in a predominantly male bastion?

13. How are you similar to or different from male colleagues? Is that a help or a hindrance?

Notes

PROLOGUE

1. The "possibilities, not obstacles" lens that these women use to see and experience life is similar to the outlook of people in other studies, such as those of Warren Bennis, who defined the Wallenda factor, and of C. Rick Snyder, who identified the hopefulness factor. See Warren Bennis, *On Becoming a Leader* (Reading, Mass.: Addison Wesley, 1990), and C. Rick Snyder, "When the Going Gets Tough, 'The Hopeful Keep Going,'" APA *Monitor* (July 1991).

2. "Reapportionment, Redistricting and Women: The Dangers and Opportunities in California," *News & Notes* (Center for the American Woman and Politics, National Information Bank on Women in Public Office, Eagleton Institute of Politics, Rutgers University) 7, no. 1 (Spring 1989): 14–15.

3. "1990 Election Credits and a Preview of Coming Attractions," *CAWP News & Notes* (Center for the American Woman and Politics, Eagleton Institute of Politics, Rutgers University) 8, no. 1 (Winter 1991): 2.

4. Ruth B. Mandel, director, Center for the American Woman and Politics, statement to the National Press Club, Washington, D.C., 8 November 1990.

5. "Nevada Politics, Women Mix," *Reno Gazette-Journal*, 11 November 1990, B1.

6. "1991 Women Officeholders, U.S. Congress and Statewide Elective Executives," CAWP fact sheet (Center for the American Woman and Politics, Eagleton Institute of Politics, Rutgers University), 13 November 1990, 1–2.

7. Jean Lipman-Blumen, "Emerging Patterns of Female Leadership in Formal Organizations: Must the Female Leader Go Formal?" in *The Challenge of Change: Perspectives on Family, Work, and*

Education, ed. Matina Horner, Carol C. Nadelson, and Malkah T. Notman (New York: Plenum Press, 1983).

CHAPTER 1

1. Karen Horney, "The Problem of Feminine Masochism," in *Feminine Psychology,* ed. H. Kelman (New York: Norton, 1967), 214–33.
2. Celinda Lake, "Campaigning in a Different Voice" (Summary, unpublished report, EMILY's List, Washington, D.C., n.d.), 2.
3. Ibid.
4. Rita Mae Kelly and Mary Boutilier, *The Making of Political Women: A Study of Socialization and Role Conflict* (Chicago: Nelson-Hall, 1978).

CHAPTER 2

1. *Random House Dictionary of the English Language,* 1970 ed., s.v. "power."
2. Barbara Booles and Lydia Swan, *Power Failure* (New York: St. Martin's Press, 1989), 51.
3. Barbara Rudolph, "Why Can't a Woman Manage More Like . . . a Woman?" *Time,* Fall 1990, 53.
4. Deborah Tannen, *You Just Don't Understand: Women and Men in Conversation* (New York: William Morrow, 1990).
5. Paula Johnson, "Women and Power: Toward a Theory of Effectiveness," *Journal of Social Issues* 32, no. 3 (1976): 99–110.
6. Althea Horner, *The Wish for Power and the Fear of Having It* (New York: Jason Aronson, 1989).
7. Ibid., 74.
8. Susan Moses, "Teen Girls Can Have 'Crisis of Connection,'" *APA Monitor* 21, no. 1 (November 1990): 27.
9. Carol Gilligan, Nona P. Lyons, and Trudy J. Hamner, eds., *Making Connections* (Cambridge: Harvard University Press, 1990).
10. Jeane J. Kirkpatrick, *Political Woman* (New York: Basic Books, 1974).
11. Jean Baker Miller, "Women and Power," *Journal: Women and Therapy* 6, nos. 1 and 2 (Spring/Summer 1987): 1–11.
12. Clarice J. Kestenbaum, "The Professional Woman's Dilemma:

Love and/or Power," *American Journal of Psychoanalysis* 46, no. 1 (1986): 15.

13. Miller, "Women and Power," 4.

14. Sherry Suib Cohen, "Beyond Macho: The Power of Womanly Management," *Working Woman*, February 1989, 77–83.

15. Miller, "Women and Power," 9.

16. Gail L. Zellman, "Women and Sex Roles: A Social Psychological Perspective," Chap. 17 in *Politics and Power*, ed. Irene H. Frieze, Jacquelynne E. Parsons, Paula B. Johnson, Diane N. Ruble, and Gail L. Zellman (New York: Norton, 1978), 351.

17. Sidney Verba, "Women in American Politics," Afterword in *Women, Politics, and Change*, ed. Louise A. Tilly and Patricia Gurin (New York: Russell Sage Foundation, 1990), 555–72.

18. Johnson, "Women and Power."

19. Anne Stratham, "The Gender Model Visited: Differences in the Management Styles of Men and Women," *Sex Roles* 16, nos. 7 and 8 (1987): 409–27.

20. Cohen, "Beyond Macho," 78.

21. Ann M. Morrison, Randall P. White, and Ellen Van Velson, "Executive Women: Substance Plus Style," *Psychology Today*, August 1987, 18–26.

22. Jean Lipman-Blumen, "Emerging Patterns of Female Leadership in Formal Organizations: Must the Female Leader Go Formal?" in *The Challenge of Change*, ed. Matina Horner, Carol C. Nadelson, and Malkah T. Notman (New York: Plenum Press, 1983), 61–87.

CHAPTER 3

1. "So What Do You Want to Be When You Grow Up? PRESIDENT!" *Life*, December 1987, 102–4.

2. Jeane J. Kirkpatrick, *Political Woman* (New York: Basic Books, 1974), 6.

3. Claudine Schneider, "First Word," *Omni*, May 1990, 6.

4. Judy Jarvis, "New Life of the Parties," *Lear's*, September/October 1988, 54–64.

5. Geraldine Ferraro, "The Future of Women in Politics" (The Goldberg Lecture, 92nd Street YM-YWHA, New York, 20 February 1991).

6. "Bringing More Women into Public Office," Center for the American Woman and Politics, Eagleton Institute of Politics, Rutgers University, June 1984, 1.

7. Kirkpatrick, *Political Woman*, 6–7.

8. Louis Harris, "The Gender Gulf," *New York Times*, 10 December 1990, D7.

9. Fred Greenstein, *Children and Politics*, rev. ed. (New Haven: Yale University Press, 1965).

10. Barbara Booles and Lydia Swan, *Power Failure* (New York: St. Martin's Press, 1989), 55.

11. Copyright © 1974 by The New York Times Company. Reprinted by permission.

12. Kirkpatrick, *Political Woman*, 20.

13. Susan and Martin Tolchin, *Clout: Womanpower and Politics* (New York: Coward, McCann & Geoghegan, 1973), 14.

14. Paula Johnson, "Women and Power: Toward a Theory of Effectiveness," *Journal of Social Issues* 32, no. 3 (1976): 108.

15. Kirkpatrick, *Political Woman*, 7, citing title of Harold D. Lasswell's book *Politics: Who Gets What, When, How*.

16. Various publications, the Center for the American Woman and Politics, National Information Bank on Women in Public Office, Eagleton Institute of Politics, Rutgers University, New Brunswick.

17. Celinda Lake, "Campaigning in a Different Voice" (Summary, unpublished report, EMILY's List, Washington, D.C., n.d.), 2.

18. Geraldine Ferraro with Linda Bird Francke, *Ferraro: My Story* (New York: Bantam, 1985), 261–62.

19. "The 'Year of the Woman'? Well, Maybe," *Business Week*, 1 October 1990, 170.

20. Deborah Tannen, *You Just Don't Understand: Women and Men in Conversation* (New York: William Morrow), 241–42.

21. Ibid., 242–43.

22. Ferraro, *Ferraro: My Story*, 243.

23. Antonia Frazier, *The Warrior Queens* (New York: Alfred A. Knopf, 1989), 7.

24. "The Power Brokers," in . . . *To Form a More Perfect Union* . . . , Report of the National Commission on the Observance of International Women's Year (Washington: U.S. Government Printing Office, 1976), 43.

25. Susan J. Carroll, "Looking Back at the 1980s and Forward to the 1990s," *CAWP News & Notes* (Center for American Women and Politics, Eagleton Institute of Politics, Rutgers University) 7, no. 3 (Summer 1990): 9.

26. Ibid.

27. Official election returns, state of New Jersey, November 6, 1990, general election.
28. Carroll, "Looking Back at the 1980s," 9.
29. "Reapportionment, Redistricting and Women: The Dangers and Opportunities in California," *CAWP News & Notes* (Center for the American Woman and Politics, Eagleton Institute of Politics, Rutgers University) 7, no. 1 (1989): 14–15.
30. Carroll, "Looking Back at the 1980s," 9.
31. Ibid., 9–10.
32. Ibid., 10.
33. Kirkpatrick, *Political Woman*, 69–83.
34. Susan J. Carroll, *Women as Candidates in American Politics* (Bloomington: Indiana University Press, 1985), 120.

PROFILE: PAT SCHROEDER

1. Pat Schroeder, with Andrea Camp and Robyn Lipner, *Champion of the Great American Family* (New York: Random House, 1989), dedication.

CHAPTER 4

1. Annie Gottlieb, "The Secret Strength of Happy Marriages," *McCall's*, December 1990.
2. Rita Mae Kelly, "Sex and Becoming Eminent as a Political/Organizational Leader," *Sex Roles* 9, no. 10 (1983): 1073–89.
3. Margaret Hennig and Anne Jardim, *The Managerial Woman* (Garden City, N.Y.: Anchor Press/Doubleday, 1977), 99–132.
4. Judith V. Jordan and Janet L. Surrey, "The Self-in-Relation: Empathy and the Mother-Daughter Relationship," in *The Psychology of Today's Woman: New Psychoanalytic Visions*, ed. Toni Bernay and Dorothy W. Cantor (Hillside, N.J.: Analytic Press, 1986), 81–104.
5. Hennig and Jardim, *Managerial Woman*, 105.
6. Rita Mae Kelly and Mary Boutilier, *The Making of Political Women: A Study of Socialization and Role Conflict* (Chicago: Nelson-Hall, 1978), 264.
7. Ronald L. Levant, Susan C. Slattery, Jane E. Loiselle, Valerie Sawyer-Smith, and Robert J. Schneider, "Non-Traditional Paternal

Behavior with School-Aged Daughters: A Discriminant Analysis," *Australian Journal of Marriage and Family* 11, no. 1, 28–35.

8. Hennig and Jardim, *Managerial Woman*, 77.
9. Kevin Leman, *Growing Up Firstborn* (New York: Delacorte, 1989), 34.
10. Kelly and Boutilier, *Making of Political Women*.
11. Stephen P. Bank and Michael D. Kahn, *The Sibling Bond* (New York: Basic Books, 1982), 200.

CHAPTER 5

1. Daniel J. Levinson, *The Seasons of a Man's Life* (New York: Ballantine Books, 1978), 91–92.
2. Mary Catharine Bateson, *Composing a Life* (New York: New American Library, 1990).
3. Carol Gilligan, Nona P. Lyons, and Trudy J. Hamner, eds., *Making Connections* (Cambridge: Harvard University Press, 1990).
4. P. Freeberg, "Self-Esteem Gender Gap Widens in Adolescence," *APA Monitor*, April 1991, 29.
5. AAUW found that at eight or nine, 60 percent of girls feel confident, assertive, and positive about themselves as compared with 67 percent of boys. Within the next eight years that figure drops to 29 percent of high school girls feeling good about themselves versus 46 percent of high school boys. It looks as though girls' stifling their DreamVoices has a high price in loss of self-esteem, resulting in a self-esteem gender gap of 17 points by age seventeen.
6. Catherine Krupnick, cited in "Lessons" by Edward B. Fiske, *New York Times*, 7 May 1990, B8.
7. Rita Mae Kelly and Mary Boutilier, *The Making of Political Women: A Study of Socialization and Role Conflict* (Chicago: Nelson-Hall, 1978).

PROFILE: ANN RICHARDS

1. Margaret Carlson, "A New Ballgame," *Time*, 10 September 1990, 41.
2. Ann Richards, with Peter Knobler, *Straight from the Heart: My Life in Politics and Other Places* (New York: Simon & Schuster, 1991), 34.
3. Ibid., 40.
4. Ibid., 152–62.

CHAPTER 6

1. Celinda Lake, "Campaigning in a Different Voice" (Summary, unpublished report, EMILY's List, Washington, D.C., n.d.).
2. Cited in Ann M. Morrison, Randall P. White, and Ellen Van Velson, "Executive Women: Substance Plus Style," *Psychology Today*, August 1987, 20.
3. Daniel M. Stern, *The Interpersonal World of the Infant* (New York: Basic Books, 1985).
4. James O'Toole, Foreword in *Leadership Is an Art* by M. De Pree (New York: Dell, 1989).
5. J. M. Burns, *Leadership* (New York: Harper & Row, 1978).
6. Geraldine Ferraro, "The Future of Women in Politics" (The Goldberg Lecture, 92nd Street YM-YWHA, New York, 20 February 1991).
7. Frank Rose, "A New Age for Business?" *Fortune*, 8 October 1990, 156–64.
8. Judy B. Rosener, "Ways Women Lead," *Harvard Business Review*, (November/December 1990): 120.
9. A. Statham, "The Gender Model Revisited: Differences in the Management Styles of Men and Women," *Sex Roles* 16, nos. 7–8, 1987. Statham, in her work on leadership style, says that "women leaders were actually equally effective [as men] in moving the group towards its goal [providing leadership] though they were perceived to be less effective because of certain style or behavioral differences they exhibited."

    Women used a communicative, task- and person-oriented style. Men used an agency-oriented style that was big on image and autonomy. Communicative styles are discounted, agency styles are valued. Consistent with these findings, other investigators studying followers' perceptions of leaders found that gender context influenced leadership perception.
10. De Pree, *Leadership Is an Art*.

CHAPTER 7

1. Dennis Kelly, "Will Finances Foreclose Tradition?" *USA Today*, 30 April 1990, 1.
2. Catherine Krupnick, cited in "Lessons" by Edward B. Fiske, *New York Times*, 7 May 1990, B8.

3. "Feminization of Power Campus Campaign," *The Feminist Majority Report* 2, no. 2 (October 1989): 5.

CHAPTER 8

1. Nancy Chodorow, *The Reproduction of Mothering* (Berkeley: University of California Press, 1978).
2. Althea Horner, *The Wish for Power and the Fear of Having It* (New York: Jason Aronson, 1989), 74.

CHAPTER 9

1. Geraldine Ferraro, "The Future of Women in Politics" (The Goldberg Lecture, 92nd Street YM-YWHA, New York, 20 February 1991).
2. D. Sisk and D. Shallcross, *Leadership* (Buffalo: Brearly, 1986).
3. J. Echergray, "Severed Heart," quoted in *Future of Motherhood* by J. Bernard (New York: Dial, 1974).
4. Harriet Goldhor Lerner, *The Dance of Anger* (New York: Perennial Library, Harper & Row).
5. Althea Horner, *The Wish for Power and the Fear of Having It* (New York: Jason Aronson, 1989), 74.
6. W. F. Sturner, *Calculated Risk: Strategies for Managing Change* (Buffalo: Brearly, 1990).

EPILOGUE

1. "Women Make Gains on the State Level," *CAWP News & Notes* (Center for the American Woman and Politics, Eagleton Institute of Politics, Rutgers University) 8, no. 1 (Winter 1991): 2.
2. Ibid.
3. Ibid.

Index